THE TRINITY IN
THE NEW TESTAMENT

THE TRINITY IN
THE NEW TESTAMENT

ARTHUR W. WAINWRIGHT

LONDON

S·P·C·K

First published in 1962
Second impression, with corrections, 1969
S.P.C.K.
Holy Trinity Church
Marylebone Road
London N.W.1

Made and printed in Great Britain by
William Clowes and Sons, Limited, London and Beccles

TO THE MEMORY OF MY FATHER

SBN 281 01285 7

CONTENTS

ABBREVIATIONS

ET   *Expository Times*

JBL   *Journal of Biblical Literature*

JTS   *Journal of Theological Studies*

LXX   *Septuagint*

SJT   *Scottish Journal of Theology*

TWNT   *Theologisches Wörterbuch zum Neuen Testament*, ed.
Gerhard Kittel, G. Friedrich

ZNTW   *Zeitschrift für die neutestamentliche Wissenschaft*

PREFACE

It is often supposed that the doctrine of the Trinity arose after the New Testament had been written, and that it is a speculative doctrine, which is not essential to the Christian message. This book has been written in the conviction that the problem of the Trinity was being raised and answered in New Testament times, and had its roots in the worship, experience, and thought of first-century Christianity. The word "problem" has been preferred to the word "doctrine", because there is no formal statement of the doctrine of the Trinity in the New Testament. But in so far as a doctrine is an answer to a problem, the doctrine of the Trinity emerges in the New Testament. The problem of the Trinity is raised there, and an attempt is made to answer it.

The fourth chapter of this book is largely drawn from an article which I contributed to the *Scottish Journal of Theology*, Vol. 10, no. 3, September 1957, and I wish to express my gratitude to the editors for allowing me to use it.

I am deeply indebted to the Reverend Doctor R. Newton Flew, who first encouraged me to investigate this subject and has commented on several of the chapters, and to the Reverend Rupert E. Davies, the Reverend Owen E. Evans, the Reverend Doctor C. Leslie Mitton, and the Reverend Professor Philip S. Watson, who have read the typescript and made many helpful suggestions.

I am also very grateful to Mrs Ena Levine for typing the work, and to my wife for helping to check the proofs and compile the indexes.

ARTHUR W. WAINWRIGHT

Manchester,
April 1962

PART I

Introduction

CHAPTER 1

THE PROBLEM OF THE TRINITY

The purpose of this work is to trace the emergence of the problem of the Trinity in New Testament times. This problem arose because Christians believed that Jesus was divine, and expressed their belief by giving him divine titles and ascribing to him functions which were usually reserved in Hebrew thought for God. This belief in Christ's divinity was expressed both in the writings of the New Testament and in the worship which was practised by the earliest Christian communities. Because the Christian Church upheld the Jewish belief in the unity of God, the belief in Christ's divinity raised a serious problem. How could Father and Son be God, and yet God be one? A further problem was raised because the Spirit was regarded as a Person, who had a decisive influence upon the lives of individuals. Was the Spirit also God, and if so, how could God be three and one?

These two questions were raised quite clearly in the second century in the writings of Theophilus, Irenaeus, and Tertullian. This is not surprising, because the statements about Father, Son, and Spirit made in the New Testament, were of such a nature as to raise the trinitarian problem for later generations of readers. It is our task to investigate whether the New Testament writers themselves were aware of the problem, either in the form of the relationship between Father and Son, or in that of the relationship between Father, Son, and Spirit. Strictly speaking, if the problem of Father and Son alone is raised, it is binitarian. But whether the problem is binitarian or trinitarian in form, the crucial issue is the relationship of Father to Son, because the problem would not have been of practical importance if there had been no Incarnation. If the Word had not been made flesh, there would have been no stumbling-block for Jewish monotheism.

3

The theme of this discussion is the problem rather than the doctrine of the Trinity. A statement of doctrine is an answer to a doctrinal problem. There is no formal statement of trinitarian doctrine in the New Testament as there is in the Athanasian Creed or in Augustine's *De Trinitate*. It will be argued that the problem of the Trinity was in the minds of certain New Testament writers, and that they made an attempt to answer it. None of their writings, however, was written specifically to deal with it, and most of the signs that a writer had tackled the problem are incidental. There was no elaborate or systematic answer to the problem. For this reason the word "problem" has been preferred to the word "doctrine". But it must be understood that the New Testament writers did not entirely neglect to answer the problem, although other matters occupied most of their attention. In so far as a doctrine is an answer, however fragmentary, to a problem, there is a doctrine of the Trinity in the New Testament. In so far as it is a formal statement of a position, there is no doctrine of the Trinity in the New Testament.

The difference between a formal statement of doctrine and an incidental or fragmentary answer to a doctrinal problem is clear when the New Testament approach to the trinitarian problem is compared with the creeds and confessions of later generations. The importance of this difference, however, can be overstressed. It is difficult to decide precisely when the doctrine first emerged. If the use of the word "Trinity" is a necessary feature of a statement of the doctrine, then it does not appear to have emerged before Theophilus (second century), who used the Greek τριάς (triad) to describe Father, Son, and Holy Spirit, or before Tertullian (late second century), who used the Latin *trinitas* for the same purpose.[1] But in these writers the words τριάς and *trinitas* do not have the depth of meaning which they later acquired,[2] and trinitarian doc-

---

[1] Theophilus, *Ad Autol.* 2.15; Tertullian, *Adv. Prax.* 3. Cf. G. L. Prestige, *God in Patristic Thought*, pp. 88, 93.

[2] Cf. Prestige, ibid., p. 94: "The word triad, then, did not originally express in any degree the unity of God. On the contrary, it emphasized the fact which constituted the main problem that Christian monotheists had to face. The term expressive of the principle of monotheism was 'monarchy'."

trine did not receive its orthodox form until over a century later. It could be argued that the doctrine emerged when Christian writers began to use philosophical methods of investigation, but it would be difficult then to decide whether these methods were present in Athenagoras and Irenaeus or first appeared in Tertullian, Clement, and Origen. Again, the emergence of trinitarian doctrine could be traced to the use of technical terms such as ὑπόστασις, οὐσία, and πρόσωπον in Greek, and *persona, substantia,* and *essentia* in Latin. But all these words have great varieties of meaning, and it would be hard to say which particular usage heralded the dawn of trinitarian theology.

In the second and third centuries a growing amount of literature was devoted to the problem of the Trinity, and the answers to the problem became more and more systematized. This gradual development of thought is more important than the introduction of technical terms. There is no clear historical boundary between the era of systematic doctrinal statement and the less reflective and less philosophical era which preceded it. The difference in style and character between New Testament writings and the works of third- and fourth-century Fathers ought not to obscure the fact that New Testament writers were aware of the trinitarian problem and made an attempt to answer it. And it ought not to obscure the fact that the problem has never been satisfactorily answered, and that the most enduring statements of the doctrine do not give complete answers to the problem but define the limits of discussion. Naturally a problem must be clarified before it can be answered. In the New Testament it is easier to see the first attempts to clarify the problem than the first attempts to answer it. But an answer begins to emerge, and it would be misleading to say that trinitarian theology is entirely post-biblical.

The trinitarian problem is not purely speculative. Biblical writers are often said to be practical rather than speculative, and to be concerned with God's activity rather than his eternal nature. Melanchthon's dictum, "To know Christ is to know his benefits", is quoted as a key to the attitude of early Christians. This interpretation of biblical thought has been carried too far. The early Christians were interested in God the Father and Christ the Son as

persons and not merely as agents of salvation. Because they loved
both the Father and the Son, they wanted to know how they were
related to each other. Nevertheless, when they discussed the nature
of God, they associated it with his activity, because of the practical
bent of their thoughts. Cullmann has observed that in the New
Testament the person of Christ is hardly ever spoken of without
an accompanying reference to his work. The Prologue of the
Fourth Gospel, for example, describes the relationship of the Word
to God ("The Word was with God, and the Word was God"), and
then speaks of the creative work of the Word ("All things were
made by him").[1] The early Christians were more interested in the
message of salvation than metaphysics, and their theology reflects
this interest. They were concerned with the activity rather than the
nature of God. In the following chapters it will be shown that they
expounded the divinity of Christ partly by describing the functions
which he fulfilled. The trinitarian problem was being presented
and answered by reference to Christ's activity towards mankind.
The New Testament writers believed that he shared in the divine
activities of creator, saviour, and judge. Although the question of
the eternal relationship of Father and Son was a very important
issue, especially for Paul, John, and the author of the Epistle to the
Hebrews, they laid the emphasis on the divine activity rather than
the divine nature.

The problem of the Trinity was from the beginning closely
connected with Christian worship. It was not the concern of the
scholar alone, but was a vital issue for the worshipping Christian.
The trinitarian pattern can be seen in the worship of the Father,
for worship was given to the Father through the Son in the Spirit.
This was the most prevalent form of worship, but even in New
Testament times Christ was worshipped as well as the Father,
though probably with less frequency. Worship of the Spirit
developed later.[2] In a subsequent age the Athanasian Creed
declared: "The Catholic Faith is this: That we worship one God
in Trinity, and Trinity in Unity." The creed acknowledges the

---

[1] Oscar Cullmann, *Die Christologie des Neuen Testaments*, p. 4.

[2] This is acknowledged in the Nicene Creed: "Who with the Father and
the Son together is worshipped and glorified."

character of a worship which was already being practised. Christian worship grew to be trinitarian in two ways: the first as the worship of the Father through the Son in the Spirit, and the second as the worship of Father, Son, and Spirit. In the New Testament, however, its trinitarian character is chiefly found in the worship of the Father through the Son in the Spirit, and, to a lesser extent, in the worship of the Son. The nature of Christian worship influenced the development of Christian thought, and, conversely, the development of thought influenced the nature of worship. Such an interplay of thought and worship helps to explain the emergence of the problem of the Trinity.

This explanation of the biblical approach to the problem of the Trinity assumes that the New Testament writers reflected on the problem. A different point of view is given by Alan Richardson in *An Introduction to the Theology of the New Testament*. He says: "There is in the New Testament no hint of a δεύτερος θεός[1] or δημιουργός[2] distinct from the God of the Old Testament revelation, nor is there any problem at all of reconciling the divinity of Christ and of the Spirit with Jewish monotheism. Christ and the Spirit are equally God in his self-determined modes of operation in the creation, redemption, and sanctification of the world."[3]

The following chapters will attempt to show that although Christ was not regarded as a Second God in the New Testament, he was regarded as God, and that the very reluctance of the New Testament writers to expound the belief that Jesus was God shows that they were aware of a problem. It will be argued that although the New Testament writers show few signs of being aware of a problem of reconciling the divinity of the Spirit with Jewish monotheism, some of them were clearly aware of the problem of reconciling Christ's divinity with monotheism.

Another point of view which differs from that which is maintained in the following pages is that of Emil Brunner in the first volume of his *Dogmatics*. Brunner says of the doctrine of the Trinity: "The starting point of the doctrine is, naturally, not a speculative one, but the simple testimony of the New Testament.

[1] Second God.   [2] Maker of the world.   [3] Pp. 122–3.

7

We are not concerned with the God of thought, but with the God who makes His Name known. But He makes His Name known as the Name of the Father; He makes this Name of the Father known through the Son; and He makes the Son known as the Son of the Father, and the Father as the Father of the Son through the Holy Spirit."[1]

Brunner's distinction between the God of thought and the God who makes his Name known is artificial. In the New Testament God makes his Name known through men's thoughts about him. Christians reflected about God from the beginning. Although their reflections did not follow the pattern of Greek philosophical thought, they were none the less reflections. Brunner's phrase "simple testimony" does not adequately describe the teaching of Paul, John, and Hebrews.

Brunner also says: "This *mysterium logicum*, the fact that God is Three and yet One, lies wholly outside the message of the Bible. . . . No apostle would have dreamt of thinking that there are the Three Divine Persons, whose mutual relations and paradoxical unity are beyond our understanding. No *mysterium logicum*, no intellectual paradox, no antinomy of Trinity and Unity, has any place in their testimony, but only the *mysterium majestatis et caritatis*; namely, that the Lord God for our sakes became man and endured the Cross."[2] While, however, the words "paradox" and "antinomy" do not occur in the New Testament, there is in the Prologue of the Fourth Gospel a clear awareness of the paradox of the relationship between Father and Son. The man who wrote "The Word was with God, and the Word was God" knew that his statement contained a paradox.

Brunner's attitude is unsatisfactory, because he makes too rigid a division between the threefold revelation which is biblical and the threefold interpretation which he believes to be post-biblical. He distinguishes too sharply between thought and preaching. His attitude is shown in a criticism which he makes of Barth, who, he says, "does not distinguish between the *problem* of the Trinity which is set us by the message of the Bible, and the doctrine of the Trinity. He does not see that the doctrine of the Trinity is the

---

[1] *Dogmatics*, I, p. 206.   [2] Ibid., p. 226.

product of reflection and not a *kerygma*."[1] It will be argued in the following chapters that the problem of the Trinity is present not only in the words of the New Testament but also in the minds of the writers, and that, whether or not they can be said to have attempted a doctrine of the Trinity, they attempted an answer to the problem.[2] It will also be shown that there is no sharp division between reflection and kerygma. In the early Church reflection led to preaching, and preaching to further reflection. Nor must it be forgotten that vigorous and authoritative utterance can also be reflective.

The New Testament basis of the doctrine of the Trinity is often the theme of an introductory chapter but rarely the theme of a book. The first volume of Lebreton's *History of the Dogma of the Trinity* deals with the New Testament and with the Hebrew and Hellenistic background. (In recent years attention has been paid to the Old Testament background, notably in two monographs, A. R. Johnson's *The One and the Many in Ancient Israel*, and G. A. F. Knight's *The Biblical Doctrine of the Trinity*.) Two reasons may be suggested for the great neglect of this theme. The first is that there has been a tendency to say without qualification that the doctrine of the Trinity is post-biblical and answers a problem which did not occur to the writers of the New Testament but only to a later generation of readers. To this point reference has already been made, and it is hoped that the argument of this treatise will refute such a view. The second reason for neglect of the theme is that it would overlap the fields of Christology and of teaching about the Spirit. This is a salutary reminder of the need for selectivity in dealing with the subject. Obviously, certain topics are common to the problem of the Trinity and the problem of Christology, and others are common to the problem of the Trinity and the problem of the Spirit. But a study of the emergence of the

---

[1] Ibid., p. 236.

[2] M. W. Wiles favours the view that the doctrine of the Trinity is an arbitrary analysis of the activity of God, which is not of essential significance in Christian thought (*JTS*, N.S. VIII, pp. 92–106). This view is not disproved if the trinitarian problem was raised in New Testament times, but it becomes difficult to maintain.

trinitarian problem need not deal with the whole of New Testament Christology nor with the whole of the New Testament doctrine of the Spirit. It must deal with Christology and the doctrine of the Spirit in so far as they imply or explicitly state that the Spirit and Christ are God. A detailed discussion of the humanity of Jesus is not relevant to our theme. Although the fact of the Incarnation is relevant, we are concerned with the divinity of Christ and especially with any statements which say that he is God. In examining the teaching about the Holy Spirit we shall be chiefly concerned with the evidence that the Spirit is a person and the evidence that the Spirit is God.

The evidence for a belief in the divinity of Christ can be divided into three groups. First there is the evidence that Jesus Christ was worshipped. The members of the Church sang doxologies to him, prayed to him, called upon him frequently as Lord and sometimes as God. Probably he was recognized as God in worship earlier than in reflective thought, but we cannot know this for certain. At any rate, it will be argued that in worship the first generation of Christians called upon Christ as God, a confession which is the distinctive and central element in the doctrine of the Trinity.

Secondly, there is the evidence that Jesus Christ was believed to perform the functions of judgement, salvation, and creation. In Hebrew thought these functions were regarded in some aspects as uniquely divine, and in these very aspects Christ was said to perform them. Christian thought about the person of Christ was practical in the sense that it considered his activity rather than his metaphysical status. In New Testament times there was no question about the way in which his nature was similar to the human and divine natures. There was no discussion of his psychological structure. Men showed their attitude to his person by describing him as one who acted in certain ways which had previously been regarded as divine.

The third group of evidence is the titles which were given to Jesus Christ. Not all these titles imply his divinity. "Master", "Teacher", "Rabbi", "Prophet", "Son of David", even the title "Messiah", do not imply divinity. "God" and "Lord" are in a different category. "God", of course, is a title which explicitly states a person's divinity. "Lord" often implies it, perhaps some-times states it explicitly. "Son of Man" and "Son of God" do not necessarily imply divinity but can be used in such a way as to refer to a unique superhuman status, which may be divine. The title "Son of God" is specially important because it raises the question of Christ's relationship to the Father. Indeed it brings us face to face with the crucial part of the trinitarian problem.

The evidence for the divinity of the Spirit is not as abundant as that for the divinity of Christ. Throughout Christian history systematic thinking about the Spirit has lingered behind that about Christology. Complaints are often heard that the Church lacks a satisfactory doctrine of the Spirit. This is a harsh criticism because the Spirit cannot easily be confined within the walls of dogma, and although Christ is greater than any dogma, the concreteness of the Incarnation makes it easier for men to dogmatize about him than about the Spirit.

A question has to be asked about the Spirit which it is not necessary to ask about Christ, namely: Is the Spirit a person? This question is not the same as: Is the Spirit *persona* in one or more of the senses used by the writers of the early Church and medieval times? The question means: Has the Spirit a nature and activities which are in certain ways analogous to the nature and activities of human beings, these points of analogy being possession of thought, feeling, and will, and existence as an individual centre of conscious-ness which is capable of relationships with other persons?

Although the biblical writers never used the terms "person", "individual", "personality", which occur frequently in dis-cussions of biblical thought, they were aware of the ideas which underlie these terms. They spoke of people and of God as if they were persons in the sense that they had thought, feeling, will, and individuality. Although they believed that families and nations had a corporate personality, they also believed that an individual could have an independent will and consciousness. And they believed that God himself had these marks of individuality.

Because God was regarded as a person, it would be fruitless to consider whether the Spirit was regarded as God, unless the Spirit was also believed to be a person. First, it will be shown that in the

New Testament the Spirit is regarded as a person. Then the evidence for his divinity will be considered. The discussion will follow the same pattern as the discussion of the divinity of Christ. What was the Spirit's place in Christian worship, and was he actually worshipped? Was he said to perform uniquely divine functions? Was he given titles which implicitly or explicitly acknowledged his divinity? In addition to these questions the relationship of the Spirit to Christ and to the Father must be discussed.

The chapters which ask the above questions about Christ and the Spirit, deal with Christology and the doctrine of the Spirit in so far as they have a direct bearing upon the doctrine of the Trinity. A discussion which co-ordinates these themes and examines their interrelations will help us to decide whether the doctrine of the Trinity, as it was formulated in later times, was an explanation imposed upon the biblical evidence from without, or a natural growth from biblical thought, a continuation of that search for an understanding of God which had already been started in the New Testament.

In recent years there has been much discussion of the doctrine of the Trinity. Some writers, notably Hodgson, have emphasized the importance of the social analogy and stressed the fact that there were three distinct persons in the Trinity.[1] Others, such as Barth and Welch, have stressed the unity of the Trinity and have revived the use of the word "mode" in their exposition of the doctrine. Welch also outlines the debate about the Trinity in the twentieth century.[2] The part of the doctrine of the Trinity in Christian worship has been discussed by Lowry.[3] C. C. Richardson has argued that the doctrine does not fittingly express the actual distinctions in the Godhead.[4] Much more attention has been paid to the doctrine in the twentieth century than in the nineteenth. In the nineteenth century there was a tendency to relegate a discussion

[1] Leonard Hodgson, *The Doctrine of the Trinity*.

[2] Karl Barth, *The Doctrine of the Word of God*; C. Welch, *The Trinity in Contemporary Theology*.

[3] C. W. Lowry, *The Trinity and Christian Devotion*.

[4] C. C. Richardson, *The Doctrine of the Trinity*.

of the Trinity almost to the place of an appendix to an exposition of Christian Theology. Schleiermacher, for example, although he calls the doctrine of the Trinity "the coping-stone of Christian doctrine",[1] devotes only fourteen of the 750 pages of *The Christian Faith* to a discussion of the Trinity, and these fourteen pages are placed in the final chapter of the work. In fairness to him it must be said that, having admitted that the doctrine contains unsolved problems, he suggests what steps should be taken to give a fuller interpretation of the doctrine. Nevertheless he does not attempt to perform this task himself. In the twentieth century, however, Barth begins his *Kirchliche Dogmatik* with an exposition of the doctrine of the Trinity. The place which he accords to the doctrine is a sign of the revival of interest in it.

An examination of the New Testament background will enable us to see how the problem of the Trinity arose, and will assist us to understand in what sense a doctrine of the Trinity can be biblical. The method of investigation which will be adopted is as follows:

1. (*a*) A discussion of the Hebrew background to the doctrine. The ideas of the one and the many in Israelite thought will be examined, and also any concepts which could have influenced the development of trinitarian doctrine. Our concern will be with the Old Testament and later Jewish influence upon the way in which the problem was stated and answered in the New Testament. (*b*) A discussion of early Christian belief in the unity and the Fatherhood of God. The New Testament writers believed firmly that God was one, and that he was Father. The evidence for these fundamental articles in the doctrine of God will be examined.

2. A discussion of the Divinity of Christ. Attention will be directed first to the evidence that Christ was the object of worship in the early Church. The titles "God" and "Lord" will be discussed because they were used of Christ in worship. After these titles have been examined, the use of quotations and doxologies about Christ and the practice of prayer to him will be discussed. The second part of this section will be concerned with the uniquely divine functions

[1] Friedrich Schleiermacher, *The Christian Faith*, p. 739.

13

of judgement, creation, and salvation, which Christ is said to have performed, and the third part deals with the relationship of Father to Son.

3. A discussion of the Divinity of the Holy Spirit. The first part of this section is about the Nature of the Spirit and his relation to Christ. In this part the person of the Spirit and the connection of the Spirit with Christ will be discussed. In the second part the Spirit's relationship to God the Father will be examined. The New Testament evidence for the belief that the Spirit is God will be considered.

4. The rise of the trinitarian problem. In this final section the evidence for the rise of the problem as a trinitarian problem will be discussed. The triadic formulae of the New Testament will be collected and examined, and it will be shown that in some parts of the New Testament the writer is aware that there is a problem about the relationship of Father, Son, and Spirit. It will also be shown that in the Fourth Gospel an attempt is made to give an answer to this problem.

CHAPTER 2

THE TRINITY IN HEBREW RELIGION

The Unity of God in Hebrew Thought

The fundamental article of the Jewish faith is that God is one. "Hear, O Israel: the Lord our God is one Lord" (Deut. 6.4), is the cry which for centuries has been recited twice each day in the Jewish liturgy. It was quoted by Jesus in his summary of the Law (Mark 12.29–30), and is echoed in the words of Paul and other writers of the early Church.[1] Monotheism had long been established in Judaism when Jesus entered the world. Although there are definite traces of polytheism in the records of early Hebrew religion, the faith had been monotheistic since the exile. The great pre-exilic prophets did not deny the existence of other gods, but they demanded a worship which was directed to Yahweh alone. The author of second Isaiah, who lived in the period of the exile, believed that Yahweh was not only the supreme God but the only God. The gods which had been fashioned by the hands of men were lifeless fabrications. Yahweh stood alone. He was the true, almighty God, who said, "I am the first, and I am the last; and beside me there is no God" (Isa. 44.6).

In the four centuries before Christ the Jewish religion was modified by many influences from East and West. The angelology of the apocalyptic literature was partly derived from Persia, and the Wisdom literature owed a debt to both Persia and Egypt. Although Greek philosophy had little or no influence upon the writers of the Old Testament, traces of it may be found in the Apocrypha. The most conspicuous Greek influence, however, is seen in the works of Philo, which were written in the first century

---

[1] 1 Cor. 8.6; Eph. 4.6; 1 Tim. 2.5; Jas. 2.19, etc.

A.D., and show how great could be the impact of Platonism upon a Jew of the Dispersion.

Some of these foreign influences were likely to weaken the monotheism of the Jews. Interest in the teaching of pagan religions could have easily led to polytheism; for the Persians were dualists, and the Egyptians believed that there was a whole family of gods. Greek philosophy, although it tended to accept monotheism or pantheism, was not always violently opposed to the traditional polytheism. In spite of these foreign influences, however, there was always a nucleus of the Jewish people which refused to allow its faith in the one God to be adulterated by any pagan accretion. The Wisdom writers, the authors of apocalyptic, and the philosopher Philo were as convinced as the rabbis of Palestine that the God of Abraham, Isaac, and Jacob was unique and almighty. Philo was never led by the allurements of Greek speculation from his belief that the God of the Hebrews was the one true God.[1]

The authors of apocalyptic, who recorded the constitution of heaven, and enumerated the orders and ranks of the angels, might easily have elevated a creature to the state of divinity. But the surviving works of apocalyptic, whatever their extravagances might have been, did not allow any other being to share the majesty of God. The same traditional emphasis is retained in the Wisdom literature. The divine Wisdom came from God, was subordinate to him and created by him.

The rabbis trod the path of orthodoxy. Although they acknowledged the existence of angels, they taught that they were creatures, subordinate to their maker. It has been argued that the rabbis personified concepts like Word and Spirit. But this is exceedingly doubtful. The terms *Memra* and *Dabar* which are translated "Word" were used for motives of reverence. The Jews thought that it was blasphemous to utter the divine name. *Memra* and *Dabar* are periphrases, which stress the majesty and do not compromise the unity of God.[2] Nor did the Jewish doctrine of the Spirit imply duality in the Godhead. It was always the Spirit of the one God.

The Jewish liturgy in the time of Jesus was thoroughly mono-

---

[1] See G. F. Moore, *Judaism*, I, pp. 361 f.

[2] Ibid., pp. 416 f.

theistic. The oneness of God was explicitly affirmed in the *Shemaᶜ*. The opposition of rabbinic Judaism to the doctrine of the Trinity was a natural reaction to a religion which appeared to deviate from an unreserved monotheism. The statement that God was one was graven deeply on the heart of every devout Jew.

Physical dangers and spiritual temptations stimulated the tenacity of the Jews, and often their orthodoxy erred on the side of rigidity. The persecutions under Antiochus Epiphanes, and the steady and persuasive pressure of Greek and Roman civilization may have caused many to waver in their faith, but the core of Judaism remained loyal to the central affirmation of the religion.

The strength of the Jewish faith is shown by the concessions which the Jewish people received from their Roman overlords. The emperors found it prudent to respect the beliefs of this stern and proud nation, and gave it the status of a *religio licita*.[1] When the governor Pilate allowed the standards which bore the emperor's image to be carried inside the walls of Jerusalem, he was, according to Josephus, breaking a law, which had been specially made out of respect for Jewish customs.[2] The ideal attitude of a Jew is to be found in the conduct of Rabbi Akiba, who in the hour of his execution continued to repeat the word "One".[3]

Akiba represents the spirit of Judaism. Whatever heresies and schisms have arisen, there has always been a strong band of Jews who have not faltered in their loyalty to the one God. The persecutions of Antiochus, the scorn and oppression of proconsuls and emperors, the dangers of their own developing theology, and finally the growth of Christianity led them to affirm more vehemently and defend more vigorously the central doctrine of their faith.

The Plurality of God in Hebrew Thought

Because the Christian religion was born in the midst of Judaism, there is a close bond between the Christian and Jewish doctrines

---

[1] Josephus, *Ant.* xiv.10; Philo, *Legat. ad Gaium*, 23.
[2] Josephus, *De Bell. Jud.* ii.9.
[3] T. J. Ber. ix.7. See Montefiore and Loewe, *Rabbinic Anthology*, pp. 269–70.

of God. Both religions agree that God is creator and judge and ruler of the universe. Both agree that he is just and merciful. Both agree that he is one. Christians have sometimes endeavoured to forge yet another link between the two religions. Some of the Fathers claimed to be able to find evidence for the doctrine of the Trinity within the pages of the Old Testament. This desire to establish a connection between the two religions is not surprising. Christianity arose in Palestine. Its first scriptures were the Old Testament. Its founder was himself a Jew. And the majority of the earliest converts were Jews of Palestine or the Dispersion. Since, however, the Fathers were inclined to seek agreement where there was in fact difference, it is necessary to ask whether they subordinated reason to desire when they found the doctrine of the Trinity in the Hebrew Scriptures.

Some of the Fathers believed that they were able to unveil truths which were hidden from less acute observers. The Jews of Jesus' day, they thought, were deceived about the nature of God. They had misinterpreted or overlooked some of the most important passages of the Old Testament. They described God in terms which were narrow and inflexible. They had not understood that the words "Let us make man in our image" were not spoken in conversation with angels, or as a plural of majesty. The Holy Trinity was speaking. Nor had they understood—with the exception of Philo—that the three men who visited Abraham by the oaks of Mamre were not only three but also one, and that the seraphim who cried "Holy, Holy, Holy" in the vision of Isaiah, were acclaiming the triune God.

There is no need to return to the early Fathers to find this type of interpretation. In our own generation scholars claim to have uncovered the seed, if not the unfolding bud, of the doctrine of the Trinity in the Old Testament. They claim that the Hebrews combined their belief in one God with an acknowledgement of the plurality of the Godhead. A. R. Johnson and G. A. F. Knight have led the way in these investigations. Johnson writes: "At any rate we can see how it was possible for a Jewish Christian to relate his Messiah so closely with the divine Being as to afford a basis for the later (and Greek) metaphysical formulation of the doctrine of the Trinity."[1] Knight goes further than Johnson: "It may be, and I would say that it is more than a possibility, that our modern study of the Nature of God as revealed in the Hebrew scriptures has opened up to us a much clearer understanding of God as a Trinity of Being than has been possible for those theologians who had only the LXX version of their scriptures as the source from which they had to draw both their concepts and their actual language when they sought to erect a systematic Christian theology."[2] If the thesis of these scholars is correct, Trinitarianism, far from being a foundling left in the porch of the Church by Greek metaphysics, is a legitimate and honourable child of Hebrew religion, whose growth was slow, and, in the years of exile, somewhat retarded, but who blossomed into vigorous manhood during the first five centuries of the Christian era.

Neither of these scholars, however, has shown that the religion of the Old Testament was trinitarian, or that there is a direct connection between the theology of the New Testament and the veiled signs of Trinitarianism which they have claimed to find in the Old Testament. Johnson approaches the problem by examining the Hebrew view of the personality of man. He argues that the ideas of "extension of personality" and "collective personality" are found in the Hebrew conception of both God and man. The first of these ideas, which is now classified as "extension of personality", is found in the story of the destruction of Achan and his household.[3] In Hebrew thought the personality of a man was not limited to his conscious life or to the events which affected his own body. It could be "extended" to include his family and servants. Because of the solidarity of the household, all its members were liable to punishment for the offence of the leader. Hence, when Achan was put to death, his family and servants and livestock were destroyed with him. In .order to wipe out Achan it was thought necessary to wipe out everything which belonged to him.

This idea of "extension of personality" lies behind the belief

---

[1] A. R. Johnson, *The One and the Many in the Israelite Conception of God*, p. 41.
[2] G. A. F. Knight, *A Biblical Approach to the Doctrine of the Trinity*, p. 4.
[3] Josh. 7.24, cf. Johnson, op. cit., pp. 6–17.

that a man's personality was communicated through his name. A dead man's brother was required to beget children by his widowed sister-in-law in order to preserve the dead man's name (Deut. 25.5). The servants of a man were so closely a part of him that they could be addressed as if they were their master himself. In so far as they carried the message of their lord, his personality was dwelling in them.[1] Even a man's words were regarded as part of his personality. When Isaac blessed Jacob he was unable to cancel his blessing. The word which he had spoken was *his* word, and yet existed in its own right. His personality had been extended beyond the realm of his own conscious being (Gen. 27.33 ff).[2]

Johnson claims that in Hebrew thought God, like men, has an extension of personality.[3] This is not a sign of anthropomorphism, for the Hebrews did not claim to describe God in human terms. They claimed to describe man in divine terms. Man was an image of God who had created him. Like God he could forgive and be angry, love and hate. They put forward a theomorphic conception of man rather than an anthropomorphic conception of God.

Not only was the likeness between God and men revealed in passions of love and hate but also in the extension of personality. God could be spoken of as one or as many. "We must be prepared", writes Johnson, "to recognize for the Godhead just such a fluidity of reference from the One to the Many or from the Many to the One as we have already noticed in the case of man."[4] Thus the Spirit of God which "rushed upon" Samson and "donned" Gideon,[5] was not an impersonal force, but an extension of the divine personality. The Spirit in the vision of the prophet Micaiah "should be thought of as an individualization within the corporate *ruah* or 'Spirit' of Yahweh's extended personality."[6] The "Word" of God must be explained in the same way. It goes forth from God's mouth and performs what he pleases (Isa. 55.11). Similarly

[1] Gen. 44.4 ff, in which Joseph's brethren address his steward as "my lord"; Judges 11.12–13, where Jephthah's messengers are addressed in the second-person singular, cf. Johnson, ibid., pp. 8–10.

[2] Cf. Johnson, ibid., p. 7. [3] Ibid., pp. 17–26. [4] Ibid., p. 20.

[5] Judges 14.6,19; 15.14; 6.34. Cf. Johnson, ibid., p. 19.

[6] Johnson, ibid., p. 20, cf. 1 Kings 22.19 ff.

the "Name" of God and the "Ark" of God are treated as if they are God himself.[1]

Johnson also claims that the Hebrews believed that a personality could be "collective". Words which described individuals were also used to describe a social group. For example *nephesh*, which is translated "life" or "breath" or "soul", refers to the life-principle in the individual, without which he cannot live. But this word is used to describe a group of people as well as the individual. According to Num. 21.4, "the *nephesh* of the people was discouraged because of the way".[2]

The word *leb* meaning "heart" is also used in both an individual and a collective sense. The individual sense is the more usual, but there are several instances in which the singular word "heart" describes the attitude and feelings of a group of people. "The heart of the people melted", according to Josh. 7.5, "and became like water."

Sometimes the nation "Israel" is regarded as a single entity, an idiom which is by no means peculiar to the Hebrew tongue.[3] The attitude behind this idiom may be responsible for the way in which the Deuteronomic laws oscillate from the second person singular to the second person plural.[4]

Johnson sees the same idea of collective personality in the word *ᵓelohim* (God), which is plural in form but in most instances singular in meaning. The plural form could be explained as a relic of polytheism. But since the Jews retained it even in their monotheistic days, it probably represents something fundamental to their conception of God. Moreover, there are several passages in the Old Testament, in which God speaks of himself in the plural. "Such a form of speech", writes Johnson, "may have come to be used ultimately as a mere matter of idiom, and may then have lost its original force."[5] But, Johnson implies, in the early days of Israelite history it may have retained its original force.

Johnson's argument has its limitations. It is concerned for the

---

[1] For the "Name" see Num. 6.22–7; Ps. 20, and for the "Ark" see Num. 10.35 f; 1 Sam. 4.5–8; 6.7–9, 20.

[2] Johnson, op. cit., pp. 11–12.   [3] Ibid., pp. 13–17.

[4] E.g. Deut. 27.2–6.   [5] Op. cit., p. 32n1.

most part with pre-exilic thought. The pericopae which provide the bulk of his evidence probably go back to a date before the exile. His arguments do not give us any information about the Jewish attitude to the unity of God at the time when Jesus was born. He has shown that, in early times at least, the Hebrew conception of the one God was capable of subtle modification. But in order to discover whether this Hebrew idea had any direct effect on early Christian thought, it will be necessary to examine the attitude of later Judaism and early Christianity to the crucial passages of the Old Testament.

First, however, we shall consider the opinions of G. A. F. Knight who agrees in many matters with Johnson, but produces some arguments which are peculiar to himself. In an argument which is intriguing but unconvincing, he contends that the "Father-Sonship principle" is part of God's essence and must exist at all points of time.[1] God attempted to reveal this relationship by giving the nation of Israel the status of sonship, and Israel was called "Son of God". This revelation was "wrecked on the sinful self-will and rebellious spirit of a stiff-necked people".[2] There is a flaw in this argument. If the "Father-Sonship principle" is part of God's essence, it can only be realized through an extension of the divine personality. If God's relationship to Israel was an instance of the "Father-Sonship principle", Israel must have been an extension of the divine personality. There is, however, no evidence that Israel was so regarded. Although God confronted his people through individual prophets and angels, the nation as a whole was not regarded as an extension of God's personality. The description of Israel as "Son of God" does not reveal a "Father-Sonship principle" but only a "Father principle" within the Godhead.

Knight launches a violent attack on the theology of the Septuagint, which he accuses of obscuring the true Hebrew doctrine of God with a veil of Greek ideas. The early Christian Fathers were led hopelessly astray by the Septuagint, and the misunderstanding has persisted until modern times. Now, however, after centuries of darkness, it seems that theologians are able, through

[1] Knight, op. cit., pp. 66–73. [2] Ibid., pp. 73.

the beneficent offices of Semitic scholars, to understand the true doctrine of God.[1]

It is not necessary here to reply to a general attack on the Septuagint, but certain facts which will be discussed in the next section show the weakness of Knight's attack. He believes that the Septuagint was largely responsible for obscuring the idea of plurality in the Godhead. Under Greek influence it stressed the unity of God to such an extent that it could not admit the modification which was characteristic of early Hebrew thought. This is only partly true. The Septuagint shows a definite tendency to eliminate suggestions of polytheism, but it retains much that does not easily harmonize with the most rigid form of monotheism. The plural verbs of Genesis and Isaiah are retained. The oscillations from singular to plural in Genesis 18 and in Deuteronomy have not been eliminated. And, strangely enough, the nearest approach to a doctrine of the Trinity in Judaism is found in the writings of Philo, who was influenced by Greek thought even more profoundly than were the translators of the Septuagint.

Old Testament Indications of Plurality within the Godhead, and their influence on New Testament Christianity

Our central problem is whether the Jews of the first century A.D. were disposed by tradition to accept the notion of a God who contained plurality within his unity. Those passages will now be examined which have been regarded as evidence for this doctrine, and an attempt will be made to discover the interpretation of them which was given in later Judaism and early Christianity. The interpretations which will be discussed are rarely accepted by modern writers, but will be examined here because they may help to indicate the climate of thought in New Testament times.

The first group of passages is Gen. 1.26; 3.22; 11.7; and Isa. 6.8. In these passages God speaks of himself in the plural. This has often been explained as a plural of majesty.[2] Johnson points out that even in the strictly monotheistic Koran the plural is used of

[1] Ibid., pp. 2–9. [2] S. R. Driver, *Genesis*, p. 14.

Allah.[1] On the other hand these plurals seemed to the Jews to require explanation.

The passages are:

> And God said, Let us make man in our image, after our likeness (Gen. 1.26).
>
> And the Lord God said, Behold, the man is become as one of us, to know good and evil (Gen. 3.22).
>
> Go to, let us go down, and there confound their language, that they may not understand one another's speech (Gen. 11.7).
>
> And I heard the voice of the Lord saying, Whom shall I send, and who will go for us? (Isa. 6.8).

The strictly monotheistic interpretation appears in the Book of Jubilees, which was written in the second half of the second century before Christ. This book gives an account of the story of Genesis, in which dogmatically objectionable statements are altered or omitted. The story of the creation is told in such a way as to dispense with the plural verb of Gen. 1.26. The creation of man is described: "And after all this he created man, a man and a woman created he them" (Jub. 2.14). But the words of God in Gen. 1.26 are not recorded. The account of the expulsion of Adam and Eve from Eden includes no verse which corresponds to Gen. 3.22. And in the story of the Tower of Babel the author of Jubilees claims that when God said, "Let us go down", he was addressing the angels. The angels are not regarded as an extension of his personality, since they call him "the Lord God" (Jub. 10.22).

Philo's comments on these passages show that they presented him with a difficulty. In his discussion of Gen. 1.26, he argues that although God was the sole agent in the creation of other things, he was assisted by subordinate powers in the creation of man. As God could create only that which was good, it was necessary that others should create the evil in man. When he said, "Let us make man", he was speaking to subordinate powers, who were his inferiors and did not impair his uniqueness.[2]

Philo gives a similar explanation of the plural verb in Gen. 11.7.

---

[1] Op. cit., p. 32n 1. Gesenius, *Hebrew Grammar*, p. 398, argues that Gen. 1.26 is a case of self-deliberation.

[2] *De Op. Mund.* 75.

God is surrounded by potencies, although he himself is one. When he spoke of "us", he was referring to these potencies. "Now we must first lay down", writes Philo, "that no existing thing is of equal honour to God and that there is only one sovereign and ruler and king, who alone may direct and dispose of all things . . . God is one, but He has around Him numberless Potencies, which all assist and protect created being."[1] It was these potencies who went down to confuse the tongues of the men who were building the Tower of Babel, since it was not fitting for God himself to inflict punishment, which was an evil.

Philo is a representative of Hellenistic Judaism. Jews of the Palestinian tradition have also commented on these passages. According to Pappias, a rabbi who lived at the end of the first century A.D., Gen. 3.22 implied that Adam had become like an angel.[2] In the Jerusalem Talmud it is argued that because Gen. 1.27 refers to one God only, 1.26 must also refer to one God.[3] The Talmud does not provide certain evidence for first-century Judaism, and may have been influenced by the desire of a later generation to defend the faith against Christianity. But there is no good reason to suppose that in this matter it is untrue to the spirit of first-century Judaism.

The Targums also show that these passages caused perplexity. The earliest of the Targums, that of Onkelos, keeps close to the original Hebrew in 1.26 and 11.7. But in 3.22 it reads: "And the Lord God said, Behold, man is become singular in the world by himself."

The Palestinian Targum attempts to explain the plural verbs by assuming that God was addressing the angels, and in 3.22 the Jerusalem Targum has a similar version.

The Jewish evidence shows a desire to interpret the passages so as to maintain the doctrine of God's unity. But in the New Testament these passages are not used in connection with the doctrine of God. The theological importance of Gen. 1.26 is recognized.

[1] *De Conf. Ling.* 170–1. (Tr. F. H. Colson.)
[2] Cf. Montefiore and Loewe, *Rabbinic Anthology*, p. 664.
[3] Berakoth, ix; cf. Oesterley and Box, *Religion and Worship of the Synagogue*, p. 180.

Paul calls man "the image and glory of God", and James speaks of men "which are made after the likeness of God".[1] But there is no reference to the plural verb "let us make . . .". Although Paul, John, and the author of the Epistle to the Hebrews teach that Christ was an agent in the creation, they do not cite Gen. 1.26 as evidence. It was not long before Christian writers seized on the verse to prove Christ's activity in creation. This type of argument occurs first in the Epistle of Barnabas, and then in Justin's *Dialogue with Trypho*.[2] Irenaeus said that God was speaking to his two hands, the Son and the Spirit, when he said, "Let us make man".[3] Thereafter these verses became acknowledged proof-texts for the doctrine of the Trinity. But there is no indication that this kind of interpretation was used by Christians of New Testament times.

Isa. 6.8 did not attract as much notice as the passages from Genesis. The Targum, however, removes the plural pronoun and reads: "Whom shall I send to prophesy, and who will go to preach?"[4] In the New Testament and the Apostolic Fathers no trinitarian doctrine is read into this verse but it is possible that Origen may have accepted a trinitarian interpretation here, as he did in verses 3–6 of the same chapter.[5]

The story of Abraham's encounter with the three men at Mamre has provoked a great amount of speculation. It contains several oscillations between singular and plural, which offer plausible support for the doctrine of the Trinity. The story begins with the statement that "The Lord (Yahweh) appeared to Abraham" (18.1). But when Abraham looked, he saw three men standing

---

[1] 1 Cor. 11.7; Jas. 3.9.

[2] Barnabas 5.5; 6.12; Justin, *Dial.* 62: 1 Clem. 33.5 quotes Gen. 1.26 ff but does not comment on the plural verb.

[3] *Contr. Omn. Haer.* IV, *Praef.* 4, xx.1.; V, i.3, vi.1, xxviii.4.

[4] J. F. Stenning, *The Targum of Isaiah*, pp. 22–3.

[5] Origen, *In Is. Hom.* iv.1, claims that the phrase "Holy, holy, holy" refers to the Trinity. He argues that Christ was the seraph who took the coal from the altar (*Hom.* iv.4). Although he says nothing about the words "Who will go for us?" in verse 8 (see *Hom.* vi.1), he describes God surrounded by the seraphim before he gives the account of Isaiah's call. He probably took it for granted that God included the seraphim in "us" when he said, "Who will go for us?"

opposite him (18.2). He addressed his visitors in the singular as "my lord" (18.3) but in the following verse spoke to them in the plural. This mysterious oscillation continues throughout the story. In chapter 19 only two angels appear, and in verse 18 Lot addresses them as "lord".

Although the Targum of Onkelos adheres closely to the meaning of the Hebrew, the Palestinian Targum tries to explain the unusual variations between singular and plural. The three men were angels, and three were sent instead of one because an angel can be sent for only one purpose at once. One angel came to announce the birth of a son to Sarah, a second to deliver Lot from the fire and brimstone, and a third to overthrow Sodom and Gomorrah. No comment is made on the fact that Abraham addressed them as "my lord", but it is probably assumed that he was speaking only to one of the men. At any rate, in verse 10 it is carefully explained that only one of the angels is speaking to Abraham. And in verse 20 it is made quite clear that "the Lord" is not to be identified with the three men, for the Targum begins the verse: "And the Lord said to the ministering angels."

A different interpretation of the incident is given by Philo. He argues that the triple vision has in reality a single object.[1] God, like an object which casts two shadows at once, may have a three-fold appearance. The three men who visited Abraham were a triple manifestation of the one God.

> The central place is held by the Father of the Universe, who in the sacred scriptures is called He that Is as His proper name, while on either side of Him are the senior potencies, the nearest to Him, the creative and the kingly. The title of the former is God, since it made and ordered the All; the title of the latter is Lord, since it is the fundamental right of the maker to rule and control what he has brought into being. So the central Being with each of His potencies as His squire presents to the mind which has vision the appearance sometimes of one, sometimes of three.[2]

This central Being, Philo argues, presents himself as one to minds which are highly purified. To those who are not initiated

[1] *De Abrahamo*, 119–31.
[2] Ibid., 121–2. (Translation by F. H. Colson, Loeb Library, *Philo*, VI, pp. 63–5.)

into the highest mysteries, he presents himself as three. To the highest class of people he appears as the eternally existent, the Father, to a second class, although he is three, he appears chiefly as the beneficent God, and to a third class he appears as the Lord, who governs the creation. These lower classes do not worship the Supreme Being for his own sake, but in order to receive his blessings or to avoid his punishments.

The Supreme Being himself is the cause only of good, and leaves the task of inflicting punishment to the potencies. Therefore only two angels took part in the destruction of Sodom. The Father abstained from this unpleasant task.[1]

Philo's exposition is not wholly consistent. The potencies are compared to shadows of the Supreme Being, and yet are said to perform actions, namely punishment, which the Supreme Being himself will not do. Paradoxes of this nature are difficult to avoid in trinitarian doctrine. According to Christian Trinitarianism, although the bond between the three persons is closer than that between any human beings, and although there is complete harmony of will and action, the Incarnate life was an activity which was appropriate to the Son alone. Philo's belief that only the inferior potencies were appropriate inflicters of punishment is a similar example of trinitarian paradox.

Philo's speculations about the nature of God, however, must not be regarded as typically Jewish. He was a Hellenistic writer who was under the spell of Plato. In two ways his doctrine does not conform to accepted Jewish tradition. First, he suggests that God and the Lord are inferior to the Supreme Being. And secondly, he claims that the Supreme Being does not himself inflict punishment on sinful men.

Since there is no comment upon Genesis 18 and 19 in the New Testament, it does not seem that the first few generations of Christians accepted the interpretation which was given by Philo. Some of the Fathers, however, regarded Genesis 18 and 19 as important. Justin Martyr and Origen give a Christological interpretation, arguing that the three men were Christ and two angels.[2]

[1] Ibid., 119–30.

[2] Justin, *Dial.* 56, cf. 86. The position of Origen is not quite so clear. It

When Abraham said, "my lord", he used the singular verb because he was speaking to Christ. The trinitarian interpretation is found in the writings of Ambrose[1] and Augustine.[2] The more comprehensive account is given by Augustine, who claims that all three persons of the Trinity appeared to Abraham, but only the Son and the Spirit to Lot. Augustine attacks the type of exegesis which had been given by Justin and Origen. If a second-century writer had produced a trinitarian interpretation of the story, there would have been a case for assuming that it was inherited from New Testament times. But there is not evidence before the fourth century that the Christians used the story to support the doctrine of the Trinity.

Although most of the Old Testament passages which we have discussed do not seem to have influenced the thought of Christians in New Testament times, three important Hebrew ideas were used by Christians to express their beliefs about the unique relationship of the Son to the Father. They are Spirit, Wisdom, and Word. These ideas give a precedent for Binitarianism rather than Trinitarianism, for they are only found separately. It is always a question of the relationship of Spirit to God or Wisdom to God or Word to God. They are important not because they offer evidence for the idea of "twoness" in the Godhead, but because they support the idea of plurality in the Godhead. Several factors contributed to the success of these terms in expounding the new doctrine. They were all rooted in Hebrew tradition. They were all keywords of Greek philosophy. And they were all sufficiently flexible to enable the Christians to formulate a lofty conception of Christ without committing themselves to polytheism.

---

is not certain but likely that *dominus* (in *Gen. Hom.* iv) refers to Christ. In that case Abraham sees Christ. In any case, for Origen the other two men are ordinary angels.

[1] Ambrose, *De Spiritu Sancto*, II, Intro. 4; *De Excessu fratris Satyri*, II, 96; cf. *De Fide*, I, xiii.80; *De Officiis Ministrorum*, II, xxi.16.

[2] Augustine, *De Trinitate*, III, 25.

THE SPIRIT

The relationship of the Spirit to God

The Spirit was thought to be of divine origin. Often he was said to come from God and to be the Spirit of God.[1] In certain passages the parallelism implies that the Spirit is identified with Yahweh.[2] In most instances, however, he is not identified with God but is so closely linked with him as to be part of him. He is God's divine power; God's breath which gives life to men, guides them, and drives them to action.[3] In no passages of the Old Testament is he explicitly identified with God.[4]

Was the Spirit regarded as a person?

The Hebrews described the Spirit in anthropomorphic terms. The Spirit was grieved.[5] The Spirit guided men[6] and instructed them,[7] caused them to rest,[8] or rushed upon them.[9] There is reason to believe that this language is more than metaphorical. Kirk points out that there is an analogy between evil spirits and the Spirit of God.[10] Both evil spirits and the Spirit of God could dominate the actions of a human being. Evil spirits are personally conceived, and this makes it reasonable to suppose that the Spirit of God also is personally conceived. Kirk also claims that the Spirit

---

[1] E.g. Judges 13.25; Isa. 32.15; 42.1; 59.21.

[2] E.g. Ps. 139.7:

> Whither shall I go from thy spirit?
> Or whither shall I flee from thy presence?

In this verse the Spirit is equivalent to the Presence, which was a term used in Judaism as a circumlocution for God.

[3] Ezek. 37.9; Judges 3.10, etc.

[4] There was a tendency in later times for the Spirit to be more closely identified with God. Yet the strict identification was never made. Cf. Büchsel, *Der Geist Gottes im N.T.*, p. 35, and E. F. Scott, *The Spirit in the N.T.*, p. 43, who writes: "With their strong sense that the Creator must stand apart from His creation—that the true attitude towards Him must be one of awe and worship, the Hebrew thinkers fall back on the idea of an intermediary power."

[5] Isa. 63.10.   [6] Ps. 143.10.   [7] Neh. 9.20.

[8] Isa. 63.14.   [9] Judges 14.6; 15.14; 1 Sam. 11.6.

[10] K. E. Kirk, *Essays on the Trinity and the Incarnation*, p. 187.

in the Old Testament has the characteristic of selective initiative which distinguishes the personal from the impersonal.

> The Spirit is not the same to all, as a *thing* or even a drug is; it chooses its recipients among men, as it (or as Yahweh) will. It is noticeable that the Fourth Evangelist, in comparing the Spirit to the wind, selects as the point of his comparison just that one feature in which the wind, as he conceives of it, is least impersonal (though in truth it is not a characteristic of the wind at all)—that it has entire freedom of initiative. As regards men, therefore, we are not going beyond the evidence if we say that the Spirit in the Old Testament is towards them as a person.[1]

It is clear, however, as Kirk admits, that in general the initiative in the Spirit's acts is Yahweh's initiative. He says that in later Judaism the Spirit was endowed with "hypostatic character" towards Yahweh; and quotes Hag. 2.5: "When ye came out of Egypt, and my spirit abode among you."[2] But even in this example there is no suggestion of interaction between Yahweh and his Spirit. It is a one-way action, God acting through the Spirit.

The word *ruaḥ* which is translated "spirit" means wind or breath, and this suggests that spirit was regarded as something material or physical.[3] In later Judaism the Spirit was regarded as a kind of light or as a sound, or as an object which has weight.[4] But although the Spirit is regarded as in some sense physical, it does not follow that the Spirit must be impersonal.[5] The personal qualities of the Spirit are the capacity to guide, to instruct, and to be grieved, qualities which do not belong to wind, breath, light, sound, or solid bodies as such. But there is no evidence that the Jews regarded the Spirit as personal in such a way as to compromise their monotheism.

The Spirit and the Messiah

In two passages of the Old Testament the Spirit is linked with the Messiah. The first of these passages prophesies the coming of a

[1] Ibid., p. 187.   [2] Ibid., p. 188.
[3] Cf. N. H. Snaith, *Distinctive Ideas of the Old Testament*, p. 143.
[4] W. D. Davies, *Paul and Rabbinic Judaism*, pp. 183–5.
[5] K. E. Kirk, op. cit., p. 186.

descendant of David who will be blessed with the sevenfold spirit:

> And there shall come forth a shoot out of the stock of Jesse, and a branch out of his roots shall bear fruit: and the spirit of the Lord shall rest upon him, the spirit of wisdom and understanding, the spirit of counsel and might, the spirit of knowledge and of the fear of the Lord (Isa. 11.1, 2).

The second passage is not clearly Messianic, although it includes the word "anointed":[1]

> The Spirit of the Lord God is upon me; because the Lord hath anointed me to preach good tidings unto the meek (Isa. 61.1).

The ethical activity of the Spirit

In the earliest records the Spirit appears as the cause of ecstatic and violent behaviour. He leapt upon Samson and enabled him to smite the thirty men of Ashkelon. He came mightily upon Saul and enabled him to cut in pieces a yoke of oxen.[2] The Spirit was an intermittent gift which departed as swiftly as it came. In later writings the idea of the Spirit as a permanent possession became more prominent. The Spirit of judgement, counsel, and might, the Spirit of grace and supplication, is an abiding gift.[3]

The old conception of an intermittent gift of the Spirit did not disappear, but ceased to be distinctive. As the Spirit was more and more regarded as a permanent, non-ecstatic possession, his ethical function grew more apparent. He guided all classes of men in the paths of righteousness and justice. This aspect of the Spirit's work was further emphasized in the New Testament and the idea was developed that the whole of life was worship and sacrifice which could be offered to God in the Spirit.[4]

---

[1] In Isa. 42.1; "Behold my servant, whom I uphold; my chosen, in whom my soul delighteth: I have put my spirit upon him", the Spirit is linked with the servant. But there is no good evidence that the servant was connected with the Messiah before the time of Christ; cf. S. Mowinckel, *He That Cometh*, pp. 410–15.

[2] Judges 14.19; 1 Sam. 11.6 ff.

[3] Isa. 11.2; Zech. 12.10; cf. E. F. Scott, op. cit., p. 20.

[4] Cf. Rom. 12.1; Heb. 13.15–16.

The expectation of the Spirit

There was a Jewish tradition that the Spirit left the Jews after the death of the prophets Zechariah and Malachi. With this tradition was connected a prophecy that there would be a future gift of the Spirit. The prophecy is contained in Joel 2.28 ff, and was believed by Christians to have been fulfilled at Pentecost.

These five aspects of the doctrine of the Spirit had great influence upon Christian doctrine. The idea of the Spirit provided a climate in which plurality within the Godhead was conceivable. It did not lead directly to doctrines about the Person of Christ, for the concepts of Wisdom and Word were preferred in Christology, and the Spirit was regarded as a Person distinct from Christ. Although this distinctiveness was not fully admitted in the New Testament except in the Fourth Gospel, the Christian experience of the Spirit was so full and remarkable that the Spirit was regarded not as an idea which could explain the nature of Christ but as a further manifestation of the nature of God which itself required explanation.

WISDOM

An important section of Jewish literature contains the idea of the Divine Wisdom, which is depicted as an effluence of God's glory, a power emanating from him, which has an existence of its own. It may be debated whether the idea of Wisdom is hypostatized, or used as a poetical metaphor.[1] But some of the language which is used seems to be more than metaphor. According to the Book of Proverbs, Wisdom cries aloud in the streets and utters her voice in the broad places. She is capable of hate and love. At the creation she was beside God as a master-workman.[2] In the Book of Ecclesiasticus she is said to praise herself and to glory in the presence of God's power.[3] The Wisdom of Solomon describes her

---

[1] Cf. O. S. Rankin, *Israel's Wisdom Literature*, pp. 222–64, and H. Ranston, *The Old Testament Wisdom Books and their Teaching*, pp. 75–81.

[2] Prov. 8.1,2,13,17,30.　　　　[3] Ecclus. 24.1,2.

as "the artificer of all things".[1] These descriptions of Wisdom, however, reveal more conscious poetic art than those of the Spirit. Although Wisdom is described as a creature, who assists God in his work, she does not give the impression of being an irresistible power which drives men to action. She gives men instruction and advice, and is more peaceful in her working than the Spirit.

The relationship of Wisdom to God is very close. This is vividly shown in the words of Wisd. 7.25 ff:

> For she is a breath of the power of God,
> And a clear effluence of the glory of the Almighty;
> Therefore can nothing defiled find entrance into her.
> For she is an effulgence from everlasting light,
> And an unspotted mirror of the working of God,
> And an image of his goodness.

Yet in spite of this close connection, she is different from God, for she makes men the friends of God and lives with God and is loved by him.[2] According to the Book of Proverbs she was formed by God, and worked with him, and rejoiced before him.[3] Thus she is more than an effluence of God. She has a conscious life of her own. She is an extension of the divine personality, an extension which suggests that there is plurality in the Godhead.

The doctrine of the Divine Wisdom was popularized in the last four centuries before Christ. It attempted to satisfy a deep need in the Jews' thought about God. After the exile they laid increasing emphasis upon the transcendence of God. He was of a different order from anything that had been created. Man could not behold him and live. Everything must tremble in awe before him. This idea of transcendence became so strong that the Jews found it difficult to account for God's presence in the world and his interest in its affairs. They could not reconcile the divine immanence with the divine transcendence. Although they were not influenced by Aristotle's theory that the perfect God has no concern for the imperfect world, they were confronted with Aristotle's difficulty. They found it hard to explain God's activity in the world. Aristotle came to the conclusion that God moved the world only by attraction. God's sublimity was not marred by the thought of men or

[1] Wisd. 7.22; cf. 8.5; 14.2.　　[2] Wisd. 7.27-8.　　[3] Prov. 8.22,30.

earthly things. The Jews rejected this answer, for they believed in a personal God, who was active in the world. They attempted to solve their problem by assuming that an intermediary power took part in the creation and maintenance of the universe. Wisdom was such a power.

The idea of Wisdom was taken over by Christian thinkers in order to explain the relationship of Christ to God. Although it was not especially connected with the Messiah in Old Testament times or in later Judaism, it was very suitable for adaptation by Christians, who wished to explain the nature of Christ. It is not surprising that the language of Wisdom literature was used by Paul and the author of Hebrews to interpret their thought about the Person of Christ.[1]

THE WORD

A third important idea in Judaism was "Word". When God wished to communicate with men, he spoke to them. Moses heard his voice from the burning bush (Ex. 3.2 ff). His word was given to the prophets.[2] When the world was created, it came into being at his spoken command.

> By the word of the Lord were the heavens made;
> And all the host of them by the breath of his mouth. . . .
> For he spake, and it was done;
> He commanded and it stood fast
>
> (Ps. 33.6,9; cf. Gen. 1.3,6).

In the Old Testament, however, the "Word" is not personified. It defines the way in which God executes his purpose. It is not itself an existent being. Even in the apocryphal writings it is not really personified. The nearest approach is Wisd. 18.15, 16:

> Thine almighty word leaped from heaven . . . bearing as a sharp sword thine unfeigned commandment; and standing it filled all things with death; and while it touched the heaven, it trod upon the earth.

This bizarre language seems metaphorical rather than literal, and provides no sure proof of the personification of the idea.

It has been argued that the concept *Memra* (Word) in the

---

[1] 1 Cor. 1.24, 30; Col. 1.15–17; 2.3; Heb. 1.1–3.
[2] E.g. Isa. 2.1; Jer. 1.4; Ezek. 2.1; Hos. 1.1; Amos 3.1, etc.

Targums was personified. *Memra* was used as a reverential substitute for God, and for that reason is often said to perform personal activities and have personal feelings. But since this and other words were employed as substitutes for the divine name *Yahweh*, there is no reason for assuming that *Memra* itself was personified.[1]

Philo makes frequent use of the term λόγος (word), sometimes in a way which suggests that it is a person. C. H. Dodd comments: "In spite of all personification, Philo is not really thinking of a personal guide and companion. The Logos is the world of ideas."[2] Nevertheless it is difficult to avoid the impression that Philo regards the Logos as a person. He says that it sustains the world and its inhabitants, and describes it as a high priest, an angel, a captain, and a steersman.[3] Although his account of λόγος is not always consistent, in many places he writes as if the λόγος were a conscious being.

Λόγος is prominent in the first chapter of the Fourth Gospel, where it is used as a title of Christ. This chapter shows the influence of the creation story of Genesis. W. F. Howard has argued that the evangelist has derived the idea of λόγος from the Old Testament and from rabbinic tradition.[4] But this does not account for the use of the term in a personified sense. John's use of λόγος in a personal sense is best explained by the influence of Philo or of Philo's unknown predecessors. Through the Hellenistic tradition the idea of "Word", like the ideas of "Wisdom" and "Spirit", helped to pave the way for Christian theology.

Two other terms of influence are "Law" and "Glory". The Law is connected in Jewish thought both with Wisdom and the Word. Ecclesiasticus 24 identifies the Law and Wisdom. And in Psalm 119 "Word" and "Law" are used interchangeably. According to rabbinic tradition the Law existed before the creation of the world and was an instrument in creation.[5]

[1] G. F. Moore, op. cit. pp. 416 f.
[2] C. H. Dodd, *Interpretation of the Fourth Gospel*, p. 69.
[3] Ibid., p. 68.   [4] *Christianity according to St John*, pp. 47–53.
[5] W. D. Davies, op. cit., pp. 170–2. In Pirke Aboth 3.23, the Law is described as "a precious instrument whereby the world was created". Cf. Sifre Deut on 11.10.

Shekinah (Glory) was used like *Memra* as a reverential substitute for the divine name. There is no hint that the rabbis regarded it as a person.[1]

Both Law and Glory were closely linked with Christ in the New Testament. He was himself the embodiment of the new Law of the Spirit.[2] He was the mediator of a new covenant, who contrasted his law with the law of Moses. He possessed a glory which he manifested at various times in his earthly life, in miracles, and at his transfiguration. In his risen state, he reigned in glory with the Father.[3]

It has been shown that the post-exilic Jews had an idea of plurality within the God-head, which was chiefly expressed through the concepts of Spirit, Wisdom, and Word. This idea of plurality is not to be found in all Jewish writings, but occurs in parts of the Old Testament, in some of the apocryphal books, and in the works of Philo.

Whereas the earlier Jews had spoken of angels as if they were extensions of the divine personality, the later concepts of Wisdom, Spirit, and Word were less obviously personal. The language of the writers often implies that these entities had a separate existence and thought and feelings like men. But Wisdom, Spirit, and Word do not appear in human form. They are more in the nature of self-conscious emanations from God. The Jews believed in angels, but angels were creatures which were of lower rank than God. Although Wisdom was a creature, she had a rank of special elevation because of her closeness to God.

The general point which Johnson and Knight have made is true. The concept of plurality in the Godhead is not strange to the Jews. It is conceivable that a trinitarian doctrine should have grown on Jewish soil. While Hellenistic thought made a great contribution to the expression of the doctrine, the idea of plurality within unity was already implicit in Jewish theology.

[1] Cf. G. F. Moore, op. cit., pp. 437–8.
[2] Cf. W. D. Davies, op. cit., pp. 169–75. Note how by saying "Take my yoke upon you", Jesus contrasted himself with the yoke of *torah*.
[3] Cf. John 1.14; 2.11; Luke 9.32; 2 Pet. 1.16, 17; 2 Cor. 3.18.

Extension and Interaction of Personality

The extension of the divine personality was not the main problem for the interpreters of the Christian doctrine of God. The doctrines of Wisdom and the Spirit were generally acceptable to Jews. Rigid monotheists did not find in them an insuperable obstacle to their faith. The problem which was presented by the Christian belief in Christ was of a different order. For Christ was no emanation from the Godhead. He was not a personified concept, an invisible idea which thought like a man or felt like a man. Christ did not resemble a man. He was a man. And because he was a man, his relationship to God was not entirely passive. He did not respond to the directions of God like a puppet. He was capable of questioning the divine commands, of praying for the avoidance of suffering, and of giving vent to expressions of despair in the moment of death.[1] When he communed with the Father it was real communion. The conversation between Jesus and his Father was not one-sided. The traffic of thought travelled both ways. Although Jesus was an extension of the divine personality, he exhibited more than extension. In his dealings with his Father there was an interaction within the divine personality. There was a dialogue within the Godhead.

Was this interaction a distinctive feature of the Christian conception of God? Or can it be found in Hebrew and Jewish writings? There is little evidence for it in the Old Testament, and only the faintest traces can be found in passages which describe the activity of the Spirit and Wisdom and the Word.

In 1 Kings 22.21 ff the lying spirit which entered into Zedekiah speaks to God in conversation:

> And there came forth a spirit, and stood before the Lord, and said, I will entice him. And the Lord said unto him, Wherewith? And he said, I will go forth, and will be a lying spirit in the mouth of all his prophets.

But since this spirit was not the Holy Spirit but a lying spirit, this is not an example of interaction within the divine personality.

Wisdom is said to live with God (Wisd. 8.3), and to make men friends of God, and to open her mouth in the congregation of the

[1] Mark 14.36; 15.34.

Most High (Ecclus. 24.2), but her conversation before God is of a purely formal type. She obeys God's commands and glories in his presence. There is no suggestion that she has any personal dialogue with him.

There is no convincing evidence of genuine interaction between the Word and God. The statement that God's word will not return to him void (Isa. 55.11) does not imply a personal relationship.

In the Old Testament there is little trace of the idea of interaction within the divine personality. The Christian's attitude to Jesus, however, begins with the fact of interaction, for Jesus first confronted his followers as a man. They first met him as one who went with them to the synagogue and the Temple. They saw him walk apart into the mountain to pray. They heard him call upon God as his Father. He even told them that there was something—namely, the day of the Son of Man—which his Father knew and he did not know (Mark 13.32). The story of Gethsemane shows Jesus pleading with his Father. And the words from the Cross show him despairing of his Father. When he was exalted, he was supposed to make intercession with the Father.[1] He was no mere extension of the divine personality. He was a separate person with a life of his own.

For the orthodox Jew, the trouble about Christ was not that he was regarded as an extension of the divine personality, but that he was believed to have been incarnate. If he had been a concept and nothing more, he would not have been a serious stumbling-block to the Jews. It was the combination of beliefs about his exalted state with the fact that he had lived a life of flesh and blood which offended the Jews. There was nothing else like it in Judaism. Although Jewish concepts were used in an attempt to explain Jesus' relationship to the Father, these concepts were not sufficient for the task. Jewish thought did not admit of this kind of plurality within the Godhead. It had no room for a second person within the Godhead, who not only did the will of the Father but conversed with him, took counsel with him, and pleaded with him. If Jesus had been just a messenger of God, his earthly appearance

[1] Rom. 8.34; Heb. 7.25; 1 John 2.1.

would have been tolerable, for he could have been described as an angel. But he had claimed the divine functions of judgement and salvation. And after his exaltation he was regarded by his followers as at least equal with the Divine Wisdom. Although Judaism provided some of the concepts, the reality was too great to be explained by the ideas of the past. Perhaps it was for this reason that in the Christology of Colossians Paul dispensed with the term "Wisdom", although he used language which was associated with Wisdom. Perhaps it was also for this reason that the Church sought help from Greek metaphysics and psychology. The idea of extension of divine personality is Hebraic. The idea of interaction within the extended personality is neither Hebraic nor Hellenistic but Christian.

CHAPTER 3

ONE GOD AND FATHER

The Jews believed in one God whom they called Father. They called him by other titles and often spoke of him by periphrases such as "the name", "the place", "the heavens". But for an understanding of the growth of the doctrine of the Trinity the title "Father" is of special importance, because in the Trinity one of the persons is God the Father. In this chapter it will be shown how the New Testament writers expressed their belief in the unity of God and described him as Father.

In the following passages God is described as one:

None is good save one, even God (Mark 10.18).

The Lord our God, the Lord is one (Mark 12.29, a quotation from Deut. 6.4).

And call no man your father on earth; for one is your Father which is in heaven (Matt. 23.9).

... if so be that God is one (Rom. 3.30).

We know that no idol is anything in the world, and that there is no God but one (1 Cor. 8.4).

Yet to us there is one God, the Father... (1 Cor. 8.6).

Now a mediator is not a mediator of one; but God is one (Gal. 3.20).

... one God and Father of all (Eph. 4.6).

Now unto the King, eternal, incorruptible, invisible, the only God, be honour and glory for ever and ever (1 Tim. 1.17).

For there is one God, one mediator also between God and men (1 Tim. 2.5).

Thou believest that God is one; thou doest well (Jas. 2.19).

One is the lawgiver and judge, he who is able to save and to destroy (Jas. 4.12).

To the only God our Saviour, through Jesus Christ our Lord, be glory, majesty, dominion, and power, before all time, and now, and for evermore (Jude 25).

And the glory that cometh from the only one ye seek not (John 5.44).
(Some manuscripts read "only God" for "only one".)

And this is life eternal, that they should know thee, the only true God, and him whom thou didst send, Jesus Christ (John 17.3).

In eight of these fifteen passages (Mark 10.18; Matt. 23.9; 1 Cor. 8.6; Gal. 3.20; Eph. 4.6; 1 Tim. 2.5; Jude 25; John 17.3) God is explicitly distinguished from Jesus Christ. In three of the passages (Matt. 23.9; 1 Cor. 8.6; Eph. 4.6) and also in the context of John 17.3, God is called Father.

The evidence shows that God was regarded as one, and that the one God was believed to be the Father of the Lord Jesus Christ. Statements of this nature hardly seem to provide fruitful ground for the growth of a doctrine of the Trinity. Yet when they are taken in conjunction with other statements in which the divinity of Christ is affirmed or implied, they lead immediately to the trinitarian problem.

The title "Father" differs from most other titles and functions of God in that it was not given to Christ. It will be argued in a later chapter that in the New Testament the title "God" itself was occasionally given to Christ. Usually, however, it refers to the Father of Christ. The title "Lord", which was given to God in the Old Testament, is used in the New Testament both of God the Father and Christ the Son. The functions of judgement, creation, and salvation are ascribed, as will be shown, to both Father and Son. But there is one title which is never given to Christ the Son, and that, as may be expected, is "Father". The application of the title "Father" to Christ would not have been impossible, for in Isa. 9.6 the future king is called "Everlasting Father". It would have been fitting for an anointed king to be called the Father of his people. But in fact the title "Father" was confined to him who was Father of Christ.

The idea of God as Father is not restricted to Christianity or even to the Hebrew-Christian tradition. It is found in many ancient religions. In early Indian religion it was believed that vegetation was the offspring of a union between Earth who was its mother and Heaven, or Dyaus, who was its father.[1]

[1] Schrenk, *TWNT*, V, p. 951.

In Greek religion Zeus, the chief of the Gods, was regularly addressed as "Father Zeus", and Homer calls him "Father of men and gods".[1] The mystery religions taught men to believe in a divine father who could give them rebirth. Mithras was called "father of the faithful". Osiris was said to be the father of Horus, and in the cult of Cybele men called upon Attis as father.[2]

The doctrine of the Fatherhood of God is also found in the writings of Greek philosophers, especially those who were influenced by Plato. In his *Republic* Plato gives the title "Father" to the Idea of the Good, which he believed to be the supreme reality and to be the necessary condition of the existence of the other ideas and of the physical universe.[3] In another dialogue, the *Timaeus*, he gives the name "Father" to the Demiurge who, he says, is creator of the world.[4] The description of God as Father is found also in later Greek philosophy. The Stoic Epictetus calls God the Father of men,[5] and the later Platonists Numenius and Porphyry say that he is Father of the Cosmos.[6]

The Christian belief in the Fatherhood of God, however, was not derived from the Greek tradition, but was indebted rather to Hebrew thought. Although "Father" is not a common title of God in the Old Testament, it occurs in many different writings, and is found at many stages of Hebrew history. As Father, God is creator of man.

> But now, O Lord, thou art our father; we are the clay, and thou art the potter; and we are all the work of thy hand (Isa. 64.8).

The title is used chiefly in connection with the election of the nation. He is the Father of Israel (Jer. 31.9; cf. Mal. 2.10). The people are his sons (Isa. 1.2; 30.1; Jer. 3.22; Isa. 45.11) and the nation collectively is his son (Hos. 11.1; Ex. 4.22). He is also described as Father of the anointed king (2 Sam. 7.14; Ps. 2.7; 89.27).

In later Judaism God was regarded as Father of the individual as well as the nation, but the emphasis was on his Fatherhood of the nation. This idea is found in the Targum and Midrash and in

[1] Od. i.28, Il. i.544; cf. *TWNT*, V, pp. 952–3.
[2] *TWNT*, V, pp. 953–4.   [3] Rep. VI.506e.   [4] Tim. 41a.
[5] *TWNT*, V, p. 956.   [6] Ibid, p. 955.

the pseudepigraphical writings. In one passage the Midrash refers to him as "Father of the whole world", but such a description is exceptional.[1] His Fatherhood is usually explained by his protective care for the Jewish race.[2]

In apocryphal writings God's Fatherhood is often connected with his Lordship, and the two titles "Father" and "Lord" are used in close proximity (Ecclus. 23.1, 4; 51.10; Tob. 13.4; 3 Macc. 5.7). A favourite rabbinic phrase was "Father in heaven".[3] This was not used to emphasize the transcendence of God but to distinguish him from earthly Fathers. The phrase was used often in worship, and God was regularly addressed as Father (e.g. Ecclus. 23.4; Wisd. 14.3; 3 Macc. 6.3, 8).

The title occurred in both Hebrew and other religions, but was given a distinctive content in Christian thought and worship. It is found in the teaching of Jesus himself, as it is recorded in the synoptic gospels. It is often assumed that one of the main features of Jesus' teaching was his emphasis on the Fatherhood of God. If the Fourth Gospel is accepted as a faithful account of the words of Jesus, the teaching about God's Fatherhood is very prominent. But in the synoptic gospels the picture is different. Indeed the sources which have the greatest claim to authenticity contain little teaching about the Fatherhood of God. In the Gospel according to St Mark, God is called Father only four times. In Q, the material common to Luke and Matthew, Jesus calls him Father eight times (four of which occur in one passage), and in the material peculiar to Luke Jesus calls God Father on seven occasions. An entirely different picture, however, is given by Matthew. In the material peculiar to Matthew Jesus calls God Father twenty-two times. In addition to this there are eight synoptic passages in which Matthew has the title "Father" where it is absent from the parallels. This shows a tendency of Matthew to introduce the title. Therefore the more reliable evidence is contained in the sayings from Mark, Luke, and Q.

[1] Midr. Prov. x.1; cf. Schrenk, op. cit., p. 978.
[2] Cf. 3 Macc. 7.6: "The God in heaven has securely shielded the Jews, as a father who always fights for his sons."
[3] Schrenk, op. cit., pp. 979–80; Dalman, *Words of Jesus*, pp. 184–9.

In Mark Jesus calls God Father in the following sayings:

For whosoever shall be ashamed of me and of my words in this adulterous and sinful generation, the Son of man also shall be ashamed of him, when he cometh in the glory of his Father with the holy angels (8.38).

And whensoever ye stand praying, forgive, if ye have ought against anyone; that your Father also which is in heaven may forgive you your trespasses (11.25).

But of that day or that hour knoweth no one, not even the angels in heaven, neither the Son, but the Father (13.32).

Abba, Father, all things are possible unto thee (14.36).

T. W. Manson points out that all these instances occur after Peter's confession of Jesus' Messiahship at Caesarea Philippi.[1] But as there is little certainty about the chronological order of Jesus' sayings, no sure conclusion can be drawn from Manson's observations.

Two important comments can be made about these four passages. First, in none of them does Jesus speak of God as the Father of both himself and the disciples together. God is either Jesus' Father (8.38) or the disciples' Father (11.25). The absolute "Father" in 13.32 is so closely linked with "the Son" that it is clear that in this verse God is regarded as Jesus' Father.

Secondly, the Aramaic word 'abba, which is retained in the Greek text of 14.36, shows how intimate was the relationship between Jesus and God. 'Abba was a familiar mode of speech which was reserved for one's own father. When men addressed God as Father, they would use the more formal 'abuna (our father), but one's own father would be addressed by using the absolute state of the noun, which is 'abba. Jews did not use this absolute form to address God, because it implied too great a familiarity. When Jesus used 'abba of God he was making a startling innovation.[2] He was claiming a relationship with God which was closer than that which was claimed by any of his countrymen. He was claiming a unique kind of sonship.

---

[1] *Teaching of Jesus*, p. 101.
[2] T. W. Manson, *Sayings of Jesus*, p. 168; Dalman, op. cit., pp. 191–2.

Of the sayings common to Luke and Matthew the following contain a reference to God as Father:

Ye therefore shall be perfect, as your heavenly Father is perfect (Matt. 5.48).

which is similar to:

Be ye merciful, even as your Father is merciful (Luke 6.36).

I thank thee, O Father, Lord of heaven and earth, that thou didst hide these things from the wise and understanding, and didst reveal them unto babes. . . . All things have been delivered unto me of my Father: and no one knoweth who the Son is, save the Father; and who the Father is save the Son, and he to whomsoever the Son willeth to reveal him (Luke 10.21–2 = Matt 11.25–7).

Our Father, which art in heaven, Hallowed be thy name (Matt. 6.9).

which is parallel to:

Father, Hallowed be thy name (Luke 11.2).

. . . how much more shall your Father which is in heaven give good things to them that ask him? (Matt. 7.11; Luke 11.13 is the same except that it has "Holy Spirit" for "good things".)

But your Father knoweth that ye have need of these things (Luke 12.30 = Matt. 6.32).

Of these passages there are five in which the title Father is used of God, four times in one of them, and once in each of the other four. In these passages, as in Mark, Jesus never links himself with other men, when he calls God Father. In Luke 10.21–2 it is "my Father" or "the Father". In the other passages it is "your Father". An exception is the Lord's Prayer, which has two forms— "Father" in Luke and "Our Father" in Matthew. If the Lukan version is original, as it is likely to be, it is another example of the intimate form of address ʾabba, and Jesus is instructing his disciples to use this mode of address. If we accept Matthew's "Our Father", "Our" does not include Jesus but refers to the disciples. "When ye pray, say 'Our Father'." "Ye" means the disciples only.

Another point of importance in these passages is that Matthew in 5.48 and 6.32 has "your heavenly Father" for Luke's "your Father". This is an example of Matthew's fondness for the form "your heavenly Father", more instances of which will be discussed later.

In the material peculiar to Luke there are the following examples of the title "Father" for God.

... I must be about my Father's business (2.49).

... it is your Father's good pleasure to give you the kingdom (12.32).

And I appoint unto you a kingdom, even as my Father appointed unto me (22.29).

Father, if thou be willing, remove this cup from me (22.42).

Father, forgive them, for they know not what they do (23.34).

Father, into thy hands I commend my spirit (23.46).

And, behold, I send forth the promise of my Father upon you (24.49).

Of these seven sayings 2.49 belongs to the infancy narratives, and 24.49 to the resurrection narratives; 23.34 is not contained in the most reliable manuscripts. The authenticity of 23.46 has often been questioned because it does not form a part of the words from the cross recorded in the other Passion narratives. Of the remaining three sayings two come from Jesus' teaching and the other from the Gethsemane story.

In three of these sayings Jesus addresses God as "Father", which is probably a translation of ʾabba. And the pronominal adjectives in the other sayings are either "my" or "your".

In Luke 15 the main point of the parable of the Prodigal Son is the comparison of God's mercy with the father's, and no reader can fail to liken the father in the parable to God. It would be artificial to confine the point of comparison to the merciful attitude of both God and the prodigal's father, and not to extend it to the fact that both God and the father exercise the paternal office.

The title "Father" is used of God forty-four times in Matthew as against sixteen or seventeen times in Luke and four times in Mark. If the instances are divided according to the sources which are suggested by the Four Document Hypothesis, they are (according to T. W. Manson)[1] Mark 4, Q.8 or 9, Matt. 22 or possibly 23, and Luke 6. These statistics show a great difference between Matthew and the other synoptic gospels in the use of the title. The nature of the evidence reveals that the evangelist had a tendency

[1] *Teaching of Jesus*, p. 99.

to introduce the title where it was not present in the original tradition. In eight passages Matthew has the title "Father" where it is not present in the synoptic parallels (Matt. 5.45; 6.26; 7.21; 10.20,29; 12.50; 20.23; 26.29). It is possible that Jesus could have uttered two similar sayings with slight variations. But the evidence mentioned cannot be explained in this way, for in no parallel does Luke have the title "Father" when it is absent from Matthew and Mark, nor does Mark have the title when it is absent from Matthew and Luke. Because of this clear tendency to introduce the title, the twenty-two occurrences of "Father" in the matter peculiar to Matthew cannot be regarded as reliable evidence for Jesus' regular use of the title.

On the other hand, the small number of instances of the title in Mark and Luke suggests that the tradition is reliable. The evidence of Mark and Luke does not imply that Jesus hardly ever called God Father. It does imply that his use of the title did not impress the disciples in such a way that it was emphasized in the earliest tradition. Moreover the use of the word ʾabba by Jesus stands out as a permanent element in the tradition. Luke's version of the Lord's prayer suggests that Jesus instructed his disciples to address God as ʾabba. At the same time the phrases "our Father" and "my Father" were used in such a way as to make a clear distinction between Jesus' relationship to God and the disciples' relationship to God. The impression is given that men can avail themselves of God's Fatherhood through their discipleship of Jesus who called God ʾabba.

The emphasis on the Fatherhood of God is taken up in the writings of Paul, who often uses "the God and Father of our Lord Jesus Christ" and similar phrases (Rom. 15.6; 2 Cor. 1.3; 11.31; Eph.1.3; Col. 1.3). God is also called "our Father" (1 Cor. 1.3; 8.6; 2 Cor. 1.2; Gal. 1.4; Eph. 1.2; Phil. 1.2; 4.20; Col. 1.2; 1 Thess. 1.3; 3.11,13; 2 Thess. 1.1; 2.16; Philem. 3).

Although he is generally regarded as the Father either of Christ or of Christian believers, in Eph. 4.6 he is described as "one God and Father of all, who is over all and through all and in all". But this idea is not a dominant theme in the writings of Paul.

Like the evangelists Paul retains the Aramaic ʾabba. Thus in

Gal. 4.6 he writes: "And because ye are sons, God sent forth the Spirit of his son into our hearts, crying Abba, Father." And in Rom. 8.15: "But ye received the spirit of adoption, whereby we cry, Abba, Father."

He agrees with the Lukan version of the Lord's Prayer in allowing the Christian believers to use the familiar form of address to God.

The title Father is given twice to God in the Epistle to the Hebrews (1.5; 12.9). In Heb. 1.5 the writer is quoting 2 Sam. 7.14 which he uses as evidence that God is Father of the Messiah. And in 12.9 God is described as the Father of spirits.

The title is rarely found in the Pastoral Epistles (1 Tim. 1.2; 2 Tim. 1.2; Titus 1.4). It is used of God three times in James (1.17, 27; 3.9), in one of which (1.17) he is called "Father of Lights". It occurs thrice in 1 Peter (1.2,3,17) once in 2 Peter (1.17), once in Jude (verse 1), and five times in Revelation (1.6; 2.27; 3.5,21; 14.1), but only three times in Acts (1.4,7; 2.33).

The title is found very frequently in the Johannine writings, in both the gospel and the epistles. Usually God is called "the Father", and there may be a trace of the Aramaic *'abba* behind this, as the absolute state could be translated in Greek by the noun with definite article. Often Jesus refers to "my Father", and on one occasion in argument with Jesus the Jews said, "We have one father, God" (John 8.41). Jesus describes God as "your Father" in only one saying (John 20.17): "I ascend unto my Father and your Father." The phrasing here makes a distinction between God as the Father of Jesus and God as the Father of Christians, a distinction which is found already in the synoptic sayings of Jesus, and is confirmed by John's contrast between Jesus the only-begotten Son of God and his followers who are children of God.

The evidence which has been considered shows that, although the title "Father" was used frequently in pre-Christian times, its use in the New Testament, especially in the sayings of Jesus and the writings of Paul and John, emphasizes that God is the Father of Jesus Christ. The title is interpreted in a distinctively Christian sense. It is rarely mentioned that he is Father of all things. Often he is described as the Father of Christian believers. But the distinctive emphasis is upon his Fatherhood of Christ. This made it possible for Christians to conceive of a Father-Son relationship within the Godhead, and to discover a plurality within the unity of God.

PART II

The Divinity of Christ

CHAPTER 4

JESUS CHRIST IS GOD

The central problem of the Trinity is that of the divinity of Christ and the relationship of Christ to the Father. The problem will be the theme of this and the following six chapters. First the names "God" and "Lord" will be discussed in so far as they are used of Christ. Then the evidence for the worship of Jesus will be considered, and his connection with the divine functions of judgement, creation, and salvation will be examined. The New Testament's attempts to explain the relationship between Father and Son will be the theme of the concluding chapter of this part.

In the course of the discussion several of the titles of Jesus will be mentioned, including "God", "Lord", "Son of God", "Son of Man", "Wisdom", "Word". There is one important omission, "Christ" or "Anointed". This title does not imply that the bearer is divine. The "Anointed" in the Old Testament, which is translated in Greek by Χριστός, can describe the king of Israel, the high priest, or a foreign conqueror such as Cyrus. In later times it refers to the eschatological Messiah, but in no way connotes divinity. The use of this title with reference to Jesus does not raise the problem of the Trinity, and therefore is not relevant to this discussion. Names and titles will be discussed which imply that Jesus is God and performs exclusively divine functions, or which are used to interpret the closeness of the relationship between God the Father and the Lord Jesus Christ.

The first title to be considered is "God". The Jews believed that there was one God, and this belief was accepted by the early Christians. Jesus himself quoted the words of the Law that "the Lord our God, the Lord is one" (Mark 12.29, from Deut. 6.4). This affirmation was repeated and never questioned by Christians of New Testament times.

53

In several verses of the New Testament, however, it seems that Jesus is described as God. The meaning of most of these verses has been disputed. Their interpretation is of crucial importance for an understanding of the early Christian attitude to Christ. Each of them will be discussed in detail, and in an additional note certain other passages will be examined in which it is possible but unlikely that Christ is being called God.

The Pauline Epistles

. . . ἐξ ὧν ὁ Χριστὸς τὸ κατὰ σάρκα ὁ ὢν ἐπὶ πάντων θεὸς εὐλογητὸς εἰς τοὺς αἰῶνας, ἀμήν (Rom. 9.5).

If there is no full stop until the end of the passage (ἀμήν), then Christ is being called God, and the passage can be translated:

. . . of whom is Christ as concerning the flesh, who is over all, God blessed for ever, Amen.

If a full stop is placed after σάρκα (flesh) or ἐπὶ πάντων (over all), then the passage does not imply that Christ is God, and may be translated in one of the following ways:

(a) . . . of whom is Christ as concerning the flesh. He who is God over all be (or is) blessed for ever, Amen.

(b) . . . of whom is Christ as concerning the flesh. He who is over all is God blessed for ever, Amen.

(c) . . . of whom is Christ as concerning the flesh, who is over all. God be (or is) blessed for ever, Amen.

As there were no punctuation marks in the original text, the translation of the passage cannot be decided by arguments about punctuation.[1] Therefore the grammar of the passage must be examined, and this favours the view that Christ is called God. Three considerations support this view.

[1] The majority of the Fathers support the view that the first full stop comes at the end of the passage. But the punctuation of some of the oldest uncial manuscripts offers slight evidence in favour of a full stop after σάρκα (flesh). Codex Vaticanus has a colon, probably inserted by a later hand, and Codex Ephraemi has a stop at this point of the passage. For a full discussion see Sanday and Headlam, *Romans*, pp. 233–4.

An attempt has been made to emend the text. If ὧν ὁ were substituted for ὁ ὤν, the passage could be translated ". . . whose is Christ as concerning the flesh, whose is God over all, blessed for ever". There is no manuscript evidence to support this emendation, which cannot be considered successful.

JESUS CHRIST IS GOD

(*a*) If the verse ended with a doxology to God the Father, we should expect εὐλογητός (blessed) to come at the beginning of the sentence. That is nearly always the word-order of the doxology in biblical Greek. The order would be changed only for some special reason. If however the doxology is addressed to Christ, εὐλογητός cannot be placed at the beginning of the clause, but naturally comes later.[1]

Moreover doxologies in the writings of Paul usually refer to someone who has been mentioned beforehand. The name of God does not occur in Romans 9 until the end of verse 5. Christ is mentioned several times. If Rom. 9.5 follows the general tendency of Pauline doxologies, it is ascribed to someone who is named in the preceding sentences. The only possible antecedent is Christ.[2]

(*b*) The words ὁ ὤν (who is) also present a problem. If the doxology is a separate sentence, the word ὤν is superfluous and it would have been sufficient to say ὁ ἐπὶ πάντων θεός (God over all). The position of ὁ ὤν suggests that it is attached to an antecedent. There are examples of similar relatival uses of the article and participle which do not refer to an antecedent,[3] but as Sanday and Headlam remark, "In this case, as there is a noun immediately preceding to which the words would naturally refer, as there is no sign of a change of subject, and as there is no finite verb in the sentence following, an ordinary reader would consider that the words ὁ ὤν ἐπὶ πάντων θεός refer to what precedes unless they suggest so great an antithesis to his mind that he could not refer them to Christ."[4]

(*c*) The words τὸ κατὰ σάρκα (as concerning the flesh) seem to expect an antithesis. Although the most probable antithesis would be τὸ κατὰ πνεῦμα (as concerning the spirit), there are

---

[1] 2 Cor. 11.31, . . . ὁ ὤν εὐλογητὸς εἰς τοὺς αἰῶνας is an example of εὐλογητός in a similar position. For a discussion of the position of εὐλογητός see Lagrange, *Epître aux Romains*, p. 227; Sanday and Headlam, op. cit., p. 236; Lietzmann, *Römerbrief*, p. 90; Cullmann, *Christologie*, p. 321.

[2] Other examples of doxologies which refer to antecedents are Rom. 1.25; Gal. 1.5. See also Lagrange, op. cit., p. 227.

[3] John 3.31; Rom. 8.5,8.   [4] Op. cit., pp. 235–6.

instances in which θεός is contrasted with σάρξ.[1] The phrase τὸ κατὰ σάρκα does not strictly require an antithesis. As Baur has shown, it can be argued that the phrase was introduced not to make a contrast with θεός but to avoid making a concession to the Judaizing Christians. Christ belonged to the Jews, but only as far as the flesh was concerned.[2] Nevertheless the passage would read more naturally if there were some kind of antithesis.

The grammatical evidence supports the view that Christ was called God. Paul would not be likely to vary his idiom, even unconsciously, unless he were making a startling statement. But those who wish to give an unusual interpretation of the language do not claim that Paul has said anything startling.

Psychological as well as grammatical arguments have been used in the discussion of this verse. Scholars claim that it is improbable or even impossible that Paul could identify Jesus with God because such an identification is inconsistent with the rest of his thought.

An example of this kind of reasoning is found in Anderson Scott's *Christianity according to St Paul*. According to Anderson Scott Jewish monotheism was so deeply ingrained in the mind of Paul that he could not have identified Jesus with God. "What we do seem to see is the Apostle being pressed by his experience and urged by his convictions up to the verge of acknowledging that Christ is God, but finally precluded from making such acknowledgement by his hereditary monotheism."[3] On these grounds Anderson Scott refuses to accept the view that Rom. 9.5 includes an identification of Christ with God.

Kirk rejects the identification for a similar reason: "So understood it is a curiously crude statement of a great truth, and singularly unlike St. Paul's general manner of dealing with such profound questions. It is difficult to imagine that if he were content to speak so frankly here he should not have done so elsewhere in his epistles, where countless opportunities for such a course presented themselves."[4]

---

[1] Luke 3.6; 1 Cor. 1.29; Col. 3.22; Philem. 16; 2 Chron. 32.8; Ps. 56. 4; Jer. 17.5; Dan. 2.11. See Sanday and Headlam, op. cit., p. 235.

[2] F. C. Baur, *Paulus*, p. 624.

[3] *Christianity According to St Paul*, p. 274.   [4] *Romans*, pp. 103–4.

Other scholars bring forth similar arguments.[1] The claim is made that, since Paul was a man of a particular character, brought up in a particular environment, he could not have made the statement that Christ was God. Or, if he had made the statement, he would have repeated it.

These arguments fail to convince. We are not in a position to say with an air of finality what was psychologically impossible for Paul. We are certainly not in a position to say that he was incapable of inconsistencies. His surviving works are small in quantity. If one or two thoughts which they contain do not seem to harmonize with the rest, we ought not to imagine that we can resolve the apparent discord only by finding a different interpretation of the Greek. Perhaps we are not fully attuned to Paul's mode of thought, which we have limited opportunities for studying because of the small quantity of his writing which has been preserved. Beliefs which are mentioned only briefly in the surviving epistles may have been expressed at greater length in works which have perished. Some thoughts, which had great prominence in his private teaching and his devotional life, may have been deliberately veiled in the epistles. It is quite possible, for example, that he believed that Christ was God, and communicated this belief privately to his followers, but was reluctant to include it in his letters because he had not yet reconciled it in thought with his Jewish monotheism. Other men have held beliefs which they could not explain rationally.

Sanday and Headlam argue that the words "who is God over all", etc., fit into the progress of thought in Romans 9: "St. Paul is enumerating the privileges of Israel, and as the highest and last privilege he reminds his readers that it was from this Jewish stock after all that Christ in His human nature had come, and then in order to emphasise this he dwells on the exalted character of Him who came according to the flesh as the Jewish Messiah."[2]

This explanation does not account for Paul's reluctance to call Christ God in other parts of his writings. Sanday and Headlam have shown how Rom. 9.5 can fit its context. They have not shown how it fits in with the rest of the apostle's thought. If he wished to introduce this clear proclamation of the divinity of Christ into his

---

[1] Cf. Baur, op. cit., p. 624; Dodd, *Romans*, p. 152.   [2] Op. cit., p. 236.

epistles, why did he not do so more often? Why did he not expand and explain the idea, instead of thrusting it forward abruptly and passing immediately to another theme? In the ninth chapter of the Epistle to the Romans nothing else is said about the Person of Christ, nothing about his relationship to the Father, nothing about his Lordship, nothing about his work in creation. While Paul may have described Christ as God in other writings which have not been preserved, the assumption that there were unknown epistles does not account for the abruptness with which he leaves this remarkable statement of the divinity of Christ undeveloped and unexplained.

The clue to the passage may well be found in Paul's emotions. When he reached the point of saying that "Christ according to the flesh" belonged to the Jews, he could have proceeded to make a statement about "Christ as concerning the Spirit". Instead of following the expected train of thought, he burst into an ascription of glory to Christ. He allowed himself to write down what he was ready to say in the intensity of worship, but was in the habit of restraining himself from writing in his letters. He acknowledged that Jesus was θεός (God) and εὐλογητός (blessed). His deep feelings, when he contemplated the rejection of Christ by the Jewish people, led him to give Christ the full honours of deity. The clause at the end of Rom. 9.5 is not part of the sequence of thought in the paragraph. It is an interjection—an outburst of praise, which the apostle allowed to remain in the epistle, perhaps because, as he surveyed what he had written, he knew that he had been writing under divine inspiration.

The Epistle to the Hebrews

πρὸς δὲ τὸν υἱόν,
ὁ θρόνος σου ὁ θεὸς εἰς τὸν
αἰῶνα τοῦ αἰῶνος   (Heb. 1.8).

This is a quotation from the Septuagint version of Ps. 45.6. There are two possible translations:

... but of the Son he saith,
Thy throne, O God, is for ever and ever. (RV)

... but of the Son he saith,
God is thy throne for ever and ever
(*or* Thy throne is God for ever and ever). (Westcott's suggestions.)

The meaning and the text of the Hebrew have been disputed but since the author of the Epistle to the Hebrews was quoting the Septuagint, these problems are not relevant to the interpretation of the passage.

The words ὁ θεός could be nominative or vocative, as the nominative of θεός usually does duty for the vocative. The translation which Westcott prefers does not express the most natural sense of the Greek. The phrase εἰς τὸν αἰῶνα τοῦ αἰῶνος (for ever and ever) is in an awkward position, if ὁ θεός is not vocative: ὁ θρόνος σου εἰς τὸν αἰῶνα τοῦ αἰῶνος ὁ θεός would be more suited to Westcott's translation.

Peake thinks that the most serious objection to the first translation is that the use of θεός and the definite article with reference to Christ is without parallel in the New Testament.[1] There is, however, a good parallel in John 20.28, where Thomas addresses Jesus as ὁ θεός μου (my God). This is also an example of the nominative used as a vocative.

Westcott suggests that a description of Christ as God would obscure the thought of the passage,[2] as the intention of the writer is to stress the eternal nature of the dominion of Christ in contrast to the mutability of the angels. In fact, however, the description of Christ as God does not obscure the thought of the passage but strengthens the contrast between Christ and the angels. The translation which implies that Christ is God, is faithful to the most natural sense of the Greek, and is to be preferred to Westcott's version.

The idea that Christ is God receives no further development in Hebrews. There are indications that he is worshipped,[3] but although he is described as Son, High Priest, and the agent in creation, no sustained attempt is made to give an account of his Deity. It is not satisfactory, however, to disregard Heb. 1.8 because it does not appear to fit in with the Christology of the

---

[1] *Hebrews*, p. 87.   [2] *Hebrews*, p. 26.   [3] Heb. 1.6, and possibly 13.21.

epistle as a whole.[1] A reasonable explanation of its presence is that, being a quotation from a psalm, it was used in Christian worship. It is introduced as if it were familiar to the readers. They would be likely to gain familiarity with it by hearing it quoted in sermons, or by singing it themselves in the psalm. The writer presupposes that Christ is regarded as a legitimate object of worship. His readers would not be unduly surprised to hear Christ addressed as God, although it may have been unusual to express the belief in writing. The writer did not amplify the statement. It was not his intention to discuss the divinity of Christ. His point in this verse is the superiority of Christ to the angels. The divinity of Christ, which is relevant but not necessary to the argument, is mentioned only in passing.

The Fourth Gospel

ἐν ἀρχῇ ἦν ὁ λόγος, καὶ ὁ λόγος ἦν πρὸς τὸν θεόν, καὶ θεὸς ἦν ὁ λόγος. οὗτος ἦν ἐν ἀρχῇ πρὸς τὸν θεόν (John 1.1–2).

In the beginning was the Word, and the Word was with God, and the Word was God. The same was in the beginning with God.

The translation "the Word of God" suggests that Christ was regarded as God. It has often been argued, however, that in this clause θεός, since it occurs without an article, is adjectival and means "divine". But if an adjective had been wanted, the word θεῖος, which occurs three times in the New Testament (Acts 17.29; 2 Pet. 1.3,4), could have been used.[2]

θεός is used with or without the article indiscriminately in the New Testament. In the Prologue to the Fourth Gospel it never has the article except in verses 1 and 2. In verses 6, 12, 13, and 18 it appears without the article. Verses 1 and 2, however, present a problem because θεός without an article occurs between two examples of θεός with the article. There is no reason to suppose that a deliberate contrast is intended. The article is absent because θεός is predicative. ὁ θεὸς ἦν ὁ λόγος would have meant "God

---

[1] See F. Scheidweiler in *ZNTW*, XLIX (1958), pp. 262–3.

[2] Origen was the first to suggest that θεός was adjectival. See Comm. in Joan. II.3.

was the Word". The Evangelist wanted θεός to be stressed. Hence he placed it at the beginning of the clause. But in order to show that it was predicative he had to omit the article.[1] The clause should be translated "the Word was God" rather than "the Word was divine".[2]

μονογενὴς θεὸς ὁ ὢν εἰς τὸν κόλπον τοῦ πατρός, ἐκεῖνος ἐξηγήσατο

(John 1.18).

The only-begotten God, who is in the bosom of the Father, he has declared him.

There is no doubt that these words identify Christ with God. But there are variant readings of the text. (ὁ) μονογενὴς θεός (only-begotten God) is supported by the weightier authorities.[3] (ὁ) μονογενὴς υἱός (only-begotten Son) is found in the Received Text. Its earliest support is in the Western Text, and it is also found in the Old Syriac version. Μονογενής (only-begotten) without a noun occurs in some codices of the Vulgate and in the Diatessaron.

Lagrange and Bousset favour the simple μονογενής (only-begotten), and argue that the nouns were added later.[4] Barrett claims that υἱός (Son) "seems to be imperatively demanded by the following clause, and is in conformity with Johannine usage".[5] Westcott and Hort accept the reading μονογενὴς θεός (only-begotten God). They argue that the substitution of the words "only-begotten Son" for "only-begotten God" would be obvious, and that the converse substitution "is inexplicable by any ordinary

[1] E. C. Colwell (*JBL*, LII (1933), 12 ff) formulates the rule that "definite predicate nouns which precede the verb usually lack the article". His views are discussed by C. F. D. Moule, *An Idiom Book of New Testament Greek*, pp. 115 ff.

[2] This verse expresses a paradox which runs through the Fourth Gospel. Jesus is one with the Father and yet the Father is greater than he. The Word is God, and yet the Word is with God. Cf. Bultmann, *Das Ev. des Johannes*, pp. 17–19.

[3] Including Codex Sinaiticus, Codex Vaticanus, Irenaeus, Clement, and Origen.

[4] Lagrange, *St Jean*, ad loc: Bousset, *Kyrios Christos*, 1st ed., p. 302.

[5] *The Gospel according to St John*, p. 141.

motive likely to affect transcribers".[1] Cullmann points out that a corrector who altered "Son" to "God" would have omitted the phrase "in the bosom of the Father".[2]

The stronger arguments are in favour of the reading μονογενὴς θεός (only-begotten God).[3] And in the first of his *Two Dissertations* Hort has justified the occurrence of this unusual title in the Prologue of the Fourth Gospel. He argues that there is a careful progress of thought in the Prologue. The introduction of the phrase "only-begotten Son" would have been abrupt, since the title "Son" had not been previously mentioned. But the word "only-begotten" and the word "God" had both been mentioned (John 1.14, and John 1.1). The words "only-begotten God" give the Prologue a roundness of form. "Verse 1 declares the Word to have been 'in the beginning'; verse 14 states that the Word, when He became flesh, was beheld to have a glory as of μονογενής; verse 18 shows how His union of both attributes enabled Him to bridge the chasm which kept the Godhead beyond the knowledge of men."[4]

ἀπεκρίθη Θωμᾶς καὶ εἶπεν αὐτῷ, ὁ κύριός μου καὶ ὁ θεός μου (John 20.28).

Thomas answered, and said to him, My Lord and my God.

The words of Thomas are addressed to Christ. They are almost certainly an instance of the nominative used in a vocative sense. Theodore of Mopsuestia suggests that this is a thanksgiving which Thomas addressed to God the Father. The context favours the view that these words were spoken to Jesus.[5]

Thomas uses the two commonest names of God in the Old Testament, "God" and "Lord", and applies them to Christ. There is no need, like Bousset, to find an origin for this saying in the Church's desire to oppose emperor-worship in the second half

[1] *New Testament*, II, p. 74.
[2] *Christologie*, p. 317.
[3] Burney's claim that the original Aramaic may have meant "only-begotten of God" is unconvincing, as it is unlikely that the translator would have mistaken the meaning. See M. Black, *Aramaic Approach to the Gospels and Acts*, 2nd ed., p. 10.
[4] Hort, *Two Dissertations*, p. 15.
[5] See Hoskyns, *Fourth Gospel*, p. 548.

of the first century.¹ But it is probable that the story was later used to oppose the demands of the emperors. Its present form may have taken shape under the influence of liturgical needs.²

Thomas may have actually uttered these words. But it is probable that the title θεός was not given to Christ immediately after the resurrection. "Jesus is Lord", not "Jesus is God", was the main confession of the primitive Church. Nevertheless the possibility cannot be entirely excluded that Thomas gave full divine honours to Jesus. The evangelist may have correctly recorded the scene in which Thomas grasped the truth of Christ's divinity "in the exaltation of his sudden deliverance from obstinate gloom to radiant faith".³

The confession of Thomas has an important place in the structure of the Fourth Gospel. The Prologue of the gospel is an account of the Incarnation of the Word of God. "The Word", says the evangelist, "was God" (John 1.1). Later, in John 1.18, Jesus is called "the only-begotten God". The Fourth Gospel begins, therefore, with a declaration of the divinity of Christ. Until the twentieth chapter there is no other open declaration of his divinity. Many things are said which imply that he is divine, but he is not called God. Then in the twentieth chapter he is openly called God by Thomas. The gospel seems to lead up to this final confession of the divinity of Christ. Since chapter 21 is probably an appendix to the original gospel, the story of Thomas may have concluded the earlier version of the gospel. The evangelist began and ended his work with a confession that Christ was God.

The Pastoral Epistles

... προσδεχόμενοι τὴν μακαρίαν ἐλπίδα καὶ ἐπιφάνειαν τῆς δόξης τοῦ μεγάλου θεοῦ καὶ σωτῆρος ἡμῶν Ἰησοῦ Χριστοῦ (Titus 2.13).

The following translations are possible:

... looking for the blessed hope, and the glorious appearing of our great God and Saviour Jesus Christ.

¹ See Bousset, op. cit., p. 301, and Bultmann, op. cit., p. 538, also Hoskyns, op. cit., p. 548. The words *dominus et deus noster*, used of Domitian (*Suet., Domit.* 13), may have heightened the significance of this passage.
² Barrett, op. cit., p. 477.
³ William Temple, *Readings in St John's Gospel*, p. 391.

... looking for the blessed hope, and the glorious appearing of the great God, and our Saviour Jesus Christ.

The crucial question is the meaning of τοῦ μεγαλοῦ θεοῦ καὶ σωτῆρος ἡμῶν. If θεοῦ (God) and σωτῆρος (Saviour) both refer to Jesus Christ, then Christ is called God in this verse, and the first translation is to be preferred. The position of ἡμῶν (our) links "God" and "Saviour", requiring the translation "our great God and Saviour". If the author had wished to make it clear that he was speaking of two persons, "the great God" and "our Saviour", he would have introduced a second definite article in front of σωτῆρος (Saviour).[1]

The better translation is the first, which says that Jesus Christ is "our great God and Saviour".[2] As Christ is not called God in any other part of the Pastoral Epistles, how is the presence of this passage in the Epistle to Titus to be explained? First, a unique statement in such a slender collection as the Pastoral Epistles ought not to cause any surprise. Secondly, both God and Christ are called Saviour independently in these epistles. A writer who could give this title to both Father and Son, might well be able to give the title "God" to Christ. Thirdly, the phrase "great God" (μέγας θεός) not only occurs in the Septuagint,[3] but also seems to have been widely current in the Hellenistic world.[4] It is possible that μέγας θεὸς καὶ σωτήρ (great God and Saviour), as Dibelius suggests, was a formula which was used of God by Jews

[1] The absence of a second article cannot be explained by supposing that the author was using a credal formula σωτὴρ Ἰησοῦς Χριστός (Jesus Christ is Saviour). There is no evidence that these words had acquired the status of a formula like κύριος Ἰησοῦς Χριστός (Jesus Christ is Lord). See Parry, *Pastoral Epistles*, p. 81.

[2] Hort, *Epistle of James*, p. 103, favours the translation: "... looking for the blessed hope and the appearing of the glory of our great God and Saviour, which glory is Jesus Christ." But the order of words favours the view that "God" refers to Christ, and the title "Saviour" has already been used of Christ in Titus 1.4. Hort's translation involves an awkward interpretation of the Greek.

[3] E.g. Deut. 10.17; Ps. 85.10; Isa. 26.4; Jer. 39.19; Dan. 2.45.

[4] See Grundmann in *TWNT*, IV, p. 546, and Deissmann, *Light from the Ancient East*, p. 269n3.

in the Dispersion, and transferred to Christ by the Christians.[1] Fourthly, if the epistle was written in the reign of Trajan, as P. N. Harrison has convincingly claimed,[2] it belongs to the same period as the letters of Ignatius, in which Christ is frequently called God. These are reasons which explain why Christ should be called God in the Pastoral Epistles.

The Second Epistle of Peter

. . . ἐν δικαιοσύνῃ τοῦ θεοῦ ἡμῶν καὶ σωτῆρος Ἰησοῦ Χριστοῦ   (2 Pet. 1.1).

There are two possible translations:[3]

. . . in the righteousness of our God and Saviour Jesus Christ.

. . . in the righteousness of our God and the Saviour Jesus Christ.

This formula is almost the same as that in Titus 2.13. As in Titus 2.13, there is only one definite article linking the two titles "God" and "Saviour". The clear meaning of the text is ". . . in the righteousness of our God and Saviour Jesus Christ",[4] and the presence of this description of Christ in an epistle which almost certainly belongs to the second century needs no explanation.

In this examination of evidence it has been argued that there are seven passages in the New Testament in which Jesus Christ is called God. They are:

. . . of whom is Christ as concerning the flesh, who is over all, God blessed for ever, Amen (Rom. 9.5).

. . . but of the Son he saith,
Thy throne, O God, is for ever and ever (Heb. 1.8).

---

[1] M. Dibelius, *Pastoralbriefe*, p. 92.

[2] P. N. Harrison, *The Problem of the Pastoral Epistles*.

[3] Although the reference to God has been omitted by some of the versions and by the uncial P, the integrity of the text has not been seriously questioned.

[4] While in Titus 2.13 ἡμῶν follows σωτῆρος, in 2 Pet. 1.1 it follows θεοῦ. But this does not mean that in 2 Pet. 1.1 "God" and "Saviour" refer to different persons. Later in the same chapter (2 Pet. 1.11) comes a similar phrase, τοῦ κυρίου ἡμῶν καὶ σωτῆρος Ἰησοῦ Χριστοῦ, in which both titles clearly refer to Jesus Christ.

In the beginning was the Word, and the Word was with God, and the Word was God. The same was in the beginning with God (John 1.1-2).

The only-begotten God, who is in the bosom of the Father, he has declared him (John 1.18).

Thomas answered, and said to him, My Lord and my God (John 20.28).

. . . looking for the blessed hope, and the glorious appearing of our great God and Saviour Jesus Christ (Titus 2.13).

. . . in the righteousness of our God and Saviour Jesus Christ (2 Pet. 1.1).

Although the interpretation of most of these passages has been seriously disputed,[1] the linguistic arguments support the view that in each of them Jesus is called God. The passages are numerous enough to ease the perplexity of those critics who are unable to accept an example when it appears to be unique in the New Testament. They will not want to dismiss an example, which has six companions, as easily as one which stands alone.

At the beginning of the second century there is a variety of extra-canonical evidence that Jesus was called God. In the Didache 10.6 the words ὡσαννὰ τῷ θεῷ Δαβίδ (Hosanna to the God of David) refer to Christ. Pliny writes in one of his letters (Ep. X. 96.7) that the Christians used to "sing a hymn to Christ as God" (carmen Christo quasi deo dicere). Ignatius frequently calls him God.[2] This form of address, this manner of description, is not likely to have suddenly sprung into being at the beginning of the second century. That there should be previous examples of the usage is not surprising. Their scarcity, not their existence, is a cause of surprise. It is only to be expected that Jesus was called God before the time of Pliny and Ignatius, since both these writers assume that this mode of speech is perfectly natural. Indeed it might have been expected that the predicate θεός would have been used of Jesus far more often in the pages of the New Testament.

An attempt must now be made to explain why these references occur in the New Testament, and why they are so few in number. There is one important characteristic which some of them, perhaps

[1] Bultmann, for example, in *Essays Philosophical and Theological*, p. 276, claims that John 20.28 is the only sure instance in the New Testament of the ascription of the title "God" to Jesus Christ.

[2] E.g. *Eph.* 1.1; 15.3; 18.2; 19.3; *Sm.* 1.1; 10.1; *Tr.* 7.1.

all of them, have in common. They have a liturgical background. Rom. 9.5 is a short ascription of praise to Christ. Its vocabulary is typical of a doxology (εὐλογητός, εἰς αἰῶνας, ἐπί πάντων). The suggestion was made that Paul wrote these words under the influence of deep emotion. They are an expression of his innermost feelings rather than an integral part of the argument. He may have written words which he was accustomed to use in his private prayers. Or he may have quoted a doxology which was used in public worship.

Heb. 1.8 is a quotation from a psalm. The author assumes that the words are well known to his readers, who will readily accept the reference to Christ. The psalm, or at any rate part of it, must have been used in the liturgy of the Christians to whom the epistle was addressed. In their worship they sang: "Thy throne, O God, is for ever." The belief that Christ is God is not the keystone of the Christology of the Epistle to the Hebrews. The author is chiefly concerned to expound the conception of the High Priesthood of Christ and his unique Sonship. The allusion to the Divinity of Christ in 1.8 does not form an integral part of the theology of the epistle. It supplies valuable evidence, however, about the liturgical background of early Christianity. Although the writer does not include the Deity of Christ within the scheme of thought which he presents in the epistle, his use of this quotation from Psalm 45 shows that he himself, and the Church to which he was writing, were prepared to acknowledge in their worship that Jesus was God.

In the Epistles to the Romans and to the Hebrews the acknowledgement of Christ's Deity is not integral to the thought but provides a clue to the liturgical background. On the other hand the Johannine references to Jesus as God, are essential to the writer's thought. The prologue begins with the statement that the Word was God, and ends with the description of the Incarnate Word as "only-begotten God". The earliest edition of the gospel ends with the story of Thomas's confession that Jesus was his Lord and his God. The evangelist implies that the Christian believer is able to discern that the risen Christ is God. The presence of these passages at the beginning and the end of the gospel proves that they are not merely passing allusions which have been introduced haphazardly. Their position in the gospel is deliberately planned.

Not only are these passages important for an understanding of the theology of the Fourth Gospel. At least one of them (John 20.28) seems to have been used liturgically.[1] The structure of the pericope in which the confession "My Lord and my God!" is included (John 20.19–29) suggests that the passage may have had a liturgical origin. C. K. Barrett claims that there is considerable evidence for this view: "The disciples assemble on the Lord's Day. The Blessing is given: Εἰρήνη ὑμῖν. The Holy Spirit descends upon the worshippers and the word of absolution (cf. v.23) is pronounced. Christ himself is present (this may suggest the Eucharist and the spoken Word of God) bearing the marks of his Passion; he is confessed as Lord and God."[2] Barrett's arguments can be supported by the frequent use of the formula κύριος καὶ θεός (Lord and God) in the Greek Old Testament and in pagan literature and inscriptions. Since the formula was so well known, it could easily have been taken over into Christian worship.

The references to Christ as God in Titus and 2 Peter may also have had their origin in liturgy. At a time when Ignatius frequently described Christ as "God", these forms of invocation and confession were probably used in many churches.[3]

The evidence which has been collected favours the view that Jesus Christ was called God in Christian worship during New Testament times. He may not have been addressed in these terms in every church of Christendom, but he was accorded this honour in the churches with which Paul, and the authors of the Fourth Gospel, Hebrews, the Pastoral Epistles, and 2 Peter, were connected. The writers of the New Testament seem to have been reluctant to commit to writing the confession that Jesus is God. The reluctance of Paul and the author of the Epistle to the Hebrews may have been caused by their inability to give an account of the relationship of this confession to the Jewish monotheism to which

---

[1] The prologue too, it has been argued, was couched in poetic form. But it must have been revised before inclusion in the gospel. The parts of the prologue which describe Christ as God are theological rather than liturgical.

[2] Op. cit., p. 477.   [3] Cf. Dibelius, op. cit., p. 92.

they continued to subscribe. Their faith outstripped their reason, and they were able to give joyful utterance to a belief which they felt incapable of expounding. But each of these writers, on one occasion, allowed himself to give expression to this deep-seated belief, and to include in the text of an epistle language which he usually confined to private and public worship.

The author of the Fourth Gospel interwove this belief into his thought. The Word, which was incarnate in Jesus Christ, was God. After the resurrection the disciple of Jesus was able to perceive this divinity as he looked at the risen Lord. Like Paul and the author of Hebrews, the evangelist was in contact with a liturgical tradition in which Jesus was hailed as Lord and God. Perhaps, by placing the confession of Thomas at the very end of the gospel, he was suggesting that it was only in the moment of worship that men were able to comprehend that Jesus was God. Only when, like Thomas, they bowed in reverence and faith before his risen majesty, could they know who he was.

NOTE:

PASSAGES WHICH PROVIDE EVIDENCE OF DOUBTFUL VALUE

There are also several passages in which it could be argued that Christ is being called God, but in which the arguments are not convincing.

1. . . . κατὰ τὴν χάριν τοῦ θεοῦ ἡμῶν καὶ κυρίου Ἰησοῦ Χριστοῦ

(2 Thess. 1.12).

There are two possible translations:

. . . according to the grace of our God and Lord Jesus Christ.

. . . according to the grace of our God and the Lord Jesus Christ.

The second translation has been preferred by the majority of translators and commentators. The chief reason in its favour is that the phrase κύριος Ἰησοῦς Χριστός occurs so often in Paul's epistles that it would be quite normal to introduce it, even in this context, without a definite article. Indeed κύριος Ἰησοῦς Χριστός seems to have been one of the earliest Christian creeds.[1]

[1] Cullmann, *Earliest Christian Confessions*, p. 41.

Two other factors may support the second translation. First, the position of the word ἡμῶν which is attached to θεοῦ seems to imply that θεοῦ and κυρίου do not refer to the same person.[1] This is not an overwhelming argument, as in 2 Pet. 1.11, and 3.18 (τοῦ κυρίου ἡμῶν καὶ σωτῆρος Ἰησοῦ Χριστοῦ) the words κυρίου and σωτῆρος both refer to Jesus Christ in spite of the presence of ἡμῶν after κυρίου.

Secondly, Frame says that the phrase ὁ θεὸς ἡμῶν rather than θεὸς πατὴρ ἡμῶν is characteristic of the Thessalonian Epistles.[2] This would explain why Paul linked two titles, one of which had the article and the other of which lacked it. The phrase θεὸς ἡμῶν without the article is also found in the Thessalonian Epistles,[3] but the examples which have the article easily outnumber this solitary reference.[4] Because of the frequency of the phrase ὁ θεὸς ἡμῶν in the Thessalonian Epistles and, above all, because κύριος Ἰησοῦς Χριστός was a credal formula, the second translation, in which Jesus Christ is not said to be God, is to be preferred.

2. . . . εἰς ἐπίγνωσιν τοῦ μυστηρίου τοῦ θεοῦ Χριστοῦ   (Col. 2.2).

These words could be translated: ". . . that they might know the mystery of the God Christ." But the better translation is: ". . . that they might know the mystery of God, even Christ." Paul means that Christ is the mystery of God, not that he is God. And a clause in verse 3, "in whom are all the treasures of wisdom and knowledge hidden", explains how he is the mystery of God.

3. αὕτη δέ ἐστιν ἡ αἰώνιος ζωή, ἵνα γινώσκωσιν σὲ τὸν μόνον ἀληθινὸν θεὸν καὶ ὃν ἀπέστειλας, Ἰησοῦν Χριστον   (John 17.3).

Bousset suggests that this should be translated in such a way as to imply that Jesus is God:[5]

And this is eternal life, that they should know thee as the only true God, and Jesus Christ, whom thou didst send, as the only true God.

To make Bousset's translation acceptable the phrase τὸν μόνον ἀληθινὸν θεόν would have to be moved to the end of

---

[1] This point is emphasized by Stauffer in *TWNT*, III, p. 106n265.
[2] *Thessalonians*, p. 242.   [3] 2 Thess. 1.1.
[4] 1 Thess. 1.3; 2.2; 3.9,11,13; 2 Thess. 1.11,12; 2.16.
[5] Bousset, *Kyrios Christos*, 1st ed., p. 301.

the sentence. The only satisfactory translation of the verse is that which treats God and Jesus Christ as separate persons:

And this is eternal life, that they should know thee, the only true God, and him whom thou didst send, Jesus Christ.

4. οἴδαμεν δὲ ὅτι ὁ υἱὸς τοῦ θεοῦ ἥκει, καὶ δέδωκεν ἡμῖν διάνοιαν ἵνα γινώσκομεν τὸν ἀληθινόν· καὶ ἐσμὲν ἐν τῷ ἀληθινῷ, ἐν τῷ υἱῷ αὐτοῦ Ἰησοῦ Χριστῷ. οὗτός ἐστιν ὁ ἀληθινὸς θεὸς καὶ ζωὴ αἰώνιος (1 John 5.20).

The Revised Version translates:

And we know that the Son of God is come, and hath given us an understanding, that we know him that is true, and we are in him that is true, even in his Son Jesus Christ. This is the true God and eternal life.[1]

Some scholars think that οὗτος (this) refers to Jesus Christ.[2] In that case Jesus would be "the true God and eternal life". This view is supported by the descriptions of Jesus as "the Life" which occur in John 11.25 and John 14.6.

On the other hand, Dodd believes that in the last clause the writer is summing up all that he has been saying about God in the epistle. οὗτος refers not to the words which immediately precede it but to the teaching about God throughout the epistle.[3]

There is, however, a more natural interpretation. οὗτος refers to τῷ ἀληθινῷ (him that is true). ἐν τῷ υἱῷ is not in opposition to ἐν τῷ ἀληθινῷ but limits the whole of the ἵνα clause. "Being in his Son Jesus Christ" is the condition upon which we are able to know and to be in the true one, who is God. In this verse, therefore, Jesus is not called God. The verse should be translated:

And we know that the Son of God is come, and hath given us an understanding that we know him that is true, and we are in him that is true, by being in his Son Jesus Christ. He is the true God and eternal life.

5. Ἰάκωβος θεοῦ καὶ κυρίου Ἰησοῦ Χριστοῦ δοῦλος (Jas. 1.1).

These words may be translated in two ways:

James, a servant of God and the Lord Jesus Christ.
James, a servant of the God and Lord, Jesus Christ.

---

[1] There are several textual variants, which attempt to make the verse easier to interpret, but they may be disregarded.

[2] Bousset, op. cit., pp. 301–2; Windisch-Preisker, *Katholische Briefe*, p. 135; Cullmann, *Christologie*, p. 318.

[3] C. H. Dodd, *The Johannine Epistles*, p. 140.

THE DIVINITY OF CHRIST

Either translation could be defended linguistically. But since the author says little about Christ in the epistle, there is no overwhelming evidence in favour of the translation which says that Jesus is God. It is possible that Christ is described as the divine glory in Jas. 2.1, but there is not sufficient evidence available to use this verse as support for the belief that New Testament Christians called Jesus God.

6. καὶ καλέσουσιν τὸ ὄνομα αὐτοῦ 'Εμμανουήλ, ὅ ἐστιν μεθερμηνευόμενον μεθ' ἡμῶν ὁ θεός (Matt. 1.23).

This can be translated in two ways:

And they shall call his name Immanuel; which is, being interpreted, God with us.

And they shall call his name Immanuel; which is, being interpreted, God is with us.

The Greek μεθ' ἡμῶν ὁ θεός is a literal translation of the Hebrew *'immanu 'el* (Isa. 7.14), which could mean either "God with us" or "God is with us". The order of words in the Greek suggests that "with us" is adverbial and that the phrase means "God is with us". But Matthew was more concerned to give a literal translation of the Hebrew than to free it from ambiguity. It is uncertain whether he meant "God with us" or "God is with us". He may not have been sure himself.

The translation "God with us" implies that Jesus is God. The translation "God is with us", however, may mean no more than that the coming of Jesus is an instance of God's activity among men. Because of its ambiguity this passage cannot be used as evidence that Jesus was called God.

7. Τῷ δὲ βασιλεῖ τῶν αἰώνων, ἀφθάρτῳ ἀοράτῳ μόνῳ θεῷ, τιμὴ καὶ δόξα εἰς τοὺς αἰῶνας τῶν αἰώνων· ἀμήν (1 Tim. 1.17).

Now unto the King eternal, incorruptible, invisible, the only God, be honour and glory for ever and ever, Amen.

C. C. Oke argues that this is a doxology to Christ.[1] He points out that θεῷ has no definite article in this verse, and that θεός without an article in John 1.1 refers to Christ. He claims that in

[1] C. C. Oke, *ET*, LXVII, pp. 367-8.

1 Tim. 1.17 θεῷ is adjectival and instead of "the only God", translates "the only divine". His argument fails to convince for three reasons.

First, the word θεῖος means "divine" and could have been used instead of θεός if the writer had intended to use an adjective.

Secondly, the doxology of 1 Tim. 6.15 f, in which similar language occurs, is given to God the Father.

Thirdly, the language of the passage itself suggests that the King in 1 Tim. 1.17 is distinguished from Jesus Christ of 1 Tim. 1.16.

In all probability, then, this doxology is given to God, and does not refer to Christ.[1]

---

[1] There are three passages to be considered in which disputed readings imply that Jesus is God.

1. ὁ δὲ νῦν ζῶ ἐν σαρκί, ἐν πίστει ζῶ τῇ τοῦ υἱοῦ τοῦ θεοῦ τοῦ ἀγαπήσαντός με καὶ παραδόντος ἑαυτὸν ὑπὲρ ἐμοῦ   (Gal. 2.20).

And that life which I now live in the flesh I live in faith, the faith which is in the Son of God, who loved me, and gave himself up for me.

Several authorities, including the Chester-Beatty Papyrus, Vaticanus, Claramontanus, and most of the Old Latin versions, support the reading τοῦ θεοῦ καὶ χριστοῦ instead of τοῦ υἱοῦ τοῦ θεοῦ. There are two possible translations of the variant reading: "God and Christ", implying that the two are separate, and "the God and Christ", implying that the two are one.

It is more likely that τοῦ θεοῦ καὶ χριστοῦ was substituted for τοῦ υἱοῦ τοῦ θεοῦ than that the opposite process took place. And in spite of the strong textual support the variant reading must be rejected.

2. ὃς ἐφανερώθη ἐν σαρκί, ἐδικαιώθη ἐν πνεύματι   (1 Tim. 3.16).

He who was manifested in the flesh, justified in the Spirit.

There is a variant reading θεός for ὅς. But this variant is almost certainly a later reading. The manuscript support is not strong (see Westcott and Hort, *New Testament*, II, pp. 132–4).

3. . . . ποιμαίνειν τὴν ἐκκλησίαν τοῦ θεοῦ, ἣν περιεποιήσατο διὰ τοῦ αἵματος τοῦ ἰδίου   (Acts 20.28).

. . . to feed the church of God, which he purchased with his own blood (*or* the blood of his own).

There is a variant κυρίου for θεοῦ, and it has good support from the "Western" text. But θεοῦ has very strong manuscript support, including Sinaiticus and Vaticanus. The reading κυρίου καὶ θεοῦ is obviously conflate. There are several other readings which have poor support (see Ropes, *Beginnings of Christianity*, III, pp. 197–9, and Westcott and Hort, *New Testament*, II, pp. 98–100).

In favour of κυρίου it has been argued that the expression "church of the Lord" is unusual and therefore has a strong claim to be authentic. But though unusual, it is not unnatural. Although it is conceivable that θεοῦ was substituted in the interests of Patripassianism, it is far more likely that κυρίου was substituted for θεοῦ in order to guard the text against heresy. Moreover, the manuscript evidence favours θεοῦ.

If the reading θεοῦ is accepted, does the verse mean that God purchased the Church with his own blood? It is difficult to imagine that the divinity of Christ should have been stated in such a blunt and misleading fashion. Two explanations may help to solve the difficulty. J. H. Moulton (*Prolegomena*, pp. 90 ff) thinks that ὁ ἴδιος may have been a title of Christ and translates: "through the blood of his own". Hort suggests that the original reading could have been τοῦ ἰδίου υἱοῦ. Alternatively, it is possible that Christ is understood as the subject of the verb "purchased" without actually being mentioned. In any case, this verse cannot be used as certain evidence that Jesus was called God.

CHAPTER 5

JESUS CHRIST IS LORD

In the New Testament the title "Lord" is given to both God the Father and Jesus Christ. In preaching, prayer, and credal confession Jesus was invoked as "Lord", and from the first century to the present day the title has been used of Christ with great frequency throughout Christendom. During the last seventy years an enormous quantity of literature has been devoted to the history of the title. The controversy about its origin and meaning has occupied the energies of many scholars. In Great Britain there is a tendency to accept the conservative view, that the title was first given to Jesus during his earthly life or during the early years of the Church's existence in Palestine. It is often assumed that the conservatives have made their case. But the radical view, that the title was first used in Hellenistic circles, continues to have influential supporters.[1]

Because of the exhaustive treatment which the subject has received, it is not necessary to enter into all the details of the problem. An attempt will be made to indicate the difficulties which have hitherto prevented and perhaps always will prevent a satisfactory solution. The fault of the protagonists on both sides of the controversy has been the ease with which they have assumed that they have unlocked the gate of truth. They have indeed unlocked gates, for they have made important discoveries. They have analysed a great quantity of evidence, and illuminated the history of Christianity and many other religions. But they have not shed a great deal of light on the area of history which lies between the end of the ministry of Jesus and the beginning of the ministry of Paul.

The main problem is the history of the title's origin and use in

[1] E.g. Bultmann, in *Theology of the New Testament*, I, pp. 121-8.

early Christianity. Was it first used of Jesus in the Aramaic-speaking community of Palestine which had its centre in Jerusalem, or in the bilingual community of Syria, the headquarters of which was in Antioch? Did the title acquire its Christian meaning under the influence of the Hebrew tradition or of Hellenistic and Oriental mystery-religions? As a prelude to the main discussion we shall examine briefly the different ways in which the title could be used in the ancient world. The word "Lord" had a great flexibility of meaning, and this explains its importance for the Church, since in Jewish circles it could convey the idea of Christ's divinity without an open denial of the treasured doctrine of monotheism.

First, the word κύριος (Lord) was used in a *possessive* sense adjectivally in both classical and Hellenistic Greek in the sense of "having power over". It was also used as a noun meaning "possessor". In this sense the word could refer to the master of a house or the owner of a vineyard. It could also describe a master in contrast to his servants.[1] The corresponding Hebrew word *ʾadon* could be used to describe the master of a house (e.g. Ex. 21.5). The Aramaic *mar* and *rab* were used of human masters. *Mar* is the title which is nearest to κύριος. It describes a man who owns or possesses something. Dalman quotes passages in which a man is called "lord" of slaves and even "lord" of a pearl or of a debt.[2]

A second usage of the word "Lord" was the *polite*. The Greek vocative κύριε was often the equivalent of the English "Sir" conveying respect without special reverence.[3] The Hebrew *ʾadoni* was used in a similar way. For example, it describes a husband (Gen. 18.12) or a prophet (1 Kings 18.7). The Aramaic *mari* (my lord) and *maran* (our lord) could also have this polite meaning,[4] and

---

[1] See W. Bauer, *Wörterbuch zum Neuen Testament*, p. 270.

[2] Dalman, *Words of Jesus*, p. 325.

[3] E. von Dobschütz, in *ZNTW*, XXX, pp. 108–9. A. Deissmann, *Light from the Ancient East*, p. 179, quotes a letter of the second century A.D., in which an Egyptian soldier greets his father as κύριε, cf. Epictetus, Dis. II, 15.15, and Seneca, Ep. iii.1. who says that strangers are greeted as "lord". Cf. Moulton and Milligan, *Vocabulary of the New Testament*, p. 365.

[4] Dalman, op. cit., p. 325. In the LXX the vocative κύριε is used in addressing Laban (Gen. 31.35), and Moses (Num. 11.28).

there is evidence in the gospels that the term was used in the polite sense both of Jesus and of his disciples.[1]

The title "Lord" had, thirdly, a *courtly* usage, in which it was applied to kings and princes and governors.[2] κύριος or *dominus* was a favourite title of the Roman emperors,[3] and Hebrew kings were addressed as *ʾadoni*.[4] The English equivalent is "My Lord" or "Your Majesty". But the ancient attitude to kings was different from the modern. In societies which officially embraced polytheism the people did not find it difficult to worship their kings. The title "Lord", when it was used of a king, had more religious content than the English "Majesty" or "Lord".

A fourth usage was *religious*. Even when the title was given to a king, it entered, as we have seen, into the sphere of religion. But the religious content was chiefly found in the ascription of the title to gods and heroes,[5] and to the cultic deities of the mystery religions.[6] "Lord" was used in this sense throughout the Middle East. It appeared in the Baal cults of Canaàn and Syria, in the religion of Attis and Adonis, in Egyptian religion, and in the local cults of Arabia.[7] In Judaism the title *ʾadonai* (Lord) became the substitute for the divine name in the reading of the scriptures, and in the Septuagint κύριος was used as the Greek equivalent.

Four different uses of the word "Lord" have been considered. They are the possessive, the polite, the courtly, and the religious. They are only roughly defined categories, which overlap at many points, but they give an idea of the flexibility of the title. The religious usage will be the chief theme of the following pages.

Although κύριος and its Latin and Semitic equivalents were used for many centuries before the birth of Jesus, the greater part of the evidence for their use as a title is no earlier than the first

[1] E.g. Matt. 8.2,6,8; Lk. 5.12; 7.6; John 12.21.
[2] Judith 2.14; Matt. 27.63; Acts 25.26, etc.
[3] Pliny, Ep. x.26; Philo, *in Flaccum*, 36 ff.
[4] E.g. 1 Sam. 22.12.
[5] W. Foerster in *TWNT*, III, pp. 1045–56.
[6] Foerster, op. cit., p. 1049.
[7] Cf. D. Nielsen, *Der Dreieinige Gott in Religionshistorischer Beleuchtung*, I, pp. 93–103, 108, and Baudissin, *Kyrios*, II, p. 258.

century B.C., which is early enough to give us a picture of the way in which they were used in New Testament times.

κύριε was used in Greece in the polite sense, and κύριος with a qualifying genitive often occurs, but there is no extant example of the absolute κύριος before the first century B.C.[1] The earliest surviving evidence of the absolute usage comes from Egypt. The god Soknopaios was called κύριος and the goddess Isis was called κύρια.[2] From Egypt also comes evidence that Ptolemy XIII was addressed as κύριος in the first century B.C. When the title was used of Ptolemy it was associated with the idea of divinity, for he was addressed as "Lord King God".[3] A generation or two later the Emperor Augustus was described in Egypt as "God and Lord Emperor".[4] During the reigns of Nero and Domitian such forms were used even more widely. In this context the title was bound to acquire the sense of divinity. It was already used to describe gods and cultic heroes. It was now being associated with the cult of the emperor. In spite of the regular appearance of θεός in company with κύριος Foerster has argued that κύριος did not refer to the divinity of the Caesar.[5] He claims that there is no evidence to prove that the title in itself expressed divinity. Such an argument is hairsplitting. If κύριος was used regularly in conjunction with θεός, and was already recognized in the East as a cultic title of deity, in the sphere of the court and the temples it would convey the idea of the emperor's divinity.[6]

The title κύριος is also found in these senses in Syria at the beginning of the first century A.D.[7] It is likely that the title had a long history in that country. In the Old Testament we encounter the Canaanite Baal, and a similar title was used in Syria.[8] But we cannot be certain that the title had a powerful influence in the popular religion at the beginning of the Christian era.

[1] Foerster, op. cit., p. 1048.

[2] Ibid., p. 1048, among other inscriptions the following are quoted: τῷ θεῷ καὶ κυρίῳ Σοκνοπαίῳ (Ditt. Or. 655, 24 B.C.) and προσκυνήσας τὴν κυρίαν θεὰν Ἴσιν (CIG 4936, 81 B.C.).

[3] Ibid., p. 1048.   [4] θεὸς καὶ κύριος Καῖσαρ.

[5] Ibid., pp. 1054-6.   [6] O. Cullmann, Christologie, p. 204.

[7] Ditt. Or. 606, see Foerster, op. cit., p. 1048.

[8] Von Dobschütz, ZNTW, XXX, p. 98.

The most striking use of the word κύριος is found in the Septuagint, where according to von Dobschütz it occurs 8,400 times. The word is used of human beings in only 400 of these instances, and of God in the remaining 8,000. Of these 8,000, 6,700 are substitutes for the tetragram Y-H-W-H. Christians who were brought up on the Septuagint would naturally associate the title κύριος with the One God of Judaism.[1]

The relationship of the Greek κύριος to the Hebrew ᵓadonai is less certain. Eventually ᵓadonai became the regular substitute for the divine name in the reading of the scriptures during synagogue worship. As von Dobschütz points out, the use of κύριος for Yahweh in the Psalms of Solomon and the Assumption of Moses, and the general character of the oral tradition of Judaism, which favoured reverential substitution, makes it possible that ᵓadonai came into use quite early.[2]

The Jewish and pagan background of the title has been examined. The evidence is varied; it is drawn from many lands and many religions. Sometimes it is fragmentary and sometimes it is as full as could be desired. When the Christian Church sprang into being, the title was already popular in both Jewish and pagan religions. Only a policy of deliberate exclusion could have prevented it from being adopted sooner or later by the Christian Church. It was certain that it would be used of God the Father. It would have been possible, however, to have refrained from using it of Christ.

[1] Von Dobschütz, ZNTW, XXX, p. 98. Dalman, Der Gottesname Adonaj, p. 59, contended that the tetragram Y-H-W-H was reproduced in the earliest edition of the Septuagint (see von Dobschütz, op. cit., p. 102), but Baudissin, pp. 12-15, has convincingly argued that κύριος was used in place of the tetragram before the beginning of the Christian era. He justifies his argument by showing that the title occurs in the Letter of Aristeas, 155, and in certain writings of Philo (e.g. de vita Mosis, II, 5-7). Moreover the use of κύριος in New Testament quotations from the Septuagint (Acts 2.21, Rom. 10.13) shows that it took the place of the tetragram for Greek-speaking Jews before the rise of Christianity.

[2] ZNTW, XXX, p. 103. In ordinary usage it was customary to employ hammaqom (the place) or hasshem (the name) as substitutes for the divine name. It is possible, however, that ᵓadonai was used as a substitute in ordinary speech as well as in worship. Otherwise it is difficult to explain how it was accepted as a liturgical substitute. Cf. Cullmann, op. cit., p. 206.

A Jew who was acquainted with the Septuagint would instinctively desire to keep the title for God the Father. But in spite of this it was used of Christ by the Jews who wrote the New Testament.

The German scholar, Bousset, argued that κύριος was first used of Christ in the Syrian Church which had its centre at Antioch,[1] the city from which Paul set off on his missionary journeys. Antioch was a great and populous commercial centre where Greek and Oriental ways of life intermingled. It was the first great Hellenistic city into which Christianity penetrated. Here the problem of interpreting the gospel to a non-Jewish world was acutely encountered. The Christians had to decide whether to shut themselves off from the pagan civilization which surrounded them or to reconcile themselves to the Gentile world without corrupting their faith. From Antioch Paul and Barnabas travelled to Jerusalem to defend their liberal attitude to the Jewish law. In Antioch the Christian Church had first to decide whether to emerge from the parochialism of Palestine and face the questions of circumcision and table-fellowship with Gentiles. Bousset argues that the church in Antioch, or at least in Syria, was the first to use the title κύριος of Jesus in worship. He claims that the practice began before Paul wrote his epistles. Bousset's theory was attacked by Rawlinson,[2] but is still accepted in a modified form by Bultmann.[3] The issue has not been finally decided, and the arguments require further consideration.

Nobody has doubted that the title κύριος was used of Christ at Antioch. The freedom with which Paul employs the title is sufficient proof. Bousset, however, tries to show that the title was not so used in the teaching of Jesus or of the earliest Palestinian church. He attempts to dispose of the evidence of the synoptic gospels, in which there are surprisingly few examples of κύριος. Of the references in Mark's gospel[4] one (Mark 5.19) refers to God the Father; another (Mark 7.28), in which the Syrophoenician woman addresses Jesus as Lord, is probably only a polite usage; and yet another (Mark 11.3), in which the disciples sent by Jesus for a colt

[1] *Kyrios Christos*, 2nd ed., pp. 76–104.
[2] *The New Testament Doctrine of the Christ*, p. 237.
[3] Op. cit., I, pp. 51–3. [4] Op. cit., pp. 78–9.

say, "The Lord hath need of him", is an example of the possessive sense, a reference to the master-servant relationship.[1]

The quotation from Ps. 110.1, which Jesus makes in Mark 12.35–7, presents a more difficult problem. The words of Jesus are:

> How say the scribes that the Christ is the son of David?
> David himself said in the Holy Spirit,
> The Lord said unto my Lord,
>   Sit thou at my right hand,
>   Till I make thine enemies the footstool of thy feet.
> David himself calleth him Lord; and whence is he his son?

If this is a genuine saying of Jesus, then Jesus himself described the Messiah as David's Lord, and this would support the theory that the title was used by the Jerusalem Church. It is not surprising that the authenticity of the saying has been challenged. Bultmann argues that these words are a rejection of the link between the Messiah and a Davidic sonship, and that if Jesus had uttered the saying, Paul would not have been able to describe him as "born of the seed of David according to the flesh" (Rom. 1.3).[2] For this reason he rejects the saying's authenticity. But Mark 12.35–7 does not imply that the Messiah cannot be David's son. It means rather that "son of David" is not an adequate description of Jesus' Messiahship. The Messiah is not only David's son but also David's Lord. He possesses an authority which is greater than David's. Hence the main argument against the genuineness of the saying is unconvincing.[3]

The title κύριος rarely occurs in the Matthaean and Lukan sayings of Jesus. The following two passages should be noted:

[1] Cf. Cullmann, op. cit., p. 210. V. Taylor, *St Mark*, p. 455, suggests that ὁ κύριος refers to the owner of the colt, who himself may have been with Jesus.

[2] *Geschichte der synoptischen Tradition*, 3rd ed., p. 146. For other views see Bultmann, op. cit., *Ergänzungsheft*, p. 21. Cullmann, op. cit., pp. 132 f, argues that Jesus is rejecting not a Davidic sonship, but the idea of a political Messiah.

[3] J. Knox, *The Death of Christ*, p. 41, rejects the saying because the quotation from the psalm would only have been needed when it was required to establish Jesus' Messiahship. But it is not unreasonable to suppose that Jesus himself made claims about his Messiahship, and that quotations were used to proclaim the gospel as well as to defend it.

Not every one that saith unto me, Lord, Lord, shall enter into the kingdom of heaven (Matt. 7.21).

And why call ye me, Lord, Lord, and do not the things which I say? (Luke 6.46).

Although these verses prove that the disciples called Jesus Lord, they do not provide evidence that Jesus himself attached any importance to the title. The disciples probably used the title in a polite or semi-courtly sense. The infrequency of these instances of κύριος is evidence of their authenticity. If Luke, who uses κύριος regularly in the narrative portions of his gospel, had wished to emphasize the origin of the title in the teaching of Jesus, he would have been tempted to introduce it on many more occasions.

Bousset rejects the evidence of the Acts of the Apostles for the early use of κύριος on the ground that the book was written late and the speeches are editorial compositions.[1] This attitude to Acts is not so much in favour as it used to be. In his book, *The Apostolic Preaching and its Development*, C. H. Dodd has claimed that the speeches ascribed to Peter in the early part of Acts are a faithful summary of the content of early Christian preaching.[2] Although these early speeches do not follow exactly the same pattern, they exhibit a certain uniformity of teaching and order of presentation which suggests that they are variations of a framework of the kerygma of the primitive Church. The early date of such a kerygma is supported by the unsophisticated nature of the theology, which shows no trace of the influence of Paul, and by the presence of Aramaisms in the text. But this evidence is not as strong as has often been imagined.[3] Even the speeches which are ascribed to Paul himself, show hardly any insight into the original and distinctive aspects of his thought. Absence of Pauline influence, therefore, may be a sign, not of an early date, but of the limitations of the author's understanding. As for the Aramaisms, they are few, and may be due to the Semitic mentality of the editor or his source. They do not in themselves prove that the passages were composed in the first decade after the resurrection of Christ. Aramaic con-

[1] Op. cit., p. 80, cf. Bousset, *ZNTW*, XV, pp. 141–62.
[2] Pp. 1–73.
[3] Cf. C. F. Evans, *JTS*, N.S., VII, pp. 25–41, for a criticism of Dodd.

tinued to be an important language after the Church spread beyond the borders of Palestine. And Christians who moved from Palestine to a Gentile milieu would continue to think in Aramaic even if they used Greek in everyday speech. The evidence of Acts for the thought of the early Church must be treated with circumspection. An attempt must be made to distinguish the content of early preaching from the interpretation of the editor of Acts.

J. C. O'Neill has shown that the editor of Acts was fond of the title κύριος, which he applied both to God the Father and to Jesus Christ.[1] The vast majority of O'Neill's examples are taken from the narrative and not from the speeches. The evidence of the speeches is not so great. And it is from the speeches that we expect to find evidence of the earliest Christian teaching.

The title "Lord" is not used of Jesus in the speeches of chapters 3, 4, 5, and 6.[2] It is, however, given prominence in Peter's speech in chapter 2. Peter claims that at his exaltation Jesus was made Lord and Christ, and quotes the words of Ps. 110.1, which Jesus himself had used (Mark 12.35-7). The idea of an exalted heavenly Lord is well in advance even of the courtly usage of the title. But it does not imply that Christ is God or the object of worship.

The final verse of the quotation from Joel presents a different problem. The verse which is quoted in Acts 2.21 reads: "And it shall be, that whosoever shall call on the name of the Lord shall be saved." Although the word κύριος is used in the Septuagint for the Hebrew Y-H-W-H, it is unlikely that by making this quotation Peter was identifying the risen Christ with Yahweh. It is indeed possible that Peter did not quote this particular verse. The main point of his making the quotation from Joel is to link the prophecy with the bestowal of the Spirit. The editor of Acts might have extended the quotation as far as this verse in order to meet his own doctrinal needs.[3] Moreover the words of Acts 2.21 do not find their fulfilment in the latter part of the speech, for the climax of the speech is the announcement of Jesus' exaltation to the Messianic Lordship of Psalm 110 and not the Divine Lordship of Joel 2.32.

[1] *SJT*, VIII, pp. 155-74.
[2] It is used of God the Father in 3.19,22; 4.26,29.
[3] Compare the same process in Luke 3.3-6.

And the words of Acts 2.21 do not find fulfilment in the subsequent events, for it was in the name of Jesus Christ and not of the Lord that converts were baptized (Acts 2.38).[1]

In spite of the difficulties in the interpretation of the speech, there is no doubt that it provides a stumbling-block to Bousset. The citation from Psalm 110 provides a link with the gospel tradition. It is not surprising that a title which Jesus accepted by implication when he quoted from this psalm was ascribed to the risen Christ very early in the history of the Jerusalem Church. The title "Lord" is given to Jesus in one other speech of Peter's. In a parenthesis of 10.36 he is described as "Lord of all". But it is surprising that the title is used so rarely in the speeches.[2]

The last words of Stephen are very important for this discussion. As he was being stoned, he cried:

> Lord Jesus, receive my spirit. . . . Lord, lay not this sin to their charge (7.59,60).

For Stephen, Jesus was more than the exalted Messiah. He was the recipient of prayer. The title "Lord" is being used in the same manner as in the mystery religions. The words of Stephen cannot be dismissed as unauthentic. They were spoken before a crowd of people, and they would be clearly impressed on the minds of those present.

Stephen goes further than Peter in his use of the title and reveals an even higher conception of the status and function of Christ. He is the first Christian who is recorded as offering prayer to Christ. The explanation may be in Stephen's Hellenistic background. The name "Stephen" is Greek. Stephen himself was a Jew, but would not be known by a Greek name unless he had a close connection with Hellenistic Judaism. Either he came from the Dispersion or he had openly expressed strong sympathies with the Dispersion. All the "seven", of whom Stephen was the leader, had Greek names, and one of them, Nicolaus, is described as a "Proselyte of

---

[1] The Western reading, found in D and some Latin and Syriac versions, is ἐν τῷ ὀνόματι τοῦ κυρίου (ἡμῶν) Ἰησοῦ Χριστοῦ. This is a doctrinal assimilation to 2.21 and 2.36.

[2] In the narrative of Peter and Cornelius, Peter says "Not so, Lord" (10.14). It is not clear whether the Lord is the Father or the Son.

Antioch" (Acts 6.5). None of the others is linked with Antioch, but almost certainly they were connected with the Dispersion, for their appointment to the office of ministering to widows was the result of complaints from Hellenistic Jews. They may have visited Antioch, especially as one of their number was an Antiochene. And they would probably know more about the religions of Hellenism than did the apostles. The evidence of Stephen's words, small and isolated as it is, supports the theory that Jesus became the object of worship under Hellenistic influence. But it supports a general Hellenistic rather than an Antiochene background.

The evidence of Acts is sketchy, not wholly reliable, and a hunting-ground for speculation.[1] It would be unsafe to build a theory upon it without support from elsewhere. Rawlinson and other scholars argue that support comes from the writings of Paul. The crucial text is 1 Cor. 16.22b: "Maranatha". This is an Aramaic phrase which has been transliterated into Greek letters. Its meaning is "Our Lord, come!"[2] Rawlinson argues that the phrase was first used in the Palestinian Church and because of its sanctity was not translated into Greek. Bousset calls this text "the highest trump-card" of his opponents. And he has made two attempts to play a higher card. In the first edition of *Kyrios Christos* he claimed that the formula was imported from Antioch and was a translation from the Greek. In *Jesus der Herr* he suggested that the phrase was a Jewish curse which invoked God to come and execute judgement.[3] In the second edition of *Kyrios Christos* he returned to his original theory with decreasing confidence, describing it as a possibility which cannot be ignored.[4] "In these suggestions", writes V. Taylor, "one hears the embarrassed advocate."[5] But embarrassment does not belong only to one party in this scholarly debate. The scarcity of evidence embarrasses everyone who attempts to

[1] O'Neill's contention (*SJT*, VIII, p. 174), that the title, when it was used of Christ, was regarded from the beginning as the equivalent of Yahweh, cannot be substantiated.

[2] The Aramaic would be either *maran 'atha* (Our Lord comes) or *marana tha* (Our Lord, come!). The latter is more likely because the same kind of invocation is found in Rev. 22.20 (Come, Lord!). The formula *maranatha* occurs also in Did. 10.6 at the end of a eucharistic prayer.

[3] P. 22.   [4] P. 84.   [5] *Names of Jesus*, p. 49.

explain the development of Christianity in this period. Bousset errs in his dogmatic exclusion of the title from the Palestinian Church. But there is no good reason to suppose that in the earliest Church the title was used regularly of Jesus, and apart from Acts 7 there is no evidence that prayer was addressed to Jesus as Lord before the time of Paul's conversion.

Bultmann claims that *maranatha*, even if it came from the Palestinian Church, was first addressed to God, and only later transferred to Christ under Hellenistic influence.[1] This is certainly possible. But since Jesus had prophesied the coming of the Son of Man, and the early Church expected his speedy return to earth,[2] the words "Our Lord, come!" could fittingly have been addressed to Christ as well as the Father. There is no doubt that they are addressed to the Son in 1 Cor. 16.22. But since this epistle was written about twenty years after the conversion of Paul, there was plenty of time for the use of the prayer to be changed, and at the time of Paul's conversion it may indeed have been addressed to the Father rather than the Son. In fact, no argument about the origin of *maranatha* is conclusive, but it is definitely possible that the invocation was addressed to Christ in the earliest Palestinian Church which expected his return to the earth.[3]

There are no other reliable traces of a pre-Pauline use of κύριος. The account of the institution of the Lord's Supper in 1 Cor. 11.23 ff includes the title "the Lord Jesus".[4] A similar account in the Gospel according to St Mark does not include the title "Lord",[5] and for this reason it would be rash to claim that the presence of "Lord" in Paul's version is sure evidence of its use by the earliest Palestinian Church.

Certain scholars believe that the hymn of Phil. 2.5–11 is pre-Pauline. The hymn ends with the affirmation that "Jesus Christ

---

[1] Op. cit., I, pp. 121–8.

[2] For an examination of New Testament teaching about the return of Jesus, see pp. 117–29.

[3] Rawlinson, *New Testament Doctrine of the Christ*, p. 237; V. Taylor, op. cit., p. 49.

[4] "... that the Lord Jesus in the night in which he was betrayed took bread" (1 Cor. 11.23).

[5] Mark 14.22–5.

is Lord to the glory of God the Father". Lohmeyer has cogently argued that the hymn is a translation from the Aramaic.[1] This, however, does not prove that it belonged to the Palestinian Church, for it could have been written in Aramaic by Paul. Although Paul's mission was chiefly to Hellenistic communities, he spent a considerable part of his life in Palestine. Perhaps while he was in prison—and Philippians seems to have been written from prison—he wrote an Aramaic hymn and translated it into Greek. If he were translating a hymn, he would not be obliged to use his normal prose style, nor in expressing Old Testament ideas would he trouble to keep to the Septuagint language. It is a great mistake to suppose that hints of an Aramaic background provide definite evidence of an early origin.

Although Bousset has failed to prove that the title "Lord" stemmed from Antioch, it is clear that the history of the title in the Palestinian Church is veiled in obscurity. In such a situation there is no alternative but to have recourse to an *a priori* argument. Von Dobschütz and Taylor argue that the introduction of a title from pagan cults would have provoked the hostility of Palestinian Christians who, if they had not already approved of the title "Lord", would not have accepted it on the authority of Hellenistic Christianity. Yet there is no trace of a Christological controversy in the first half-century of the Church's history. There are different emphases in Christology, and there are seeds of later divisions, but there is no indication that Christology was openly debated.[2] This point seems to have escaped the notice of Bousset, who has tried to anticipate most of the criticisms which have been levelled against him. He claims that the doubling of the object of faith and worship would have been impossible in Palestine. The Church in Jerusalem could not have given divine honours to anyone but Yahweh. Yet he never shows why the worship of Christ in Hellenistic Christianity should have failed to provoke criticism amongst the Jewish Christians.

It now remains to sketch the outline which can dimly be

[1] *Philipperbrief*, pp. 90 ff, cf. A. M. Hunter, *Paul and his Predecessors*, pp. 45–61.
[2] Von Dobschütz, op. cit., p. 106. Taylor, op. cit., p. 48.

discerned in this obscure period of history. The early Christians called Jesus *mari* or *maran*, a title which had often been given to Rabbis. It was not merely the equivalent of "Sir" but was nearer to the English "My Lord". Jesus himself did not reject the title but did not encourage the use of it although he quoted the famous opening of Psalm 110 and by implication claimed the title for himself. After Pentecost the apostles used this psalm, which Jesus had quoted, in order to support their belief in his exaltation. The polite use of the word was definitely transformed into the courtly. But homage paid to an exalted heavenly Lord cannot easily remain courtly. By a natural development the heavenly Lord became the object of prayer and worship; Stephen at his death was praying to the ascended Lord. Whether or not he thus influenced the Church in Antioch we cannot say. The Church of Antioch was early in existence. And it is significant that a Jew with Hellenistic associations should be the first who is said to have prayed to Christ.

After his conversion Paul, to whom Jesus was revealed as Lord, went into the region of Arabia. This was the country bordering on Damascus and not far from Syria. Gal. 1.17–18a implies that Paul spent a considerable amount of time in Damascus and Arabia. It is likely that he was influenced in this period by the Christianity of Syria rather than Palestine. In the Epistle to the Galatians he stresses the fact that he had very few dealings with the Church in Jerusalem. It was not long before he established his headquarters in Antioch, which he used as a base for his journeys.

Syria was a more suitable soil for the development of the doctrine of the Person of Christ than Palestine. And Bousset has made a valuable contribution to Christian history by stressing this fact. In Syria it was no crime for the Christians to describe Christ by the title which was already accorded to the deities of the mystery religions and to the Roman Emperor. By ascribing this title to Christ the Hellenistic Christians affirmed that he meant as much to them as the deities of other religions meant to their devotees. The title was already in use in the Palestinian Church. But it is extremely likely that in Syria its meaning was extended along the lines indicated by Stephen in his dying prayer. Through the writings of Paul the idea of the risen Lord underwent a great development. It meant more for him than any corresponding idea in mystery religions. Although the cultic deities were the chief recipients of worship in these religions, they were members of a pantheon. For Paul, however, there was one God and one Lord Jesus Christ.

In the Dispersion, where the Septuagint was used, κύριος was the substitute for Yahweh. If it was used of Jesus in worship, a Jew would think that the doctrine of monotheism was being threatened. Yet there are indications that Christians consciously transferred the title from God to Christ in such a way as to suggest that Christ was almost identical with God.

Joel 2.32, "Whosoever shall call on the name of the Lord shall be saved", is quoted in Acts 2.21 and Rom. 10.13. In the Old Testament the Lord is Yahweh. In Acts 2.21, as we have mentioned already, it is uncertain whether Peter actually identified the Lord in Joel with the Christ. But it is clear that Rom. 10.13 refers to Christ, and this is the clearest evidence that the divine title was consciously applied to Christ where Jews would normally have applied it to Yahweh.[1]

There are other passages in which the connection with Yahweh is slightly veiled. They are Phil. 2.9–11, Eph. 4.8, and John 12.40.

1. Wherefore also God highly exalted him, and gave unto him the name which is above every name; that in the name of Jesus every knee should bow . . . and that every tongue should confess that Jesus Christ is Lord, to the glory of God the Father (Phil. 2.9–11).

This passage is dependent on Isa. 45.23, "that unto me every knee shall bow, every tongue shall swear". Although in the Hebrew text the words "Yahweh" and "God" do not occur, there is no doubt that Yahweh is the object of worship. And the Septuagint refers to God (θεός). Where the prophet was thinking of Yahweh Elohim, Paul speaks of Jesus Christ. Moreover it is likely that for Paul the "name which is above every name" was "Lord", the name of God himself.

2. When he ascended on high,
   he led captivity captive,
   And gave gifts unto men (Eph. 4.8).

[1] The influence of Joel can also be detected in 1 Cor. 1.2 and 2 Tim. 2.22.

The Hebrew of Ps. 68.18, upon which this verse is based, does not mention Yahweh. But in the last clause of Ps. 68.18 God is called *yah ʾelohim*. Words which were spoken of Yahweh in the psalm are used of Jesus in Ephesians.

> 3. He hath blinded their eyes, and he hardened their heart;
> Lest they should see with their eyes, and perceive with their heart,
> And I should turn,
> And I should heal them (John 12.40).

These words are based on Isa. 6.10, and the evangelist's comment is: "These things said Isaiah, because he saw his glory; and he spake of him" (John 12.41). The evangelist means that Isaiah was speaking of Jesus. Yet Isaiah was speaking of the Lord God.

The above quotations show the tendency of early Christians to refer Old Testament passages to Jesus, although they had originally been referred to Yahweh. They provide evidence that Jesus received honours which had been given in the Hebrew tradition to Yahweh.

There are signs of a similar process in the use of the words ἐγώ εἰμι ("I am") in the Fourth Gospel. ἐγώ εἰμι is used in the Septuagint to translate *ʾani hu* ("I am he"), which is often used by Yahweh of himself.[1] There is a close parallel between Isa. 43.10: "... that ye may know and believe me, and understand that I am he (ὅτι ἐγώ εἰμι)", and John 8.24: "For except ye believe that I am (ὅτι ἐγώ εἰμι), ye shall die in your sins." The frequent use of ἐγώ εἰμι in the Fourth Gospel suggests that Jesus appeared with the authority and power of Yahweh. Most impressive are the absolute uses of ἐγώ εἰμι, in 8.24, quoted above, and in 8.58: "Before Abraham was, I am." Other sayings are: "I am the bread of life" (6.35, cf. 6.41,48), "I am the light of the world" (8.12; 9.5), "I am the door (of the sheep)" (10.7,9), "I am the good shepherd" (10.11,14), "I am the resurrection and the life" (11.25), "I am the way, and the truth, and the life" (14.6), and "I am the (true) vine" (15.1,5). All these sayings emphasize the uniqueness of Jesus' activity, and the evangelist may well have had

[1] Cf. Deut. 32.39; Isa. 41.4; 43.13; 46.4; 48.12. Cf. Barrett, *St John*, pp. 282–3, and Bultmann, *Johannesevangelium*, p. 248.

the Hebrew *ʾani hu* in mind.[1] He may also have been thinking of Ex. 3.14, in which God describes himself as "I am" (LXX ἐγώ εἰμι). There is a resemblance too to the "I" sayings in Proverbs 8, in which Wisdom speaks about herself. The "I am" sayings, however, in the Fourth Gospel do not directly imply that Jesus is linked with Yahweh. It is rather a case of undefined suggestion.[2]

Another link between Jesus and Yahweh is in the use of the idea of the bridegroom. In several passages of the Old Testament the relationship of Yahweh to Israel is said to be that of bridegroom to bride. In Hos. 2.20 Yahweh says: "I will even betroth thee unto me in faithfulness: and thou shalt know the Lord." According to Isa. 54.5: "For thy Maker is thine husband; the Lord of hosts is his name."[3] Rabbinic sayings connect the marriage-time with the Messianic age.[4] In the New Testament the same marriage metaphor is used to describe the relationship of Christ to the Church.[5] The idea has a basis in a saying of Jesus himself:[6]

> Can the sons of the bride-chamber fast, while the bridegroom is with them? as long as they have the bridegroom with them, they cannot fast. But the days will come when the bridegroom shall be taken away from them, and then will they fast in that day (Mark 2.19–20).

In the following passages the idea is further developed:

> For I espoused you to one husband, that I might present you as a pure virgin to Christ (2 Cor. 11.2).

> Husbands, love your wives, even as Christ also loved the church, and gave himself up for it (Eph. 5.25).

> He that hath the bride is the bridegroom: but the friend of the bridegroom, which standeth and heareth him, rejoiceth greatly because of the bridegroom's voice (John 3.29).

[1] Cf. also 8.18: "I am he that beareth witness of myself", and 8.23: "I am from above." ἐγώ εἰμι also appears in Mark 14.62 as Jesus' reply to the high priest's question about his Messiahship and his Divine Sonship.

[2] See Barrett, op. cit., pp. 242–3, for a full discussion.

[3] Cf. Isa. 62.4,5; Jer. 2.2; 3.14; Ezek. 16.8; Mal. 2.11.

[4] Cf. Taylor, op. cit., p. 88.

[5] Ibid., pp. 87–8.

[6] The idea is implicit in the parables of the Marriage Feast (Matt. 22.1–14) and the Wise and Foolish Virgins (Matt. 25.1–13).

The marriage of the Lamb is come, and his wife hath made herself ready (Rev. 19.7, cf. Rev. 21.9; 22.17).

In these passages Christ is the bridegroom and the Church, or the Christian people, is the bride. In John 3.29 John the Baptist is likened to the friend of the bridegroom. This idea of Christ as the bridegroom is further evidence of the tendency to set Christ in the place of Yahweh.

In spite of the way in which Jesus was called Lord, and in spite of the tendency to transfer to him ideas and quotations which originally referred to Yahweh, it must not be assumed that he was openly and directly identified with Yahweh. Other passages stress the difference between the Lord and God. For example the greetings of the Pauline letters include the formula "God the Father and the Lord Jesus Christ", and in 1 Cor. 8.5,6 Paul says that although in pagan religions there are "gods many and lords many", the Christians have "one God and Father . . . and one Lord, Jesus Christ" (cf. Eph. 4.5,6).

The New Testament writers did not consistently identify Christ with Yahweh. Caution restrained them. In worship they probably gave the title "Lord" the same implications as the title "God". The two titles are combined in Thomas's confession, "My Lord and my God!" (John 20.28), and such a confession would be appropriate for use in worship. But even the Fourth Evangelist, who planned his gospel so that the confession of Jesus Christ as Lord and God should come as a climax, exercised restraint. He reserved the statement that Christ was Lord and God until the twentieth chapter because he believed that in the moment of worship the truth about Christ was apprehended. The other New Testament writers were reluctant to call Jesus God, and the title "Lord" had the advantage of flexibility of meaning. It could not offend a monotheist in the same way as the title "God". Hence, a distinction is made by Paul between the Lord Christ and God the Father, and this emphasis balances those passages in which it seems that Christ is being identified with Yahweh.

CHAPTER 6

THE WORSHIP OF JESUS CHRIST

In the last two chapters it has been argued that Jesus Christ was given the divine titles "God" and "Lord", and that in so far as he was called by these names, he was the object of worship. Further evidence will now be examined, much of which confirms the view that Jesus was worshipped by Christians of the first century. This evidence is divided into four sections: doxologies ascribed to Christ; prayers offered to Christ; quotations from the Old Testament which are transferred from Yahweh to Christ; the use of the Greek equivalents of the word "worship" in connection with Christ.

Doxologies ascribed to Christ

In many passages of scripture praise and blessing are given to God. These passages are often couched in liturgical form and may have been composed primarily for use in worship. There are many of these doxologies in the New Testament. Most of them are addressed to God the Father, as, for example, the great hymn of Rom. 11.33ff, the epilogue of Romans (16.25–7), the doxologies of 1 Pet. 1.3–5, Jude 24–5, and many passages in the Book of Revelation.

There are two clear examples in the New Testament of doxologies which are ascribed to Christ. They are:

> But grow in the grace and knowledge of our Lord and Saviour Jesus Christ. To him be the glory both now and for ever. Amen (2 Pet. 3.18).

> Unto him that loveth us, and loosed us from our sins by his blood; and he made us to be a kingdom, to be priests unto his God and Father; to him be the glory and the dominion for ever and ever. Amen (Rev. 1.5b, 6).

A further example is Rom. 9.5 ("Christ . . . who is over all, God blessed for ever. Amen"). This has been examined in an earlier chapter.[1]

[1] See pp. 54–8.

In two other passages it is not immediately clear whether the doxology is in honour of the Father or of Christ.[1]

Now the God of peace, who brought again from the dead the great shepherd of the sheep with the blood of the eternal covenant, even our Lord Jesus, make you perfect in every good thing to do his will, working in us that which is well-pleasing in his sight, through Jesus Christ; to whom be the glory for ever and ever. Amen (Heb. 13.20–1).

From a grammatical point of view the doxology is more likely to have been given to Christ than to God, since the relative "to whom" (ᾧ) immediately follows the word "Christ". On the other hand, since "God" is the subject of the main verb "make you perfect", it is possible that the doxology is ascribed to God. This second consideration is more important than the former, and in all probability the doxology was addressed to God the Father.

The Lord will deliver me from every evil work and will save me unto his heavenly kingdom: to whom be the glory for ever and ever. Amen (2 Tim. 4.18).

The interpretation depends on whether "Lord" refers to God or to Christ. In several passages of the Pastoral Epistles "Lord" is clearly used of Christ.[2] In other passages it could possibly refer to God the Father,[3] but in all these examples the title could also refer to Christ. A clue to the interpretation of 2 Tim. 4.18 is provided by the description of the Lord as "the righteous judge" (2 Tim. 4.8).[4] This "righteous judge" is Jesus, because at the beginning of the chapter (2 Tim. 4.1) there is a reference to "Christ Jesus, who shall judge the quick and the dead". Moreover, in 2 Tim. 4.1 "his appearing and his kingdom" refers to Christ's appearing and Christ's kingdom, and this suggests that "his heavenly kingdom" in 2 Tim. 4.18 means "Christ's heavenly kingdom". The evidence of 2 Tim. 4 as a whole favours the view that the doxology of 2 Tim. 4.18 is addressed to Christ.

---

[1] On pp. 72–3 it has been argued that the doxology of 1 Tim. 1.17 refers to God the Father and not to Christ.

[2] 1 Tim. 1.2,12,14; 6.3,14; 2 Tim. 1.2,8.

[3] 1 Tim. 6.15; 2 Tim. 1.16,18; 2.7,14,19,22,24; 4.8,14,17,18,22.

[4] Cf. 2 Tim. 4.14: "The Lord will render to him according to his works."

As a result of the preceding discussion it is possible to say that there are four examples in the New Testament of doxologies to Christ: 2 Pet. 3.18; Rev. 1.5b, 6; Rom. 9.5; and 2 Tim. 4.18. There are also two doxologies in the Book of Revelation, which are addressed to both Father and Son.

> And every created thing which is in the heaven, and on the earth, and under the earth, and on the sea, and all things that are in them, heard I saying, Unto him that sitteth on the throne, and unto the Lamb, be the blessing and the honour, and the glory, and the dominion, for ever and ever (Rev. 5.13).
>
> Salvation unto our God which sitteth on the throne and unto the Lamb (Rev. 7.10).

Since the New Testament is not a Book of Common Prayer, we cannot expect to find a large number of doxologies in its pages. Few are given to the Father and few to the Son. But the presence of even a small number in the New Testament shows that they had won general acceptance in the cultus. The words of John 5.23 were being fulfilled: "That all may honour the Son, even as they honour the Father."

An insight into the importance of Christ in Christian worship can be obtained by comparing the ᶜalenu prayer of the Jewish liturgy with certain Christian parallels.[1] This ᶜalenu prayer, which now concludes the daily morning service, may be pre-Christian in origin.[2] If so, it would be known to the first Christians.

Several parts of the prayer are reflected in New Testament descriptions of Christ. Language, which was used about God in the synagogue, was used about Christ in the Church. The ᶜalenu prayer opens:

> It is meet that we should praise the Lord of all; that we should ascribe greatness to Him who formed (the world) from the beginning.

The first part of this verse is reflected in the title "Lord of all", which is given to Christ in Acts 10.36. The second part of the verse is reflected in those parts of the New Testament in which

---

[1] Cf. W. O. E. Oesterley, *The Jewish Background of the Christian Liturgy*, pp. 68–70. Oesterley's translation of the prayer is used.

[2] Cf. J. H. Hertz, *The Authorized Daily Prayer Book with Commentary*, Part I, p. 208.

Christ is described as one who assisted in the creation of the world.[1] Later in the prayer come these words: "We worship before the King of the kings of kings." A similar title, "king of kings", is given to Jesus in Rev. 17.14 and 19.16. Although this title is found in the Old Testament,[2] it is likely that it was chiefly imprinted upon the minds of Jewish Christians by its regular use in the synagogue. The last four verses of the prayer are:

That to Thee every knee must bow, every tongue swear.
Before Thee, O Lord our God, let them bow and fall down; and to the glory of Thy great Name let them give honour.
And let them take upon themselves the yoke of Thy Kingdom, and do Thou reign over them for ever and ever.
For the Kingdom is Thine, and for ever and ever shalt Thou reign in glory.

The first two of these verses are based on Isa. 45.23, and contain language similar to that which is used of Christ in Phil. 2.10–11. The language of the Philippians seems to be derived from the ᶜ*alenu* prayer rather than Isaiah, since there is a reference to "glory" in both the ᶜ*alenu* prayer and Philippians, but not in Isaiah. The prayer reads: "and to the glory of Thy great Name let them give honour"; and Philippians reads: "and that every tongue should confess that Jesus Christ is Lord to the glory of God the Father."

While the ᶜ*alenu* prayer, following Isaiah, says that every knee must bow and every tongue must swear to God, Philippians says that every knee must bow in the name of Jesus and every tongue must confess that Jesus Christ is Lord.

The third verse of this concluding section of the prayer, "And let them take upon themselves the yoke of Thy Kingdom", may have been in Jesus' own mind when he said: "Take my yoke upon you and learn of me" (Matt. 11.29). The prayer speaks of the yoke of God's kingdom. Jesus invites men to take his own yoke upon them.

The second part of the third verse and the fourth verse are prayers that God will reign for ever and ever. This is an Old Testament theme, which is taken up in Revelation in which it is

[1] John 1.3; Col. 1.16; Heb. 1.2.
[2] Ezra 7.12; Ezek. 26.7; Dan. 2.37; cf. Hos. 8.10 ("king of princes"). In none of these O.T. examples is the title used of God, but only of earthly kings.

said that not only God but also the Son and the saints will reign for ever and ever (Rev. 11.15; 22.5).

The *alenu* prayer is only one part of the Jewish liturgy. Other sections of the liturgy also may have had their influence on Christian worship. The parallels which have been mentioned above are sufficient to show that it is possible that Christians were influenced by synagogue worship. The evidence is by no means conclusive, since most of the parallels may be explained by a common dependence on the Old Testament. But it has been shown that Philippians is closer to the *alenu* prayer than to Isaiah. It is likely that the words which have been quoted were specially impressed upon the mind of a Jew because they were repeated frequently in the liturgy. These words would naturally spring to the minds of Christians when they expressed their faith by hymns and doxologies. But they were not content simply to borrow the formulae of Judaism. They applied to Christ many of the ancient formulae which had formerly been reserved for God.

Prayer to Christ

This section is concerned with petitions and intercessions to Christ. In the broadest sense of the word the *alenu* prayer is a prayer. But it is a doxology rather than a petition or intercession, and for that reason has been considered in the preceding section. The passages which will now be examined show that Christians of the first century prayed to Jesus both for themselves and for others.

In the Acts of the Apostles there is one example of prayer to Jesus. When Stephen was being stoned to death, he cried: "Lord Jesus, receive my spirit. . . . Lord, lay not this sin to their charge" (Acts 7.59–60).

In the epistles of Paul there are several petitions and intercessions to Christ. The invocation *maranatha* (1 Cor. 16.22), which is Aramaic for "Our Lord, come!", is probably an ancient Christian formula which was taken over by Paul.[1] The invocation, "Come, Lord!" (Rev. 22.20) may spring from the same origin.

Another probable example of petition to Christ is found in 2 Cor. 12.8. In a description of his religious experiences Paul says

[1] See pp. 85–6.

that once he "besought the Lord" about a thorn in his flesh. "The Lord" probably refers to Christ for the following reason. The Lord's reply to Paul's prayer was: "My power is made perfect in weakness" (2 Cor. 12.9). In this context "my power" seems to be "Christ's power", because in the same verse Paul says: "Most gladly therefore will I rather glory in my weaknesses, that the power of Christ may rest upon me." The identification of Christ with the Lord is not certain in this passage, but is implied by the most natural interpretation.

Other prayers in the Pauline Epistles are couched in the form of benedictions. Three of these are found in the Epistles to the Thessalonians:

> Now may our God and Father himself, and our Lord Jesus, direct our way unto you: and the Lord make you to increase and abound in love one toward another, and toward all men, even as we also do toward you (1 Thess. 3.11,12).

> And the Lord direct your hearts into the love of God, and into the patience of Christ (2 Thess. 3.5).

> Now the Lord of peace himself give you peace at all times in all ways. The Lord be with you all (2 Thess. 3.16).

In the first of these three passages (1 Thess. 3.11–12) there are two sections. The first speaks of both the Father and the Lord Jesus. The second speaks of the Lord. The two passages from the Second Epistle to the Thessalonians (2 Thess. 3.5 and 3.16) are both about "the Lord". There is good reason to believe that in this epistle the title "Lord" always refers to Christ. In any case since the title "the Lord Jesus Christ" appears three times in this chapter (2 Thess. 3.6, 12,18) it is highly probable that the absolute title "Lord" is also used of Christ.

Bultmann classifies these as prayers,[1] but they are not directly addressed to God or the Lord, and are better classified as benedictions. With them may be linked the benedictions in which Paul prays that the grace of the Lord Jesus Christ may be with his readers.[2]

[1] *Theology of the New Testament*, I, pp. 126 ff.

[2] Rom. 1.7; 16.20; 1 Cor. 1.3; 16.23; 2 Cor. 1.2; 13.14; Gal. 1.3; 6.18; Eph. 1.2; 6.24; Phil. 1.2; 4.23; Col. 1.2; 1 Thess. 5.28; 2 Thess. 1.12; 3.18; Philem. 3,25. Similar formulae occur in 2 John 3; 1 Tim. 1.2; 2 Tim. 1.2; Titus 1.4.

There is yet one more passage in the New Testament which shows that prayer was made to Christ. In John 14.14, according to the most reliable textual authorities, Jesus says: "If ye shall ask me anything in my name, that will I do." Some authorities omit the word "me".[1] Since the practice of prayer to Christ had already emerged in New Testament times it cannot be argued that the word "me" was introduced under the influence of a later and more developed cultus. The best manuscripts support the inclusion of the word "me", and the passage is evidence that Christ was an object of prayer in the place where the Fourth Gospel was written.

In spite of the wide and varied evidence of prayer to Jesus, Bultmann has argued that prayer was offered to him only in private and not in public liturgies.[2] Bultmann makes a distinction between doxologies and invocations on the one hand, and prayers on the other.[3] The doxologies which have already been discussed and invocations such as *maranatha* and Stephen's dying cry are not reckoned by Bultmann as prayers. This is an unwarrantably narrow attitude to prayer. When Paul said *maranatha* ("Our Lord, come!") he was praying to Jesus to return to the earth. This cry was not only an invocation but also both an intercession and a petition, for Paul was praying that Christ would return to the aid of both his fellow-Christians and himself.

Bultmann admits that private prayer was addressed to Christ, and believes that the three passages which have been quoted from the Epistles to the Thessalonians are examples of this kind of prayer. Bultmann's distinction between public and private prayer is too rigid. There is no reason why Paul should not have used in public the kind of prayer which he included in the Epistles to the Thessalonians. Indeed, since he incorporated prayers into his epistles, he expected them to be read to the assembled congregation.

---

[1] In John 14.14 με is omitted in A D L and the Old Latin Versions. The omission was probably caused by assimilation to verse 13 (so Bultmann, *Ev. Joh.* p. 473) or by a desire to avoid contradiction of 16.23 (so Barrett, *St John*, p. 384). The whole of the verse is omitted by a few authorities including Old Latin b.

[2] *Theology of the New Testament*, I, p. 128.   [3] Op. cit., pp. 126–7.

Moreover, in public extempore prayer Paul would be likely to utter some of the petitions and intercessions which he made in private prayer. Bultmann admits that there was extempore prayer in the early Church but thinks that it soon acquired a "cultic" character. Nevertheless he does not deny that Paul himself used free prayer. And if Paul used free prayer in public, no rigid distinction can be made between the language of his private and public prayer.

The readiness of first-century Christians to pray to Christ is strong evidence of their belief in his divinity. But it is not absolutely conclusive, for in Judaism prayers were offered to others besides God. For example, many Jews believed that there were angels whose function was to make intercession to God. They made petitions to these angels to pray for them.[1] But the prayers to Christ which have been quoted in this chapter are not petitions that he will intercede to the Father. In several parts of the New Testament, Christ is regarded as a heavenly intercessor.[2] But his function extended beyond that of mere intercession to the Father. The prayers which have been quoted show that he received prayer in his own right and was believed to have power to answer the requests which were made to him. Since Christians addressed their prayers only to the Father and to Christ, and avoided praying to angels or patriarchs, the fact that Christ was thought worthy to

[1] Evidence for this belief in angelic intercessors is found in Zech. 1.12; Job 5.1; 33.23; 1 Enoch 9.3; 15.2; 71.1–6; Test. Dan 6.2; Test. Levi 3.5. It is likely that petitions were made to these intercessors. Moore, *Judaism*, I, p. 439, quotes a saying of R. Judan (fourth cent.) in which men are told to cry to God and not to Michael or Gabriel. Moore, op. cit., III, p. 134, argues that this saying does not prove that petitions were made to angels. But it is extremely likely that the Rabbi was attacking an actual practice.

[2] Rom. 8.34; Heb. 7.25; 1 John 2.1. The Spirit is also said to make intercession in Rom. 8.26. It may be inferred from the parable of the Rich Man and Lazarus that prayer was made to Abraham after his death (Luke 16.19–31). The rich man cries in his torment to Abraham, and asks him not only to have mercy on himself but also to send Lazarus to warn his surviving brother. Because, however, this is an imaginary dialogue between men in the after life, it has no direct bearing on the practice of prayer on earth. There is no evidence in the New Testament that prayer was offered by Christians to any of the patriarchs.

receive prayers in the same way as his Father, suggests that his followers ranked him with the Father.

Quotations from the Old Testament which are transferred from Yahweh to Christ

The New Testament is richly stocked with Old Testament quotations, some of which are repeated by several authors. Prophecies and hymns, which were believed to foretell the coming of the Messiah, were eagerly adapted for use in the Church. Rendel Harris has contended that these quotations were taken from a collection of Christian testimonies which was circulated through a large part of the Church.[1] Another theory is that of Selwyn, who argues that these quotations were used in early Christian hymns. He cites examples of Jewish hymns which were mosaics of Old Testament texts, and suggests that Christians made similar collections.[2]

A number of Old Testament quotations have already been examined.[3] These were used of Yahweh in the Old Testament and of Christ in the New Testament. They are evidence that Christ was honoured as God in the worship of the Church. Other quotations of this type will now be examined.

A catena of quotations about "the stone" was circulated in the early Church. There are traces of it in the synoptic gospels, Acts, Romans, Ephesians, and 1 Peter.[4] Hence it seems to have had a wide currency in the Church. The only quotation which is relevant to our discussion is Isa. 8.13, 14:

> The Lord of hosts, him shall ye sanctify; and let him be your fear, and let him be your dread. And he shall be for a sanctuary; but for a stone of stumbling and for a rock of offence to both the houses of Israel.

These words of Isaiah are quoted in two writings of the New Testament, Romans and 1 Peter. The words quoted are:

[1] J. Rendel Harris, *Testimonies*.

[2] E. G. Selwyn, *First Epistle of Peter*, pp. 275–7.

[3] Acts 2.21; Rom. 10.13; Phil. 2.9–11; Eph. 4.8; John 12. 40. See pp. 89–90.

[4] Mark 12.10, 11 (cf. Matt. 21.42; Luke 20.17); Luke 20.17–18; Acts 4.11; Rom. 9.33; Eph. 2.20; 1 Pet. 2.4, 8. See Selwyn, op. cit., pp. 270–1.

Behold I lay in Zion a stone of stumbling and a rock of offence (Rom. 9.33).

He became the head of the corner and A stone of stumbling and a rock of offence (1 Pet. 2.7, 8).

Isaiah called Yahweh "a stone of stumbling", but Paul and Peter gave this title to Jesus. The way in which they used the quotation suggests that it was part of a hymn or liturgical formula, and lends weight to the belief that the title was applied to Christ in worship, and was part of a common tradition which did not spring from any particular apostle.

But sanctify in your hearts Christ as Lord (1 Pet. 3.15).

This is a reminiscence of the Old Testament rather than a quotation from it. The Old Testament passage is:

. . . they shall sanctify my name: yea they shall sanctify the Holy One of Jacob, and shall stand in awe of the God of Israel (Isa. 29.23).

Although this is not an exact quotation, it is likely that the writer was aware of the Old Testament background and was transferring to Jesus an honour which had formerly been given to Yahweh.

And let all the angels of God worship him (Heb. 1.6).

καὶ προσκυνησάτωσαν αὐτῷ πάντες ἄγγελοι θεοῦ.

These words are based on a clause of Deut. 32.43 which appears in the Septuagint but not in the Massoretic text. The LXX reads: καὶ προσκυνησάτωσαν αὐτῷ υἱοὶ θεοῦ. (Some authorities read πάντες ἄγγελοι for υἱοί.)

The writer of Hebrews may have been influenced by the Septuagint version of Ps. 97.7, which is: προσκυνήσατε αὐτῷ πάντες οἱ ἄγγελοι αὐτοῦ

The quotation is used in Hebrews to show the superiority of Christ to the angels, and may have been part of a series of proof texts, or may even have been a liturgical formula, since it is included in a group of quotations with which it is assumed that the readers are familiar.

Greek equivalents of the word "worship"

There are two Greek verbs which are specially connected with
worship.[1] They are προσκυνεῖν and λατρεύειν. λατρεύειν is
not of great importance for this discussion. In the Septuagint it is
used almost exclusively of service to God or to heathen deities.[2]
In the New Testament it is never used of service or worship given
to Christ. It is used of the service of God in the earthly temple and
in the heavenly sanctuary. Phil. 3.3: οἱ πνεύματι θεοῦ λατρεύοντες
is capable of two interpretations, (a) "those who worship in the
Spirit of God", and (b) "those who worship the Spirit of God".
Arguments will be brought forward later to show that the first of
these interpretations is preferable.[3] In any case there is no instance
of λατρεύειν which has Christ as object.

The word προσκυνεῖν occurs far more frequently in the
New Testament than λατρεύειν. In the Septuagint προσκυνεῖν
generally translates the Hebrew shahah, which denotes bowing
down or worship. It is not always used of God but can describe
the attitude of one man to another. In the New Testament too it
denotes bowing down or worship.

In the sayings of Jesus προσκυνεῖν is used to describe an
attitude which men should have to God alone. When the devil
offered Jesus all the kingdoms of the world on condition that he
should worship him, Jesus replied: "Thou shalt worship
(προσκυνήσεις) the Lord thy God, and him only shalt thou
serve" (Matt. 4.10=Luke 4.8).

The evangelists, however, use the word προσκυνεῖν to describe men's attitude to Jesus. In Mark the word describes the
attitude to Jesus of the Gerasene demoniac, who, when he saw
Jesus, "ran and worshipped (προσεκύνησεν) him from afar"
(Mark 5.6). Again, in Mark 15.19, the mocking soldiers are said to
have fallen on their knees and worshipped (προσεκύνουν) Jesus.
This is an ironical use of the word προσκυνεῖν, but in the former
example the demoniac offered genuine worship.

[1] The word λειτουργεῖν is used of religious or secular service and is not confined to the service of God. It occurs rarely in the New Testament and does
not have Christ as object.
[2] Cf. Strathmann in Kittel, *TWNT*, IV, pp. 59 ff.   [3] See pp. 227–8.

In Luke the verb προσκυνεῖν occurs only three times, twice in the dialogue with Satan (Luke 4.7, 8), in which Jesus says that worship is to be given only to God, and once at the end of the gospel (Luke 24.52), when the disciples are said to have worshipped Jesus after he was carried up into heaven. Luke does not record any worship of Jesus before the time of his resurrection.

In Matthew the use of προσκυνεῖν is less restrained than in Mark and Luke. The wise men worship the infant Jesus (Matt. 2.2,8,11), and this may be genuine worship rather than polite obeisance. But when a varied collection of people, including a leper, a ruler, a Canaanite woman, a slave, and the mother of the sons of Zebedee, are all said to worship the adult Jesus during his ministry,[1] it is certain that the word προσκυνεῖν is being used to describe polite obeisance. On the other hand when the men in the boat saw Jesus walking on the water (14.33) and worshipped him and called him the Son of God, their attitude was perhaps one of real worship. Certainly Matthew cannot be used as evidence that Jesus was not worshipped until after his resurrection.

The only person who is said to worship Jesus in the Fourth Gospel is the blind man whose sight he restored (John 9.38). In Heb. 1.6 ("Let all the angels of God worship him") Christ is the object of worship.[2] And in the Book of Revelation Christ receives worship together with God, according to 5.14.[3] There are no further instances of the use of προσκυνεῖν to describe the worship of Christ in the New Testament.

The examples of προσκυνεῖν which have been discussed do not greatly strengthen the evidence for the worship of Christ. The ambiguity of the word προσκυνεῖν, which can be used of oriental obeisance as well as actual worship, makes it impossible to draw any certain conclusions from the evidence.

[1] Matt. 8.2; 9.18; 15.25; 18.26; 20.20.   [2] See p. 102.

[3] In Rev. 3.9 the object of worship is the members of the Church in Philadelphia. Probably the word προσκυνεῖν should be translated "bow down to" in this context.

CHAPTER 7

JESUS AND JUDGEMENT

In the three previous chapters Jesus was shown to have been the object of worship in the Church of New Testament times. In the next three chapters it will be argued that he was believed to perform the divine functions of judgement, creation, and salvation. It was typical of the Jewish mentality of early Christian writers that beliefs about Jesus were expressed in terms of his activity rather than his metaphysical nature. Activities were ascribed to Jesus which were generally regarded in Judaism as belonging to God alone. While his divinity was being acknowledged in worship, it was being expounded in terms of the divine activities which he performed.

The first function to be discussed is judgement. It is being taken first because it was claimed by Jesus for himself. Although in Jewish teaching judgement is not regarded in every sense as an exclusively divine function, some aspects of it seem to have been confined to God alone. The aim of this discussion is to discover whether Jesus was believed to perform that kind of judgement which was regarded in Judaism as an exclusively divine function.

The Israelite and Judaistic Background

In Hebrew religion God's holiness was revealed in his justice. The prophets taught about a God whose power was not capricious but controlled by ethical standards. "His Lordship", writes Herntrich,[1] "expresses itself in the dispensation of justice, and in his dispensation of justice one recognizes that he is the Lord." His sphere of

---

[1] *TWNT*, III, p. 923.

authority is the whole earth.[1] Judgement and righteousness are of the essence of his majesty and holiness.[2]

It is not surprising that Judaism developed into a legalistic religion. At its heart was the idea that God was judge over his people. His supreme revelation had been given in the form of law. Although he used the services of human judges and human courts, he was himself the judge *par excellence*.

Four chief aspects of God's judgement can be discerned in Hebrew and Jewish thought: the daily task of administrative justice, which was often performed by human agents; the judgement which was executed upon nations by conquerors, who were often unconscious servants of God and did not act within the framework of the Jewish legal system; the judgement which was to be effected on the Day of the Lord, and with few exceptions is ascribed in Jewish literature to God alone; the judgement which was pronounced upon the inward attitude of the individual, and was rarely entrusted to a man.

The Daily Task of Administrative Justice

In ancient Israel justice was meted out in two ways, by *torah* and by *mishpat*. *Torah* was a decision which was not passed upon precedent. The Pentateuch itself was *torah*, since it was given by God to Moses and appealed to no other legal pronouncements. The same word *torah* was used to describe particular legal decisions, provided there was no recourse to precedent. If a judgement was based on precedent, it was called *mishpat*.[3]

In both *torah* and *mishpat* men were acting on behalf of God. They were exercising the divine function of judgement. They were not serving him blindly, but were making conscious and deliberate decisions. God was regarded as the author of a judgement. For if a decision was *mishpat*, it was based on *torah*, and if it was *torah*,

[1] Cf. Gen. 18.25: "Shall not the Judge of all the earth do right?" Cf. Ps. 94.2.

[2] Cf. Isa. 5.16: "The Lord of hosts is exalted in judgement, and God the Holy One is sanctified in righteousness." Cf. Deut. 32.4.

[3] Cf. N. H. Snaith, *Distinctive Ideas of the Old Testament*, p. 75.

it had been given by God. In order to discover *torah* men consulted lots or the divine oracle, and if they were prophets, they relied upon visions. Although these methods of establishing *torah* depended on circumstances which were beyond the control of human beings, they included an element of reflection and inter-pretation. Human judges were not puppets in the hands of God. They used their own minds. God had entrusted them with authority to interpret and apply his laws and oracles.

The task of judgement was not limited to a single class of men. Priests, prophets, and state officials all sat in judgement on behalf of God. The early rulers of Israel were actually called "Judges". This was quite consistent with Hebrew teaching about judgement. The day-to-day administration of the state, and the hearing of particular problems and disputes were not separate activities. The ruler was continually passing judgement. A divine task had been entrusted to a man.

The Judgement which was Executed upon Nations by Conquerors

God judged the nations through foreign conquerors. The Assyrian was the rod of his anger with which he punished Jerusalem and Samaria (Isa. 10.5). Cyrus was the shepherd of God, his Anointed, before whom he subdued nations and loosed the loins of kings (Isa. 44.28; 45.1). These pagan kings who were ignorant that they were agents of Yahweh, had a different relationship to God from that of the judges and kings of Israel and Judah. While foreign conquerors executed the divine justice unwittingly through the victories which they won and the havoc which they spread, the judges and kings consciously fulfilled a mission to which they had been appointed by God.

The Judgement which was to be Effected on the Day of the Lord

The expectation of the "Day of Yahweh" is given frequent expression in Jewish literature. The teaching about this day is often ambiguous. In early times the people believed that on the Day of the Lord they would win a decisive victory over their enemies.

But Amos warned them that it would be a day of punishment, a vindication not of God's people but of God's justice.[1]

A generation later Isaiah uttered a similar warning: "For there shall be a day of the Lord of hosts upon all that is proud and haughty, and upon all that is lifted up; and it shall be brought low" (Isa. 2.12). The Day of the Lord was not to be the occasion of an ordinary judgement. It had an air of finality. It was the climax to which the drama of history was moving. The Day may have been identified with the devastation wrought by invading armies, but whatever its precise form would be, there was no doubt that it was the Day of the Lord. The hand which controlled the dreadful events was God's. A pagan monarch might be the divine executioner, but could not be the divine judge. He did not pass sentence. He did not acquit or condemn.

After the exile the Day was described in more colourful terms. It was "the great and terrible day of the Lord" (Joel 2.31, Mal. 4.5). Malachi believed that it would be a day of judgement and punishment which would inaugurate an era of peace and blessedness (Mal. 4.1–3). In Joel 2.30 ff the signs that will precede the Day are described in apocalyptic language: "And I will shew wonders in the heavens and in the earth, blood, and fire, and pillars of smoke. The sun shall be turned into darkness, and the moon into blood, before the great and terrible day of the Lord come."

In these writings it is assumed that Yahweh will be the judge on this "great and terrible day". According to Malachi, God described it as "the day which I do make" (4.3), and on which "I will come near to you and to judgement" (3.5). Although the righteous will tread down the wicked, they will not actually pass the judgement. God alone will be judge.

The teaching about a Day of Judgement was developed and often highly elaborated in later Judaism. But with few exceptions it is made clear that God is the judge. Even where a Messiah is introduced, he does not pass sentence. He may carry out the punishment

---

[1] "Woe unto you that desire the day of the Lord!
wherefore would ye have the day of the Lord?
it is darkness, and not light." Amos 5.18.

on the Day of the Lord and execute administrative justice in the Messianic kingdom, but he does not actually pass the sentence at the Last Judgement.

According to the Psalms of Solomon 17 and 18, the Messiah will be a righteous king, pure from sin, and a descendant from David. He will gather together the scattered tribes and make Jerusalem holy. He will destroy the ungodly nations by the breath of his mouth. These psalms do not say that the Messiah will judge the people when these tremendous events are taking place. He will only judge them afterwards, when he exercises administrative justice in the Messianic kingdom.[1]

According to the Testament of Levi, after punishment has been inflicted on the sinners, a priestly Messiah will arise. The judgement which he will exercise belongs not to the law court but to the council chamber.[2]

In the Ethiopic Enoch, God, who is "Lord of the sheep" presides over the judgement. There is an obscure reference to "the other" (90.20), who took the sealed books and opened them before the Lord of the sheep. But the actual judgement is pronounced by God.

According to the Wisdom of Solomon the righteous will judge the nations. At first sight this seems to be an exception to the tendency to ascribe judgement to God alone. But when the verse is studied as a whole, there is no doubt that it refers to an administrative justice which the righteous will exercise.

They shall judge nations, and have dominion over peoples;
And the Lord shall reign over them for evermore (Wisd. 3.8).

---

[1] "And he shall gather together a holy people, whom he shall lead in righteousness,
And he shall judge the tribes of the people that has been sanctified by the Lord his God." Ps. Sol. 17.28–9.

[2] "And after their punishment shall have come from the Lord, the priesthood shall fail.
Then shall the Lord raise up a new priest.
And to him all the words of the Lord shall be revealed;
And he shall execute a righteous judgement upon the earth for a multitude of days." Test. Levi 18.1–3.

Some Judaistic writings state very forcibly that God alone will pass the final judgement. Three very important passages will be quoted.

1. Jub. 23.31, in which the future of the righteous is described:

> And their bones shall rest in the earth and their spirits shall have much joy, and they shall know that it is the Lord who executes judgement.

2. Ass. Moses 10.7:

> For the Most High will arise, the Eternal God alone,
> And he will appear to punish the Gentiles,
> And he will destroy all their idols.

The author of this work idealizes Moses in such a way that there is no place for a Messiah. The whole task of judgement and punishment is performed by God without the assistance of a Messiah or of angels. It is "the Eternal God alone" who accomplishes the work. This emphasis may have been made in order to attack the belief that some other person than God presided over the judgement. If Charles is right in dating the book between A.D. 7 and A.D. 30, the author cannot have been attacking Christianity.[1] He must have been referring to a belief which was already held in Judaism.

3. 4 Ezra 6.6:

> . . . and through me alone and none other were they created; as also the End (shall come) through me alone and none other.

This statement with its repetition of the words "alone" and "none other" seems also to be an attack on unorthodox views.

Two Jewish writings suggest that others beside God were believed to pass the final judgement. They are the Book of Daniel and the Similitudes of Enoch.

In Daniel there is a description of the judgement, in which according to one interpretation the saints perform the judicial office. Dan. 7.22 is the only verse in the book which could mean

[1] *Assumption of Moses*, p. lviii

that the saints exercise judgement on the day of judgement. The interpretation of this verse is disputed. The Revised Version reads: ". . . and judgement was given to the saints of the Most High". This implies that the saints executed judgement. But the margin of the Revised Version reads: ". . . and judgement was given for the saints of the Most High". This marginal reading means that judgement was given in favour of the saints. It does not imply that they themselves were appointed judges.

Charles emends the text to read: "Judgement sat, and dominion was given to the saints of the Most High."[1] He also argues that the Almighty is surrounded by angelic assessors.[2] "The saints do not judge", he writes, "but God alone. They are His assessors." He claims that in the sentence "Judgement was set" (7.10), the word "judgement" means "those who judge". Yet he emends 7.22 so that it does not mean that the saints were judges.

There are several weaknesses in his discussion of the vision. The notion of an assessor is not appropriate. An assessor is a legal adviser whom the judge consults on difficult points of law. It is doubtful whether the author of Daniel seriously meant that God needed the advice of angels on difficult points of law. A further difficulty in Charles's account is his identification of the angels in 7.10 with the "saints of the Most High". For in the interpretation of the vision the saints are compared with "one like unto a son of man", who in the vision is distinct from the ministering angels.

The ambiguity of 7.22 makes it impossible to decide whether the saints were expected to be judges on the Day of Judgement. When they were given dominion they would exercise administrative justice. But it is uncertain whether they were supposed to be judges upon the great day itself.

In the Similitudes of Enoch there is clearer evidence that another being than God was judge on the Day of Judgement. The Son of Man will be judge of both angels and men. This Son of Man is a heavenly being who performs the task of Messiah. The conception of the Messiah is supernatural and much more exalted than anything in earlier Jewish literature.

---

[1] *The Book of Daniel*, ad. loc. [2] Ibid., p. 193, cf. p. 184.

The work of this Son of Man is described in the following passage (Enoch 62.1–3):

> And thus the Lord commanded the kings and the mighty and the exalted, and those who dwell on the earth and said:
>> 'Open your eyes and lift up your horns if ye are able to recognize the Elect One.'
>
> And the Lord of Spirits seated him on the throne of his glory.
> And the spirit of righteousness was poured out upon him,
> And the word of his mouth slays all the sinners,
> And all the unrighteous are destroyed from before his face.
> And there shall stand up in that day all the kings and mighty,
> And the exalted and those who hold the earth,
> And they shall see and recognize
> How he sits on the throne of his glory,
> And righteousness is judged before him,
> And no lying word is spoken before him.

In this passage the Son of Man is described as the judge who presides at the Day of Judgement. The Lord of Spirits, that is, God, has delegated to the Son of Man or the Elect One the judicial function.

The Son of Man again appears as judge in 69.27:

> And he sat on the throne of his glory,
> And the sum of judgement was given unto the Son of Man,
> And he caused the sinners to pass away and be destroyed from off the face of the earth,
> And those who have led the world astray.

The sense of these passages is beyond dispute. The Messiah is expected to be the judge. But in the same section there is another passage in which God is the judge and the angels carry out the punishment to which he sentences the offenders (62.9–11):

> And all the kings and the mighty and the exalted and those who rule the earth
> Shall fall down before him on their faces,
> And worship and set their hope upon that Son of Man,
> And petition him and supplicate for mercy at his hands.
> Nevertheless the Lord of Spirits will so press them
> That they shall hastily go forth from his presence,
> And their faces shall be filled with shame,
> And the darkness grow deeper on their faces.

And he will deliver them to the angels for punishment,
To execute vengeance on them because they have oppressed his children
and his elect.

As in the New Testament, the thought of the Messiah as judge
alternates with the thought of God as judge.

Because the Similitudes of Enoch are of uncertain date, their
importance for a study of the New Testament has been questioned.
Charles claims that they were written in the first century B.C.,[1] but
J. Y. Campbell argues that there is no clear indication of the date.[2]
The Similitudes at least provide a picture of a kind of thought
which was current in Judaism at the beginning of the Christian
era. Even if the text of the work has been influenced by Christian
tradition,[3] it is likely that the idea of the heavenly Son of Man, who
would pronounce and execute judgement, was being taught before
the birth of Jesus. The Similitudes of Enoch are influenced by the
Book of Daniel. Probably they misinterpret the Book of Daniel in
assuming that the Son of Man will be the judge. But their dependence on Daniel suggests that their central theme arose independently
of Christianity and indeed before the Christian era.

Three passages have been quoted (Jub. 23.31; Ass. Mos. 10.7;
4 Ezra 6.6), in which it is emphatically stated that God alone will
judge. They were probably written in condemnation of the belief
that angels or a Messiah would exercise judicial functions. The kind
of teaching which occurs in the Similitudes of Enoch seems to have
been well known to the writers of these works, and would therefore be pre-Christian. Whereas the bulk of Jewish teaching supported the view that only God would exercise judgement on the
Day of the Lord, the Similitudes of Enoch are evidence of a belief
that God would delegate this task to the Messiah.

The Judgement which was Pronounced upon the Inward Attitude of the Individual

There is a fourth aspect of divine judgement. God is the judge
of a man's inner life. This idea is often expressed in the Psalms:

Judge me, O Lord, for I have walked in mine integrity:
I have trusted also in the Lord without wavering.

[1] *Book of Enoch*, p. 108.   [2] *JTS*, XLVIII (1947), pp. 146-8.
[3] Cf. Dodd, *Interpretation of the Fourth Gospel*, p. 242.

> Examine me, O Lord, and prove me:
> Try my reins and my heart.
> For thy loving kindness is before mine eyes;
> And I have walked in thy truth (Ps. 26.1–3, cf. Ps. 7.8,9, 17.3, 139.23).

The idea is also found in the following:

> For God shall bring every work into judgement, with every hidden thing, whether it be good or whether it be evil (Eccles. 12.14).

> The Lord knoweth the hearts of all . . . who shall render to every man according to his deeds (Prov. 24.12, LXX).

> And he shall assuredly judge those who are in this world, and shall visit in truth all things by means of their hidden works. And he shall assuredly examine the secret thoughts, and that which is laid up in the secret chambers of all the members of man, and shall make them manifest in the sight of all, with reproof (Apoc. Bar. 83.1 ff; cf. also Ecclus. 1.30).

Although this inner searching is generally described as the work of God alone, according to the Similitudes of Enoch it is performed by the Elect One (61.9):

> And when he shall lift up his countenance
> To judge their secret ways according to the word of the name of the Lord
> of Spirits,
> And their path according to the way of the righteous judgement of the Lord
> of Spirits,
> Then shall they all with one voice speak and bless,
> And glorify and extol and sanctify the name of the Lord of Spirits.

The writer who believed that the Messiah would pass the final judgement on the destinies of God's creatures, found no difficulty in regarding him as the judge of men's secret thoughts.

In the foregoing pages it has been shown that the Jews believed that God was supreme judge over the affairs of men. His authority covered the daily administration of the state and also the final judgement. He passed judgement on both the outward actions of men and their inward attitudes.

From the earliest times he was believed to delegate the power of judgement to men. Sometimes men were said to act consciously under his guidance. At other times they seemed to be blind instruments of his will. When men judged on his behalf, they were executing the daily task of administrative justice or inflicting military defeat on sinful nations. The final judgement and the judgement on men's inner attitudes were to be carried out by God alone. An exception occurs in the Similitudes of Enoch, in which the Son of Man is described as both judge on the last day and judge of men's inner attitudes.

John the Baptist

John the Baptist prophesied the coming of a strong one, who would perform the sifting process which was essential to judgement.

> ... whose fan is in his hand, and he will throughly cleanse his threshing-floor; and he will gather his wheat into the garner, but the chaff he will burn up with unquenchable fire (Matt. 3.12 = Luke 3.17).

His prophecy about baptism with fire also refers to judgement:

> ... he shall baptize you with the Holy Ghost and with fire (Matt. 3.11 = Luke 3.16).

John the Baptist believed that the Coming One would be a judge. But who was the Coming One? The synoptic evangelists, and, according to their report, Jesus himself, thought that the Coming One was the Messiah. John the Baptist, however, seems to have expected that Elijah would be the Coming One. In *The Mystery of the Kingdom of God*[1] Schweitzer contends that the Baptist combined elements from the thought of both Malachi and Joel. Joel prophesied an outpouring of the Spirit before the arrival of the great and terrible day of the Lord, and Malachi prophesied the coming of Elijah before the great and terrible day of the Lord (Joel 2.28 ff; Mal. 4.5). The Baptist linked the outpouring of the Spirit with the coming of Elijah, and foretold that Elijah would baptize with the Spirit. Schweitzer's view is supported by the fact that the Baptist did not mention a Messiah but only a Coming One. Moreover, when the Baptist sent his disciples to ask Jesus "Art thou he that cometh, or look we for another?" (Matt. 11.3; Luke 7.19) they did not suggest that they were looking for a Messiah.[2]

[1] P. 152.

[2] The prophecies of baptism with fire and the burning of the chaff also suggest that John expected the coming of Elijah. They are reminiscent of passages in Malachi, where the Lord God himself is likened to a refiner's fire (Mal. 3.3), and is said to burn up the proud and the wicked like stubble (4.1).

John the Baptist regarded himself as the Voice which is mentioned in Isa. 40.3: "The voice of one that crieth, Prepare ye in the wilderness the way of the Lord." This verse is cited as a prophecy of the coming of the Baptist in all four gospels (Matt. 3.3; Mark 1.3; Luke 3.4; John 1.23). G. S. Duncan claims that "we may trace an undeniably genuine tradition" behind John 1.19 ff in which the Baptist denies that he is Elijah and affirms "I am the voice of one crying in the wilderness".[1] And this is consistent with the evidence of the synoptic gospels.

Jesus corrected the opinion of the Baptist. He said that the Baptist was Elijah (Mark 9.11–13; Matt. 11.14) but he himself was the Messiah. For our present purpose the most important factor in the Baptist's teaching is that he expected a man to come as judge. He believed that Elijah would perform this divine function. In this respect he was out of tune with the main theme of Jewish belief,

---

How did the Baptist come to assign this work to Elijah? The best explanation of the introduction of this idea is that John the Baptist supposed that the judgement described in Mal. 3.2 ff was to be executed by Elijah. The opening verses of Malachi 3 contain a striking ambiguity. The crux of the problem is found in verse 1, which is divided into three sections.

1a. The messenger who prepares the way: "Behold, I send my messenger, and he shall prepare the way before me."

1b. The coming of the Lord: "and the Lord, whom ye seek, shall suddenly come to his temple."

1c. The coming of the messenger of the covenant: "and the messenger of the covenant, whom ye delight in, behold, he cometh, saith the Lord of hosts."

Verses 2 and 3 describe the coming of someone to sit in judgement. This judge could not be the messenger of 1a who only prepares the way. He could be either the Lord of 1b or the messenger of the covenant of 1c. Smith in his I.C.C. Commentary on Malachi (p. 63) claims that the Lord of 1b and the messenger of the covenant of 1c are the same person. It would, however, be easy for the Baptist to assume that judgement was passed by a messenger of the covenant who was not identical with the Lord. When he had made that assumption, the next step would be to link the messenger of 1c with the messenger of 1a. Since the messenger was to prepare the way, he could easily be identified with Elijah of Mal. 4.5 who was to come before the great and terrible day of the Lord.

[1] *Jesus, Son of Man*, p. 85.

but provided Jesus with an idea which could be adapted to fit his conception of himself as Messiah and judge.

The Synoptic Gospels

The next task is to determine whether Jesus believed that he himself would preside over the Day of Judgement. The most graphic picture which the synoptic gospels provide of the final judgement is the story of the separation of the sheep from the goats (Matt. 25.31–46). In this story the Son of Man presides over the judgement and executes it (25.31–3):

> But when the Son of man shall come in his glory, and all the angels with him, then shall he sit on the throne of his glory; and before him shall be gathered all the nations; and he shall separate them one from another, as the shepherd separateth the sheep from the goats: and he shall set the sheep on his right hand, but the goats on the left.

T. W. Manson contends that the Son of Man represents the people of the saints of the Most High, as in the Book of Daniel, and that the King is the Messiah who acts as the representative of the saints.[1] It is difficult to read this distinction into the story. In verse 33 the Son of Man sets the sheep on the right hand and the goats on the left. In verse 34 the story continues: "Then shall the King say unto them on his right hand. . . ." The narrative reads as if the King was the same person as the Son of Man.

Jesus was speaking about himself when he used the titles "King" and "Son of Man". And the words "Come, ye blessed children of my Father" imply that the Son of Man was also Son of God. The passage contains much information about Jesus' idea of his own person, and one of the most important features of the passage is that he describes himself as judge. G. S. Duncan claims that the story is not strictly a picture of the Last Judgement. Men judge themselves daily by their reaction to Jesus, and it is this truth which the story is intended to convey.

> The body of the story, therefore, is in no sense the description of a Final Judgement; it is rather a pictorial explanation of the eternal principles in accordance with which judgement is enacted.[2]

[1] *Sayings of Jesus*, pp. 249–50. [2] Op. cit., p. 197.

Duncan goes on to argue that the Son of Man is not depicted in this passage as a judge:

> If the picture is not one of Judgement it is scarcely accurate to say, as is so often done, that the Son of Man appears here as Judge. He is never so described in the narrative. He appears indeed in glory, with the splendour and the authority of a king; he is seated, too, on a throne, with the angels in attendance. But what he does is not so much to judge those who are marshalled before him as to separate them into two classes according to a test against which there is no appeal, and then to declare to them their inevitable fate. And he speaks and acts throughout as the representative, firstly of him whom he calls "my Father", and secondly of those whom he calls "my brethren".[1]

If Duncan does not believe the functions described in the narrative are those of a judge, what does he expect a judge to do? The Son of Man sits on a throne, divides men into two classes, and sentences them to punishment or grants them a reward. This is the work of a judge. Duncan claims that the Son of Man is acting as the representative of his Father and his brethren. But he is none the less a judge. His Father does not stand beside him and whisper instructions into his ear. The Son of Man comes in his own glory and passes judgement himself.

The story of the Sheep and the Goats is recorded only in Matthew. Dodd dismisses it with the remark that "there is however no direct confirmation of this in our other sources".[2] But the absence of parallels does not justify the rejection of the evidence of Matthew's special source. Moreover, the occupation of the Son of Man as judge is found elsewhere in the synoptic gospels. According to Mark 8.38 Jesus said:

> For whosoever shall be ashamed of me and of my words in this adulterous and sinful generation the Son of man also shall be ashamed of him, when he cometh in the glory of his Father with the holy angels.[3]

There is a similar saying in Matt. 10.32–3 = Luke 12.8–9.

---

[1] Ibid., p. 197.   [2] C. H. Dodd, *Parables of the Kingdom*, p. 85.
[3] Matthew reproduced this saying in such a form that it is even clearer that the Son of Man is passing judgement:
For the Son of Man shall come in the glory of his Father with his angels; and then shall he render to every man according to his deeds (Matt. 16.27).

Matthew does not mention the Son of Man, but the Lukan version is as follows:

> Everyone who shall confess me before men, him shall the Son of man also confess before the angels of God: but he that denieth me in the presence of men shall be denied in the presence of the angels of God.

Dodd claims that in the original form of the saying the Son of Man appeared not as a judge but as an advocate.[1] The Q form of the saying (Matt. 10.32-3 = Luke 12.8-9) represents the Son of Man as an advocate and the angels of God as judges. But it could equally well represent Jesus as judge and the angels as an audience. The Markan saying certainly depicts the Son of Man as judge, and even if the two sayings have different meanings Jesus may well have uttered them both.

Dodd says that as there is no reference to the Son of Man in the Matthaean form of the Q saying (Matt. 10.32-3), there was probably no reference to him in the original saying. But this argument applies only to the Q saying and does not exclude the reference to the Son of Man in the Markan saying.

T. W. Manson contends that in the Markan saying the Son of Man "stands for the Remnant, the true Israel of which Jesus is the head".[2] He explains the saying thus:

> In the final consummation the confessors and deniers on earth will be confessed and denied by the Son of Man, that is, by the true spiritual Israel speaking through Christ its King.

This view is supported by the alternative reading "whosoever shall be ashamed of me and mine" in which "words" is omitted. In Manson's opinion "me and mine" refers to the Son of Man.

If Manson is right, the saints execute judgement. We have seen that it is uncertain whether the saints execute judgement in Daniel 7. And neither Messel nor Manson has proved that the Son of Man is a collective title in the Similitudes of Enoch.[3] Manson's theory has already been examined in connection with the story of the Sheep and the Goats. It does not carry conviction. The title

---

[1] Op. cit., p. 85n2. [2] Op. cit., p. 109.

[3] V. Taylor, *Jesus and His Sacrifice*, pp. 24 ff; *Names of Jesus*, pp. 25 ff; T. W. Manson, *The Teaching of Jesus*, pp. 211 f; N. Messel, *Der Menschensohn in den Bildenreden des Henoch*.

"Son of Man" in the gospels refers to one person, as it does in the Similitudes of Enoch. Judgement will be executed by Jesus' disciples not at the Last Judgement but in the Messianic kingdom, when the judgement which they will exercise will be administrative: ". . . and I appoint unto you a kingdom, even as my Father appointed unto me, that ye may eat and drink at my table in my kingdom; and ye shall sit on thrones judging the twelve tribes of Israel" (Luke 22.29–30).

The sayings in Matt. 25.31–46 and Mark 8.38 provide the clearest evidence of Jesus' belief that he would come again as judge. The explicitness of these sayings has aroused the suspicion that they are the product of editorial revision. But there are other passages in which the meaning is not so explicit, and which have certainly not been altered in the tradition.

In Luke's Gospel the phrases "Day of the Son of Man" and "Days of the Son of Man" replace the Old Testament phrases "Day of the Lord" and "great and terrible day of the Lord". This change of terminology means that the Son of Man was expected to play the part which was ascribed to Yahweh in the Old Testament.

In Luke 17.22–37 there is a prophecy about the coming of the days of the Son of Man. The days will come suddenly like the lightning. They will take men unawares, as did the flood in the time of Noah, and the fire and brimstone when it suddenly rained upon Sodom. It will be a time when one man is separated from another.

> I say unto you, in that night there shall be two men on one bed; the one shall be taken and the other shall be left. There shall be two women grinding together; the one shall be taken and the other shall be left (Luke 17.34–5).

This is the only passage in which the phrase "Day of the Son of Man" appears. "Day of the Lord" occurs nowhere in the synoptic gospels, but "the Day" is often mentioned, usually in the sense of "Day of Judgement" (e.g. Mark 13.32; Matt. 12.36; Luke 10.12). Dodd minimizes the importance of these sayings:

> There is no independent interest in the Day of Judgement as such, or in the fate of the Gentiles in the judgement. The time-honoured image of a Last

Judgement is simply assumed, and used to give vividness and force to solemn warnings.[1]

The gospels, however, give the impression that Jesus had a definite interest in the Day of Judgement. A considerable proportion of his teaching is concerned with the advent of the Son of Man and with judgement.[2]

Jesus regarded judgement as a verdict on a man's inward attitude as well as on his deeds. In the Sermon on the Mount he says that anger and lust can bring men into danger of judgement (Matt. 5.21–32). In Mark 8.38 he says that if a man is ashamed of him and his words, he will be ashamed of that man. Shame is an attitude of mind. Jesus' judgement penetrates behind men's actions to their thoughts and feelings.

Forgiveness is closely related to judgement, and forgiveness was believed by the Jews to be within the power of God alone. "The prophet", writes Abrahams, "whether John the Baptist or another—might bring men to forgiveness; he did not bring forgiveness to men; it was not his to bring. The mediatorial idea—suggested by the allegorising interpretation of scripture on the one hand and by the inroad of angelology and the doctrine of ancestral virtue with its mediatorial appeal on the other—was not altogether absent from later Rabbinic theology, but on the whole it is true to assert that the principle was left intact that God and God alone is the object of worship and the sole and immediate source of forgiveness."[3] Jesus claimed this divine power, and pronounced forgiveness to the sinner.[4] In his own teaching and actions he showed that divine justice included mercy.

[1] Op. cit., p. 83.

[2] John Knox, *The Death of Christ*, p. 65, argues that Jesus would never have claimed to be the heavenly Son of Man, because "a sane person, not to say a good person, could not think of himself in such a way". Knox thinks that such a claim would have compromised the humanity of Jesus. But this does not follow. The humanity of Jesus was shown by his need of contemporary religious ideas to express the unique fact of his relationship to the Father. "Son of Man" was such an idea.

[3] I. Abrahams, *Studies in Pharisaism and the Gospels*, I, p. 140.

[4] Mark 2.5: "And Jesus seeing their faith saith unto the sick of the palsy, Son, thy sins are forgiven."

Luke 7.48: "And he said unto her, Thy sins are forgiven."

The Acts of the Apostles

There are only three references to judgement in the Acts of the Apostles:

> And he charged us to preach unto the people, and to testify that this is he which is ordained of God to be the judge of quick and dead (10.42).

> . . . inasmuch as he hath appointed a day, in the which he will judge the world in righteousness by the man whom he hath ordained (17.31).

> . . . he reasoned of righteousness, and temperance, and the judgement to come (24.25).

The first two of these passages show that in early Christianity Jesus was expected as judge. This theme does not hold a constant place in the reports of preaching in Acts. There is much less attention paid in Acts to the final judgement than there is in the synoptic gospels. But when the judgement is mentioned, Christ is described as judge. This gives a clear indication of the belief of the early Christians.

Paul

Paul offers abundant evidence that he believed that Jesus Christ would come as a judge. He stresses this theme more in the earlier than the later epistles. In the First Epistle to the Thessalonians he says that the Lord Jesus will come with his saints. The Thessalonians are exhorted to be blameless "to the end that he may stablish your hearts unblameable in holiness before our God and Father, at the coming of our Lord Jesus Christ with all his saints" (1 Thess. 3.13). Later in the same epistle Paul writes: ". . . and may your spirit and soul and body be preserved entire, without blame at the coming of our Lord Jesus Christ" (1 Thess. 5.23b). Both these passages refer to the coming of Jesus in judgement. The emphasis on the need for blamelessness and holiness makes this clear. According to the Second Epistle to the Thessalonians the Lord Jesus will be revealed from heaven "with the angels of his power in flaming fire, rendering vengeance to them that know not God, and to them that obey not the gospel of our Lord Jesus: who shall suffer punishment, even eternal destruction from the face of the Lord and from the glory of his might, when he shall come to be glorified in his saints . . ." (2 Thess. 1.7–10).

In the First Epistle to the Corinthians Paul writes that the Lord will come as judge: "For I know nothing against myself; yet am I not hereby justified: but he that judgeth me is the Lord. Wherefore judge nothing before the time, until the Lord come, who will both bring to light the hidden things of darkness, and make manifest the counsels of the hearts; and then shall each man have his praise from God" (1 Cor. 4.4,5). The word "Lord" in this passage refers to Christ, as the Day of Judgement is called "the day of the Lord Jesus" in 1 Cor. 5.5, and the phrase "day of our Lord Jesus Christ" occurs in 1 Cor. 1.8.[1]

He speaks again of "the day of our Lord Jesus" in the Second Epistle to the Corinthians (1.14), and affirms that "we must all be made manifest before the judgement-seat of Christ; that each one may receive the things done in the body, according to what he hath done, whether it be good or bad" (2 Cor. 5.10).

In the later epistles Paul says little about the final judgement. Christ is regarded as the goal to which all things proceed,[2] and this idea takes priority over any teaching about judgement. An exception to this tendency in the later epistles is found in Philippians, in which it is said that "The Lord is at hand" (Phil. 4.5). He comes, however, as Saviour rather than Judge: "For our citizenship is in heaven; from whence also we wait for a Saviour, the Lord Jesus Christ" (Phil. 3.20).

Although he usually speaks of Christ as judge, Paul does not exclude the idea that God the Father passes judgement: "for we shall all stand before the judgement-seat of God" (Rom. 14.10). In the First Epistle to the Corinthians he even says that the saints will execute judgement: "Or know ye not that the saints shall judge the world? and if the world is judged by you, are ye unworthy to judge the smallest matters? Know ye not that we shall judge angels? how much more, things that pertain to this life?" (1 Cor. 6.2,3). This idea may be based partly on Dan. 7.22 and

---

[1] In 1 Cor. 5.5 the word "Jesus" is omitted by much of the textual evidence. But the unquestioned reading of 1 Cor. 1.8 shows that "the day of the Lord" means "the day of the Lord Jesus Christ".

[2] "All things have been created through him, and unto him" (Col. 1.16, cf. Eph. 1.10).

partly on Jesus' promise that his disciples would share in judgement (Matt. 19.28; Luke 22.30).

Paul assumes that judgement extends to the secrets of a man's heart, whether it is passed by God or by Christ: ". . . in the day when God shall judge the secrets of men, according to my gospel, by Jesus Christ" (Rom. 2.16). "Wherefore judge nothing before the time, until the Lord come, who will both bring to light the hidden things of darkness, and make manifest the counsels of the hearts" (1 Cor. 4.5).[1]

It is indeed surprising that Paul gives as much space as he does to the theme of Final Judgement. His doctrine of justification shifts the emphasis from the future to the present. The important part which the doctrine of the Last Things continues to play in Paul is sure evidence of its place in early Christian belief. Paul was expounding a tradition which he himself had received from others.

Paul is not concerned with all the manifold details of the Final Judgement. He does not indulge in fanciful descriptions but prefers to stress the central fact that Christ will act as judge. It has often been contended that Paul's high Christology was developed in the later epistles, in which Christ is portrayed as the author and goal of all things. But in the earlier epistles Paul describes Christ as the judge, and this is the mark of a developed Christology. Paul had already accepted a high Christology in the earlier writings, for a high Christology was taught by Jesus himself and handed down by the early Church, the Christology which spoke of Christ as the judge.

The Johannine Writings

The Fourth Gospel contains a number of passages in which the evangelist describes Jesus as the judge.

> For neither doth the Father judge any man, but he hath given all judgement unto the Son (5.22).

[1] Cf. H. A. A. Kennedy: *St Paul's Conception of the Last Things*, p. 205: ". . . it is evident that the idea which stands out most sharply before him in connection with the *process* of judgement, is the revelation of the secrets of human souls to themselves and probably to others, the testing of human character by a severe experience, which he symbolises by fire."

And he (the Father) gave him (the Son) authority to execute judgement, because he is the Son of man (5.27).[1]

I can of myself do nothing: as I hear, I judge: and my judgement is righteous; because I seek not mine own will, but the will of him that sent me (5.30, cf. 9.39).

Elsewhere in the gospel the Evangelist writes as if Jesus were not the judge:

For God sent not the Son into the world to judge the world; but that the world should be saved through him (3.17).

Ye judge after the flesh; I judge no man (8.15).

And if any man hear my sayings, and keep them not, I judge him not: for I came not to judge the world, but to save the world.

He that rejecteth me, and receiveth not my sayings, hath one that judgeth him: the word that I spake, the same shall judge him in the last day (12.47, 48).[2]

Of these sayings 8.15 may be discounted, for Jesus is merely contrasting his behaviour with the Pharisees' censoriousness. He is not making a statement about his present or future mission.

John 3.17 does not imply that Jesus does not exercise judgement. It states that the real purpose of his coming was to save and not to judge. But even if judgement was not the purpose of his coming, it was part of the work which he performed.

John 12.47–8 says that men will be judged by their reactions to the words of Christ. The word judges men because it is the word which Jesus has been given by the Father.

The Fourth Evangelist seems to teach by paradoxes. The Father does not judge, because he has given authority to the Son. Yet it is not the Son who judges, but the word which the Father

---

[1] R. H. Charles, *The Book of Enoch*, p. 48, thinks that John 5.27 is almost a quotation from Enoch 69.27:

And he sat on the throne of his glory,
And the sum of judgement was given to the Son of Man.

There is however, no sure evidence that the Fourth Evangelist knew the Similitudes of Enoch, and the similarity of language may be only a coincidence. The Evangelist would find a source for his ideas in the teaching of Jesus, for the picture of Son of Man as judge is common to the Synoptic and Johannine Gospels.

[2] Cf. also John 5.45 which implies that not Jesus but the Father is judge.

has given him. At one time the evangelist gives the impression that men are judged by their reaction to Christ, and that Christ does not judge actively. At another time he gives the impression that Christ himself actively executes judgement.

These paradoxes are the result of a tension between a present and a future judgement. When the Fourth Gospel speaks of the present judgement, it lays the emphasis on the judgement of men by their reaction to Christ, especially to Christ exalted on the cross. But the gospel also refers to a future judgement:

> ... for the hour cometh, in which all that are in the tombs shall hear his voice, and shall come forth; they that have done good, unto the resurrection of life; and they that have done ill, unto the resurrection of judgement (John 5.28–9).

Bultmann argues that these verses are a later interpolation because they are inconsistent with the realized eschatology of the gospel.[1] But the Fourth Evangelist was not conscious of an inconsistency between the two types of eschatology. The two exist side by side, as, for example, in 6.54:

> He that eateth my flesh and drinketh my blood hath eternal life; and I will raise him up at the last day.

Realized eschatology does not exclude a belief in a future judgement, but emphasizes that men are judged now by their reaction to Christ. In the future he will pass judgement actively at the Last Judgement. Such teaching is not inconsistent, but is responsible for the apparent contradictions which are found in the gospel's account of Christ the Judge.[2]

[1] *Ev. Joh.*, p. 196.

[2] According to John 16.7–11, the Spirit also does the work of a judge: "Nevertheless I tell you the truth; it is expedient for you that I go away: for if I go not away, the Comforter will not come unto you; but if I go, I will send him unto you. And he, when he is come, will convict the world in respect of sin, and of righteousness, and of judgement: of sin, because they believe not on me; of righteousness, because I go to the Father, and ye behold me no more; of judgement, because the prince of this world hath been judged." This passage is perplexing because "sin", "righteousness", and "judgement" are not really parallel terms. The Comforter will convict the world because of its sin, in vindication of righteousness, and as part of the process of judgement, which has already reached its culmination in the judgement which was passed

The First Epistle of John, which we assume to have been written by the author of the Fourth Gospel, makes little contribution to the subject of judgement. There will be a "day of judgement" (4.17), and a manifestation of Christ (3.2), but it is nowhere suggested or implied that Jesus will be the judge.

Other New Testament Writings

There are several passages in other New Testament writings, where God is described as judge:

> For we know him that said, Vengeance belongeth unto me, I will recompense. And again, The Lord shall judge his people. It is a fearful thing to fall into the hands of the living God (Heb. 10.30–1).
>
> ... God the Judge of all (12.23).
>
> ... for fornicators and adulterers God will judge (13.4).
>
> And if ye call on him as Father, who without respect of persons judgeth according to each man's work ... (1 Pet. 1.17).
>
> ... who, when he was reviled, reviled not again; when he suffered, threatened not; but committed himself to him that judgeth righteously (2.23).

In 2 Peter it is implied that God will be judge at the Final Judgement. He committed the angels to "pits of darkness, to be reserved unto judgement" (2 Pet. 2.4).

In the Epistle of Jude, 14–15, he is said to execute judgement:

> And to these also Enoch, the seventh from Adam, prophesied, saying, Behold, the Lord came with ten thousands of his holy ones, to execute judgement upon all, and to convict all the ungodly of all their works of ungodliness which they have ungodly wrought, and of all the hard things which ungodly sinners have spoken against him.

Cf. Jude 9:

> But Michael the archangel, when contending with the devil he disputed about the body of Moses, durst not bring a railing judgement, but said, The Lord rebuke thee.

---

upon Satan when Christ was crucified. The Spirit is judge in this passage. Dodd (*Interpretation of the Fourth Gospel*, p. 414) argues that according to St John the coming of Christ is mediated by the Spirit, and so the Last Judgement is also mediated by the Spirit. He also claims that παράκλητος means "Advocate" as in 1 John 2.1. Then the Spirit would be both judge and counsel.

Certain passages may refer to either Christ or God the Father as judge, e.g. 1 Pet. 4.5; Jas. 5.8–9; 2 Tim. 4.7,8. But apart from the Book of Revelation the remaining writings of the New Testament have little to say about Christ's work as judge. According to the Epistle to the Hebrews Christ's coming will coincide with the judgement (9.27–8; 10.37) but Christ himself is not described as judge. For this writer Christ is the heavenly intercessor.

In the Second Epistle to Timothy it is said that Christ will pass judgement when he appears again:

> I charge thee in the sight of God, and of Christ Jesus, who shall judge the quick and the dead, and by his appearing and his kingdom . . . (2 Tim. 4.1).

Apart from the very probable allusion in 2 Tim. 4.8 there is no other reference to Christ as judge in the Pastoral Epistles.

The Apocalypse frequently speaks of Christ as judge. There are three types of judgement which are described in the book. First there is present judgement. "Every visitation of the churches," writes Charles, "every divine judgement upon them, is regarded as a spiritual advent of Christ."[1] Threats of this advent are found in Rev. 2.5,16,22–3; 3.3,20.

A second type of judgement will take place at the final advent of Christ, which in the view of the writer is close at hand:

> Because thou didst keep the word of my patience, I also will keep thee from the hour of trial, that hour which is to come upon the whole world, to try them that dwell upon the earth. I come quickly: hold fast that which thou hast, that no one take thy crown (Rev. 3.10, 11).

> Behold, I come quickly; and my reward is with me, to render to each man according as his work is (Rev. 22.12; cf. 22.20).

When Christ comes he will reap the harvest with a sharp sickle (Rev. 14.14–16), and tread the winepress of God's wrath (14.17–20; 19.15). The date of this judgement will be the "great day of God" (16.14).

A third type of judgement precedes the Millennium, and seems to be given to the saints (20.4). But in the final events Christ himself exercises the judgement.

[1] *Eschatology*, p. 405.

Conclusion

The evidence which has been discussed shows that Jesus claimed that as Son of Man he would be the judge at the last day. The apostolic Church accepted his claim, Paul and the author of the Fourth Gospel developed it, and the writer of the Apocalypse gave it great prominence. Paul also claimed that the saints would judge men and angels, but apart from this isolated instance the New Testament confined the task of passing the final judgement to Father and Son.

These facts are very important for an understanding of the doctrine of the Person of Christ. Jesus claimed for himself a divine function which hitherto—with one or two exceptions—had been regarded as the sole prerogative of the Almighty. The Christian Church accepted his claim. "And he shall come again with glory to judge both the quick and the dead" became an article of faith.

CHAPTER 8

JESUS AND THE CREATION

It would seem natural to discuss creation before judgement, but the chapter on creation is placed after the chapter on judgement because the Christian belief in Jesus as judge arose earlier and developed more quickly than the belief in Jesus as creator. It has been shown that with some exceptions the final judgement was regarded by Jews as the special task of God, but that the Christians soon began to describe Jesus as judge, a doctrine which was supported by the sayings of Jesus himself. We shall now inquire if a similar process occurred in the Christian belief about Jesus' function in the creation of the world. The discussion will lead to the conclusion that Paul, John, and the author of Hebrews believed that the Christ was an agent in the creation of the world, that this doctrine is not found in Jesus' own teaching or in the earliest preaching of the Church, but that the words of Jesus and the earliest preachers enable us to understand how the doctrine developed. Before the New Testament evidence is examined it will be shown that there were two conflicting views in Judaism about the uniqueness of God's activity in creation. Some writers taught that there were mediators in creation. Others taught that God alone performed the work. Those who held the second view would assume that Christ was being treated as God when he was described as an agent in creation.

First, it is necessary to define the area of our investigation. There are four aspects of God's creative activity, but only one, the creation of the world, will be the theme of the main part of this chapter. The other aspects of his creative activity, which will be discussed in the concluding section of the chapter, are: first, the sustaining and maintenance of the created universe; secondly, the leading of the created universe to an end or goal; and thirdly, the new creation. The major part of the chapter, however, will be concerned with the creation of the world, and the problem of whether God was assisted by others in this act. In order to avoid a confusion which could arise from the ambiguity of the word "creation", it will be used to mean "creating" but not "that which is created". In this chapter "creation" will always mean the act of bringing the world into being.

The Old Testament and Later Judaism

In the beginning God created heaven and earth. The Hebrews did not agree with each other about all aspects of the doctrine of the creation, but they accepted the belief that God was the creator. There were differences of opinion about the origin of created things. In earlier times it was assumed that God had formed the world out of a watery chaos.[1] Later, however, men began to believe that he had created the world from nothing.[2] There were differences of opinion about the function of the angels at the creation, as we shall see in the following pages, but none of these differences of opinion affected the belief that God was the creator, who had formed the sun and moon and stars, who had made the sea and the dry land, who had caused the trees and fruits and flowers to spring forth, who had given life to animals and birds and fishes, and, to crown his work, had created man in his image after his likeness.[3]

This doctrine was expressed in all its grandeur by Second Isaiah, the prophet of the exile, who described how God had created the heavens and stretched them forth and spread abroad the earth and given breath to the people upon it.[4] The doctrine is found also in the eloquent poetry of the Psalms. The heavens are the work of God's fingers, and he ordained the moon and stars.[5] In the final chapters of the Book of Job the wonder of God's handiwork is portrayed. He laid and fastened the foundations of the earth,

[1] Gen. 1.1 ff.
[2] 2 Macc. 7.28; cf. Rom. 4.17: "God . . . who calleth the things that are not, as though they were." Cf. also Heb. 11.3.
[3] Gen. 1.1—2.3.   [4] Isa. 42.5; cf. 40.12–31; 48.13; 51.9–16.
[5] Ps. 8.3; cf. 33.6–9; 148.5 f.

determined its measures, shut up the sea with doors, made the cloud a garment for it, and the thick darkness a swaddling band for it.[1]

This belief in God the Creator, which was so firmly rooted in Hebrew thought, was accepted without question in later Judaism. Whether embellishments were added or rigidly avoided, the hard core of the doctrine was treasured and guarded.

The belief that other agents assisted God in the creation of the world had great popularity amongst the Jews and took several forms. The beings which are said to have been agents in the creation can be divided into two categories. First, there are conceptual emanations from the Godhead, such as Wisdom, Word, and the Spirit. Secondly, there are angelic beings who are different from the emanations in two important respects. The first difference is that the angels have definite personal characteristics while the emanations are not so clearly persons. The second difference is that angels are often described as members of a great company of angels, but the emanations are rarely linked together and usually stand alone. Either Wisdom or Word or the Spirit is said to be the mediator, but not all three together.

The first group, the emanations from Godhead, will now be considered. They are described here as emanations. This term has been chosen because it leaves open the question of the being's personality. It does not prejudice us in our investigation whether the being was regarded as a person or not. The most important of these emanations are Wisdom, Word, and the Spirit. In the discussion of the Word, however, the concept of the Law will be mentioned, since it is closely akin to that of the Word.

In Hebrew thought the idea of the Divine Wisdom was frequently linked with the creation. According to the Book of Proverbs, when God established the heavens and marked out the foundations of the earth, Wisdom was "by him, as a masterworkman".[2] In the Wisdom of Solomon the Divine Wisdom is called the "artificer of all things". She is said to choose God's works for him. Man was formed by her.[3] These passages from

---

[1] Job 38.1—42.6.   [2] Prov. 8.30.
[3] Wisd. 7.22; 8.3,4; 9.1,2; cf. Ecclus. 24.3, which recalls Gen. 1.2.

Proverbs and the Wisdom of Solomon portray Wisdom as a conscious being who acted with God in the creation of the world.

Another important concept was Word. The world was created by God's word. The story of Genesis is punctuated by the creation formula which is repeated over and over again: "And God said ..."[1] The same theme is echoed in the Psalms: "By the word of the Lord were the heavens made."[2] But the Word was not personified in the Old Testament nor even in rabbinic thought.[3] The only writer who clearly treats the Word as a person is Philo, and even he is not consistent. We have argued already that Dodd goes too far when he claims that Philo never regarded the Word as a person.[4] Since Philo describes the Word in anthropomorphic terms such as "high priest" and "sea captain", he did not always regard it as impersonal. But he does not describe the Word as a person when he is writing about the creation of the world. "God sealed the universe", he says, "with an image and idea, his own Logos."[5] Here the Word is not an agent or mediator, but rather, in Dodd's phrase, "the medium of the creation of the world".[6] Philo makes his position even plainer when he calls God "the cause by which the world has come into being", and the Word "the instrument through which it has been fashioned".[7] The Word was not God's fellow-worker but the tool which he used.

The idea of Law is closely connected with that of Word. Although the Law was never properly personified, it was often described in highly picturesque language. A rabbinic passage calls

---

[1] Gen. 1.3,6,9, etc.   [2] Ps. 33.6.

[3] Isa. 55.11 ("So shall my word be that goeth forth out of my mouth: it shall not return unto me void") is no exception. It is the metaphorical language of poetry in which God asserts that he will always accomplish his will.

Even in the apocryphal writings the idea is not truly personified. The nearest approach is Wisd. 18.15,16. ("Thine almighty word leaped from heaven.") This too is probably a vivid poetical fantasy.

It has been suggested that in the Targums the Word (*Memra*) was personified. The *Memra* of God was used as a reverential substitute for "God", but this usage did not imply personification. G. F. Moore, *Judaism*, I, p. 417, argues that the substitution is adequately explained by the motive of reverence.

[4] See p. 36: cf. Dodd, *The Interpretation of the Fourth Gospel*, p. 69.

[5] De Somn. ii.45.   [6] Op. cit., p. 68.   [7] De Cher. 127.

the Law the Firstborn through whom God created heaven and earth.[1] On the other hand, according to the Pirke Aboth, the Law was no more than an instrument with which the world was created.[2] And in the Scriptures themselves there is no indication that the Law was active at the creation.

The Holy Spirit is linked with creation in Gen. 1.2 in which it is said that the Spirit brooded upon the face of the waters. This idea, however, is not followed up in the Old Testament, except in Ps. 33.6:

By the word of the Lord were the heavens made;
And all the host of them by the breath of his mouth.

In this verse the word *ruah* could be translated "Spirit" instead of "breath". Apart from these two references the Spirit is not said to have taken part in the creation.

The entities which have been discussed, Wisdom, Word, Law, and Spirit, are sometimes described in language which suggests that they are persons, but they are not said to have appeared in human form. Nor are they said to have acted in liaison with each other. Each is regarded as a sole and sufficient mediator of the divine activity. They are not described as fellow-members of a family of supernatural beings. Each, taken by itself, is an extension of the divine personality. Each alone fulfils the need for a mediator of the transcendent God.

It is otherwise with the second type of intermediary, the angels. The Jews believed that angels were personal beings, and often described them as members of a large family. Some of the angels spent their whole time in the presence of God, ministering to him. Others acted as the intermediaries of God to men. In the Old Testament there are many accounts of the visits of individual angels to men, but angels are not mentioned by name until the Book of Daniel in which the angel Gabriel is the messenger of God and the angel Michael is the supernatural prince of Israel.[3] In the apocryphal Book of Tobit the angel Raphael is mentioned.[4]

According to the apocalyptic writings which have survived,

[1] Gen. Rabb. i.1. [2] Pirke Aboth, iii.19.
[3] Dan. 8.16; 9.21; 10.13,21; 12.1. [4] Tob. 3.17; 5.4; 8.2, etc.

angels play a prominent part in God's dealings with man, but are connected with the government and final judgement of the world rather than creation. Certain rabbinic writers, however, say that God consulted the angels when he created the world.[1] And Philo says that when God made man he took fellow-workers with him.[2] It seems that these fellow-workers were angels.

The belief that angels assisted in the creation of the world was probably more widespread than the positive evidence suggests. For the doctrine gained enough support to arouse opposition. According to Genesis Rabbah the angels were not created on the first day, in order that no one might say that "Michael and Gabriel helped to stretch out the canopy of heaven, which was the work of God alone".[3] This opposition proves the popularity of the doctrine which it attacks. It is likely that many people were attracted by speculative and bizarre descriptions of the activities of angels. But we cannot be certain how opinion was divided and we cannot discover the relative strength of the conflicting views. All we know is that there was a division of opinion.

The evidence which has been reviewed shows that at least some Jews believed that God was assisted by other beings in the creation. Of the concepts Wisdom, Word, Law, and Spirit, only Wisdom can confidently be said to have been regarded as a personal agent in the creation, a belief which is found in the Book of Proverbs and the Wisdom of Solomon. Other writers spoke of the angels as agents in creation, and yet others affirmed the belief that God created the world without assistance from anyone else.

Against this background of thought emerged the Christian doctrine of the Person of Christ. In our consideration of the New Testament three facts which have arisen from this discussion should be specially remembered.

1. Jews who opposed the doctrine of angelic agency in creation regarded creation as a function which belonged to God alone. In their eyes the claim that Jesus was an agent in creation was a claim that he was God.

[1] Palestinian Targum, Gen. 1.26; 3.22; 11.7; Jerusalem Targum, Gen. 3.22.
[2] *De Op. Mund.* 75.
[3] Gen. Rabb. i.3: cf. Moore, *Judaism*, 1, p. 381 and 4 Ezra 6.6.

2. Concepts such as Wisdom and Word provided a framework of thought within which Christians could attempt to express their beliefs about Christ.

3. Christ was different from all concepts such as Wisdom, Word, Law, and Spirit because he had been seen with the eyes and had walked the earth as a man. He was different too from angelic beings because his life on earth was human. He shared the common human experiences and submitted to the daily routine of human life.

These three points will help us to discern both the continuity of thought between Old and New Testaments and the uniqueness of the Christian belief about Christ.

The Synoptic Gospels

Since John the Baptist has not left any teaching about the creation of the world, the discussion passes immediately to the sayings of Jesus in the synoptic gospels. Jesus accepted the belief that God was the creator who had made the human race both male and female and had clothed the grass of the field.[1] The sayings of Jesus show that he had an intense interest in the world of nature and a reverence for everything which God had brought into existence. In none of his sayings, however, does he claim to be God's agent in creating the world. While the belief that Jesus would return as Judge was based upon his own prophecies, there is no indication in his words that he had been creator.

A theory has been put forward, however, by P. W. Schmidt that Jesus identified himself with the Divine Wisdom.[2] If Jesus made this identification, it does not follow that he believed himself to have been active in the creation of the world. He might not have been thinking of that particular aspect of Wisdom's work. Nevertheless, if he did identify himself with Wisdom, he gave his followers the opportunity to inquire into the implications of his claim, and to draw conclusions which were not in his mind when

[1] Mark 10.6; Matt. 6.30; Luke 12.28.

[2] P. W. Schmidt, *Menschheitswege zum Gotteskennen*, pp. 195 ff, discussed by A. E. J. Rawlinson, *The New Testament Doctrine of the Christ*, p. 260, cf. W. D. Davies, *Paul and Rabbinic Judaism*, pp. 156–7.

he uttered the saying, the conclusion, for example, that he was active in the creation of the world.

Schmidt's theory is based upon three passages from the synoptic gospels: Luke 11.49; Matt. 11.16–19=Luke 7.31–5; Matt. 11.25–30 (cf. Luke 10.21–2). These passages will now be examined.

1. Therefore also said the wisdom of God, I will send unto them prophets and apostles . . . (Luke 11.49).

In a parallel passage in Matt. 23.34f it is Jesus, not Wisdom, who says: "Therefore, behold, I send unto you prophets, and wise men, and scribes. . . ."

Luke would not have inserted this reference to the Wisdom of God if his tradition had been the same as that recorded by Matthew, but although Luke's tradition is probably genuine, it does not prove that Jesus identified himself with Wisdom. "It is best to take the words", writes Creed, "as a periphrasis for God: 'God, in his wisdom, said, I will send . . .'."[1] Creed's explanation is convincing. The difference of wording in Matthew may be traced back to Jesus himself who may have introduced the same saying on different occasions in different ways. Alternatively his saying may have been reported in two ways from an early date. In any case the saying does not give strong support to the view that Jesus identified himself with Wisdom.

2. Matt. 11.16–19=Luke 7.31–5.

These passages have more or less the same form in both gospels, but their endings differ as can be seen below:

Matt. 11.19b: καὶ ἐδικαιώθη ἡ σοφία ἀπὸ τῶν ἔργων αὐτῆς.

And wisdom is justified by her works.

Luke 7.35: καὶ ἐδικαιώθη ἡ σοφία ἀπὸ πάντων τῶν τέκνων αὐτῆς.

And wisdom is justified by all her children.

The preposition ἀπό is better translated as "by" than as "of" or "from", but these last two translations have been favoured by some scholars. For example "of" is used in the Revised Version of Luke 7.35.

[1] *St Luke*, p. 167.

Matthew has "works" (ἔργων) where Luke has "children" (τέκνων). This variation may have been caused by the ambiguity of the Aramaic equivalent which can mean either "works" or "children".[1] If Matthew's rendering ("Wisdom is justified by her works") is accepted, there are two possible interpretations. According to the first, the works of Jesus prove that he is the Divine Wisdom. Since, however, the context is not only about Jesus but also about John the Baptist, the second interpretation is more plausible, according to which Jesus and John the Baptist are children of Wisdom and vindicate her by their works.

If Luke's version ("Wisdom is justified by all her children") is accepted, the children of Wisdom are those who obey her, namely, the men and women who have followed Jesus and John the Baptist and will justify the Divine Wisdom by their conduct and speech.

Neither the Matthaean nor the Lukan version supports the view that Jesus claimed to be the Divine Wisdom. There remains one more passage upon which Schmidt bases his argument. And this will provide much stronger evidence for his theory than the two sayings which have already been examined.

3. Matt. 11.25–30 (cf. Luke 10.21–2).

Schmidt argues that in this passage Jesus is using the fifty-first chapter of Ecclesiasticus.[2] In chapter 51 the son of Sirach offers a thanksgiving to God, and then reveals a mystery about the Wisdom of God and appeals to his readers to lay hold upon her. There is a large degree of similarity between the words of Jesus in Matt. 11.25–30 and sections of the chapter of Ecclesiasticus. It does not appear to be an example of direct quotation but rather of reminiscence. There are a few close verbal agreements between Matt. 11.25–30 and Ecclesiasticus 51. Other similarities, which are not verbal, suggest that the writer of the gospel was not using the Septuagint translation of Ecclesiasticus but an independent transla-

---

[1] See A. H. McNeile, *The Gospel according to St Matthew*, p. 159.
[2] Op. cit., pp. 195 ff.

tion.[1] This independence of the Septuagint confirms the belief that Jesus actually uttered Matt. 11.25–30.

While the whole of Matt. 11.25–30 has often been discussed in great detail, our main interest is in verses 28–30:

> Come unto me, all ye that labour and are heavy laden, and I will give you rest.
>
> Take my yoke upon you, and learn of me; for I am meek and lowly in heart: and ye shall find rest unto your souls.
>
> For my yoke is easy, and my burden is light.

The authenticity of these verses does not depend on that of the preceding verses (25–7), for 28–30 may well be a separate saying, since it does not occur in the Lukan parallel.[2] The chief argument

[1] In the earlier part of the saying (Matt. 11.25–7) only ἐξομολογοῦμαί σοι, πάτερ, κύριε (11.25) is reminiscent of Ecclus. 51, verse 1 of which reads: ἐξομολογήσομαί σοι. And since they are the opening words of a prayer, the similarity does not prove dependence, for only a limited number of opening phrases would be available. The rest of the similarities occur in verses 28–30. The close verbal correspondences are as follows:

Matthew 11	Ecclesiasticus 51
28. οἱ κοπιῶντες . . . ἀναπαύσω	27. ἐκοπίασα.
29. καὶ εὑρήσετε ἀνάπαυσιν ταῖς ψυχαῖς ὑμῶν	27. καὶ εὗρον ἐμαυτῷ πολλὴν ἀνάπαυσιν.
	26. καὶ ἐπιδεξάσθω ἡ ψυχή ὑμῶν παιδείαν.

The following similarities are not verbal, but suggest that the translator of the Matthaean saying had not consulted the Septuagint version of Ecclus. Hence it is likely that the saying existed first in Aramaic or Hebrew. This is good evidence for the early date of the saying.

Matthew 11	Ecclesiasticus 51
28. δεῦτε πρός με.	23. ἐγγίσατε πρός με.
29. ἄρατε τὸν ζυγόν μου ἐφ' ὑμᾶς, καὶ μάθετε ἀπ' ἐμοῦ.	26. τὸν τράχηλον ὑμῶν ὑπόθετε ὑπὸ ζυγόν, καὶ ἐπιδεξάσθω ἡ ψυχὴ ὑμῶν παιδείαν.

There is no strong case against the authenticity of the saying. It is probable that Jesus uttered it himself.

[2] Norden, *Agnostos Theos*, pp. 277–308, claims that there is a similarity of pattern between Ecclesiasticus 51 and Matt. 11.25–30. The absence, however, of the verses 28–30 in the Lukan parallel, suggests that the latter verses may not have been in the original saying. W. D. Davies, op. cit., p. 157, claims that

against the authenticity of 28–30 is its dependence on Ecclesiasticus, but this echo of Ecclesiasticus, which does not reveal a knowledge of the Septuagint version, is not a convincing reason for the spuriousness of the saying.

What are the implications of the saying about Christ's claims for himself? It seems that he was aware of the text of Ecclesiasticus. That is the best explanation of the similarity between the saying and Ecclesiasticus 51. T. W. Manson argues that Jesus may not have been dependent on Ecclesiasticus. "If the author of Ecclesiasticus could think of such words", he writes, "so might Jesus."[1] The closeness of the similarity, however, between the two passages makes it more than likely that Jesus was making deliberate use of Ecclesiasticus 51. And if Jesus was consciously thinking of Ecclesiasticus, then he was deliberately applying to himself language and ideas which had been used with reference to Wisdom. Rudolf Otto claims that Jesus was speaking as a representative of Wisdom.[2] But this is not true, for a comparison of the two passages shows that Jesus was contrasting himself with Wisdom rather than speaking on behalf of Wisdom. The son of Sirach appealed to men to come and learn about Wisdom,[3] but Jesus invited them to come and learn about himself. The son of Sirach directed his appeal to the unlearned, but Jesus called those who laboured and were heavy-laden. According to Ecclesiasticus the man who learns about Wisdom will obtain a rest which consists of material prosperity, but Christ offered rest to the souls of men. There is no parallel in Ecclesiasticus to the words "For I am meek and lowly in heart". Indeed these words of Jesus are in complete contrast to the self-glorification in which Wisdom is supposed to indulge according to another part of Ecclesiasticus. The difference in spirit between the two passages is well illustrated by the way in which God is addressed. The son of Sirach describes God as King, but Jesus calls him Father.

---

if verses 25–30 do not belong integrally to verses 25–7, the case for direct dependence on Ecclesiasticus 51 falls to the ground.

[1] *The Sayings of Jesus*, pp. 186–7.
[2] *The Kingdom of God and the Son of Man*, pp. 137 ff.
[3] Ecclus. 51.23–30.

In Matt. 11.28–30 Jesus is contrasting himself with the Jewish conception of Wisdom. He offers gifts more precious than those which Wisdom is said to give. If men desire true knowledge of God and wish to submit themselves to the yoke of the true law, if they long for perfect rest, they should come to Jesus.

He was making tremendous claims for himself, but their importance must not be exaggerated. In none of these passages which have been examined does Jesus say that he existed before his birth or that he assisted in the creation of the world. When he contrasts himself with Wisdom, he is speaking of God's present relationship to men and not of the original act of creation. Nevertheless, once he had implied that he was greater than Wisdom, he had opened the way for later developments in thought about his person. If he was greater than Wisdom in one respect, was he not greater in others? Could he not be called an agent in the creation of the world? Was it not he rather than Wisdom who had stood beside God as a wise master-workman?

It is not known whether Paul and John and the author of Hebrews knew the contents of Matt. 11.28–30, but if they did, they would have regarded the passage as consistent with their expositions of the work of Christ in creation. Indeed the attitude which Jesus adopted in this saying may have been one of the chief reasons why his followers used the idea of Wisdom to elucidate their beliefs about him.

The Acts of the Apostles

The Acts of the Apostles have nothing to say about Jesus' part in the creation of the world. But two titles which are used of him in the Acts would confirm the belief in his pre-existence and his activity in creation. The first of these titles is "Lord" which has already been discussed. This title was given to God by the Jews, and although it could be used of earthly rulers, the frequent application to Christ encouraged a belief in his divinity, and consequently in his pre-existence and his agency in creation. The second title is ἀρχηγός which may be translated "captain" or "author". It occurs twice in the Acts, in 3.15 where Jesus is called ἀρχηγὸς τῆς ζωῆς (captain—or author—of life) and in 5.31 where he is called ἀρχηγὸς καὶ σωτήρ (captain—or author—and saviour).

The word is used in three ways in Greek. First, it can refer to the founder or eponymous hero of a city or colony.[1] Secondly, it may describe the creator of something, for example of life or of nature.[2] The third meaning is "prince" or "chief" or "captain".[3] The first of these meanings does not apply to the two instances of the word in Acts, and a choice must be made between the last two meanings. The third usage, "prince", "chief", or "captain", is often found in the Septuagint, but in popular Hellenistic usage the second meaning, "author" or "creator", prevailed. It is this second meaning which is most appropriate in the other two New Testament passages in which ἀρχηγός occurs (Heb. 2.10 and 12.2).

Are we then to translate ἀρχηγός in Acts as "author" or as "captain"? The modern practice is to base Greek translations upon the Septuagint usage, a commendable practice when a word is found frequently in the New Testament. But ἀρχηγός occurs only four times in the New Testament. If the writers had been conscious of the Old Testament background of ἀρχηγός, they might have used the word more often. Since they use it rarely, they are not likely to have had the Septuagint usage in mind. They were probably thinking of the popular usage, "author" or "creator". Moreover, the context of Acts 3.15 favours the translation "author". The title is given to Jesus in a speech which follows the healing of a lame man. The theme of the speech is that Jesus has made the lame man strong. It is therefore appropriate that he should be called "author of life". In Acts 5.31, however, since there is no qualifying genitive after ἀρχηγός, the translation "author" or "creator" would be awkward, and "captain" or "prince" would be more suitable. There is only one passage in which Christ is described as "author" or "creator" and this does not refer to the creation of the world but to the restoration of life to a diseased limb.

This use of the word ἀρχηγός and the ascription of the title

---

[1] See Delling, *TWNT*, I, p. 485.   [2] Cleanthes, Fr. 537/2.
[3] See Moulton and Milligan, *Vocabulary of the Greek Testament*, p. 81.

"Lord" to Christ are signs of the way in which the Church's thought was developing. Christ was regarded as the giver and Lord of life, but was not yet linked with the act of creation. The Church was waiting for a genius to unfold the doctrine which was hidden beneath its phrases of praise and adoration. The flower of later Pauline Christology had not emerged but the bud was slowly opening.

Paul

The first statement that Christ was active in creation is found in the writings of Paul. It occurs in the Epistle to the Colossians (1.16):

> For in him (ἐν αὐτῷ) were all things created, in the heavens and upon the earth, things visible and things invisible, whether thrones or dominions or principalities or powers; all things have been created through him (δι' αὐτοῦ), and unto him (εἰς αὐτόν).

The phrases ἐν αὐτῷ (in him) and δι' αὐτοῦ (through him) describe Christ's activity in the creation of the world. Linguistically the prepositions ἐν and διά could refer to an instrument rather than an agent.[1] But Paul is speaking of a person. He always regards Jesus Christ as a person, and in Col. 1.16 he means that Christ's part in creation was a conscious deliberate activity. Christ had walked the earth as a man, and in his risen state had personal contact with men. In this passage Paul affirms his belief that Christ also had an active and intelligent part to play in creating the world.

Because this is the only passage in which Paul has written about Christ's agency in creation, it has been rejected by some scholars as an interpolation. There is no textual ground for this attitude. Since the thought and language of the section are greatly dependent on earlier Jewish writings, there is no good reason to reject it as a Hellenistic interpolation. Our task is not to dictate what Paul ought to have written but to explain what he wrote.

The above passage is the only one in which Paul describes Jesus as active in the creation of the world. 1 Cor. 8.6 ("and one Lord

---

[1] For διά expressing instrumentality see Acts 5.12; 2 John 12: and for ἐν in this sense see Luke 22.49; Acts 11.16; 1 Cor. 3.13 etc.: cf. C. F. D. Moule, *An Idiom Book of New Testament Greek*, pp. 56-7, 77.

Jesus Christ, through whom (δι' οὗ) are all things, and we through him (δι' αὐτοῦ)") refers to Christ's present activity in maintaining or sustaining the created universe. The preposition διά "through" is used in 1 Cor. 8.6 as well as in Col. 1.16, but in 1 Corinthians the word διά does not imply that Christ created all things. The preposition ἐκ which occurs in the first part of 1 Cor. 8.6 describes the creation and ascribes this act to God the Father: "Yet to us there is one God, the Father, of whom (ἐξ οὗ) are all things and we unto him (εἰς αὐτόν)."

A saying of Marcus Aurelius resembles 1 Cor. 8.6. When he is speaking of Nature, Aurelius says, "Of thee are all things, in thee are all things, unto thee are all things".[1] This resembles even more closely some words in Romans in which Paul is speaking not of Christ but of God the Father: "For of him, and through him, and unto him, are all things."[2] Paul was not of course indebted to Aurelius who wrote his Meditations long after Paul's death. But the saying may represent a common Stoic outlook, and Aurelius may have been quoting an older formula, which may have influenced Paul's mode of expression and even his thought.

If Paul could quote Aratus at Athens, he must have been acquainted with Stoic teaching.[3] The travelling philosopher was a frequent sight in the lands of the Eastern Mediterranean. Paul would meet such men in towns and villages and on the highways. But although Stoic teaching may have influenced his mode of expression and that part of his thought which dealt with the idea of all things being "unto" God and Christ, he did not derive his teaching about the creation of the world from this source. He inherited his belief in God as creator from the Jews.

The source of Paul's belief that Christ was active in creating the world was not Hellenistic. It was Jewish. He knew of the Jewish teaching about Wisdom, Word, and Law, and he applied this teaching to Christ. He actually calls Christ the "wisdom of God",[4] although he does not lay great stress upon this as a title. And there are several other passages in which he is influenced by Wisdom

---

[1] ἐκ σοῦ πάντα, ἐν σοὶ πάντα, εἰς σὲ πάντα (Meditations, IV,23).
[2] ὅτι ἐξ αὐτοῦ καὶ δι' αὐτοῦ καὶ εἰς αὐτὸν τὰ πάντα (Rom. 11.36).
[3] Acts 17.28.   [4] 1 Cor. 1.24,30.

literature in his exposition of the activity of Christ. He never says that Christ is the Word, but he is influenced by Philonic teaching in part of his description of Christ's work.

Paul refrained from emphasizing that Christ was Wisdom or Word, because he believed Christ's work to be greater than anything ascribed to these entities. It was not because he refused to give an account of his nature. If this had been so, he would not have allowed himself to call Christ "the wisdom of God". His reluctance to use these titles is caused by his awareness of the surpassing greatness of Christ's person and work.

Although Jewish ideas and language were the vehicle of Paul's thought, his beliefs about Christ and creation were formed by the application of Jewish and Christian tradition to his own experience. There was the Jewish tradition of Wisdom and Word. There was the growing belief amongst Christians that Jesus was Lord. There was the comparison with Wisdom made by Jesus himself in Matt. 11.28–30. There was the title "author of life" applied to him in the early kerygma which is recorded in Acts. All these traditions and practices opened the way for Paul to give expression to his own experience of Christ as the creator of new life within him. First and foremost Christ was the bringer of a new creation which renewed a man inwardly. And if he was the new creator, then it was reasonable to suppose that he was the creator when first the world was made. Paul was slow to give expression to this idea, for it was a bold thought. It does not occur till Colossians, which is one of the latest of his epistles. The different trains of thought which can be traced in the earlier epistles merge in this great passage from Colossians.

Paul had early accepted the belief that Jesus was the preexistent Son of God. Jesus, though he was rich, for our sakes became poor (2 Cor. 8.9). He was the rock which accompanied the Israelites in the wilderness (1 Cor. 10.4). Paul also believed that Christ maintained the universe which God had created. All things were through him (1 Cor. 8.6). And he believed that if any man was in Christ a new creation had taken place. "If any man is in Christ, he is a new creature" (2 Cor. 5.17). These thoughts did not lead with irrefutable logic to the belief that Christ was creator of the world, but they made it easier for Paul to accept that belief.

If Christ was the Son of God who existed before his incarnation, if he was the giver of the Spirit which renewed life within the believer, and if he was the Lord who ruled over God's universe, then it was reasonable to suppose that he had taken part in the creation of the world. In this doctrine Paul passes beyond the immediate theme of redemption which is his chief message. The doctrine of Col. 1.16 is not one of the cardinal doctrines of *saving* faith. It belongs more to the realm of speculation. On the other hand it is an implicate of the belief in the divinity of Christ. It is an implicate of a doctrine, which was not yet clearly formulated by Paul, but which is included within the saving faith, the doctrine that Christ is "true God of true God". The appearance of this belief that Christ was creator shows how Paul's theological account of his beliefs and experiences was crystallizing. He must have already given considerable thought to the problem of Christ and creation, and when he was confronted with the practical issue of the Colossian heresy that the world was created by angels, he made his beliefs public.

The Epistle to the Hebrews

This epistle owes a considerable debt to Wisdom literature and to the allegorical type of exposition which is found in the writings of Philo. The phrase "effulgence of his glory" (Heb. 1.3) has a clear parallel in Wisdom 7.25–6:

For she is . . . a clear effluence of the glory of the Almighty . . .
For she is an effulgence from everlasting light.

The description of Christ as a High Priest after the order of Melchizedek is reminiscent of Philo's statement that the Logos is a Priest after the order of Melchizedek. Because of the link with Wisdom literature it is not surprising that the author of the epistle has a high Christology and describes Christ as an agent in creation. Christ is called "heir of all things, through whom also he [God] made the worlds" (Heb. 1.2).

The writer of Hebrews may not have read Paul's writings, but his teaching about Christ's rôle in creation suggests that he was acquainted with Paul's thought. It is possible, however, that the development was made independently of Paul, and that the author of Hebrews, using Jewish and Christian traditions to interpret his own beliefs and experience, reached the same conclusion as Paul.

The Johannine Writings

In the Fourth Gospel it is acknowledged that Christ was pre-existent. He is the Word which has been in existence from the beginning (John 1.1, cf. 1 John 1.1). He existed before Abraham (John 8.58), and he is described as an agent in the creation. Through him all things were made. Without him nothing was made that has been made (John 1.3).

The source of this doctrine in John, as in Paul, is the writer's own belief and experience together with the background of Jewish and Christian tradition. John was specially influenced by Jewish teaching on the theme of the Word, and although it is not certain that he was deeply versed in the Stoic and Philonic philosophies he probably knew something about them, and was deliberately attempting to expound the gospel in terms which would appeal to men and women who had been reared in the Hellenistic tradition. The term λόγος (Word) was used frequently both by Philo and by the Stoics, and its appearance in the Fourth Gospel cannot be dismissed as a coincidence. Undoubtedly the evangelist was influenced chiefly by the biblical tradition about the Word, but he would also be thinking of readers who knew as much about popular Hellenistic philosophy as about the beliefs of the Hebrews.

The main influence, however, was the evangelist's own awareness of the power of Christ, who was the giver of life, and who breathed the Spirit upon the disciples to inaugurate a new creation. This Saviour, who brought the new creation, had also been active in the first creation. Like Paul, the Fourth Evangelist was sensitive to the best Hebrew thought and conscious of the mental outlook of the people among whom he worked. This alertness of mind enabled him to write in language which awakened the hearts of men of widely different cultures. But his inspiration was found not in the traditions which he had inherited or discovered but in the Christian experience which he shared and the gospel story which he interpreted.

The Implications of the belief that
Christ was active in the Creation of the World

In the preceding sections it has been shown that Paul, John, and the author of the Epistle to the Hebrews believed that Christ was active in the creation of the world. These are the only three writers in the New Testament who state this doctrine openly. The doctrine is not found in the synoptic gospels or the Acts of the Apostles. But there are sayings of Jesus and phrases of the early Christian kerygma which foreshadow the later developments of doctrine.

The function of creation was regarded by many Jews as a unique function of God. But opinion about this matter was not unanimous. Some Jews believed and others vigorously opposed the doctrine that the angels were agents in creation. The suspicion which was cast on the belief in angelic mediation gives an indication of the reaction which many Jews would have to the Christian belief that Christ had been active in the creation. The claim that he not only existed before his birth but had also occupied a unique position as God's fellow-worker in creation would cause the deepest offence to many Jews.

On the other hand there is plenty of evidence that concepts such as Wisdom, Word, and Spirit were used to describe a mediating agent in the creation. They do not seem to have caused as much trouble as teaching about angelic mediation, because they were so closely related to God as not to shake men's belief in God's unity. But they became a stumbling-block when they were applied to Christ, because Christ was a person who had lived on earth. When it was taught that Christ had taken part in creation the question of his divinity had to arise sooner or later.

These new teachings which occur in Paul, John, and Hebrews were not infallible signs of a belief in Christ's divinity. But the functions which were ascribed to him were so exalted and so inimical to the cherished convictions of many a Jew that the New Testament writers would have written in this strain only in order to show that Christ had a unique relationship to God, for which no human precedent could be found. They hesitated to say outright that Christ was God. They preferred to use the ideas of Wisdom and Word in an effort to reconcile their belief about the Son to their conviction that God was one. But these ideas were not sufficient to achieve this purpose, because in the Old Testament they had not been used to describe a man. This explains why Paul rarely describes Christ as the Wisdom of God but makes frequent use of the language of wisdom. It also explains why John only uses the title Word at the beginning of the Gospel and the First Epistle. The writers themselves were aware of the inadequacy of these concepts to express the mystery which they believed. But when they describe Christ as judge and creator, they are describing the activities of one whom they believe to be God. They do not attempt a systematic exposition of the doctrine of Christ's person. But the way in which they write about his activities shows that their convictions, though not precisely formulated, were taking definite shape. As this process continued, the problem of Christ's relationship with the Father came more into the foreground.

Other Aspects of Creative Activity
Sustaining and Maintenance of the Universe

The Jews did not regard God as a creator who had abandoned the universe after he had formed it. His work of creation could not be divorced from his continual watch over the universe. The Old Testament is a record of God's activity in history. It describes his deliverance and protection of his people, his punishment of their sins and his reward for their faithfulness. It describes also his control of the destinies of Gentile nations, and his power over the world of nature. This task of sustaining the created universe was not uniquely divine. Kings and princes, prophets and priests were God's ministers in this work. But none of them is said to exercise the universal control which is attributed by Paul to Christ in the words "all things are through him" (δι αὐτοῦ), and which is claimed by Jesus for himself when he says "All authority has been given to me in heaven and on earth" (Matt. 28.18).

One of the avenues through which early Christians approached their belief that Christ was agent in creation was the doctrine of

Christ's Lordship over all things in heaven and on earth. We have already examined the use of the title "Lord" in the New Testament. Paul believed that God had put all things in subjection under Christ's feet (Eph. 1.22; 1 Cor. 15.27). In virtue of this power Christ sustained the created world. There is "one Lord Jesus Christ, through whom are all things and we through him" (1 Cor. 8.6). "In him all things consist" (Col. 1.17). The Lordship of Christ is not merely a title by which he received tributes of service and adoration. He gives life to the world which is held together by him. A doctrine such as this goes beyond the belief that Christ was a divine servant who came to perform special tasks in the world as did prophets and kings. His ministry is not confined to a particular people or generation. His Lordship is universal.

The same idea occurs in the Epistle to the Hebrews, the author of which speaks of Christ "bearing all things by the word of his power" (1.3). But although Christ is often given the title Lord and although his power over the life of individual Christians is generally acknowledged, nothing is said except in the Pauline writings and Hebrews about his function of maintaining the whole world. The silence of other writers may have been caused by the difficulty of expounding the doctrine.

Other Aspects of Creative Activity
The leading of the created universe to an end or goal

One of Paul's original contributions to Christian thought is his doctrine that Christ is the end or goal of history. This is not, strictly speaking, a doctrine about creation. It is mentioned here because in Paul's mind it is linked with his belief that Christ was active in creating and sustaining the world. In Col. 1.16 he says all things are "unto him". The theme is elaborated in Eph. 1.9 ff in which God's good pleasure is said to be "to sum up all things in Christ, the things in the heavens, and the things upon the earth". And in Eph. 4.15 God's purpose is said to be that we "may grow up in all things into him, which is the head, even Christ".

Jewish literature was full of speculations about the last things but there is a distinctiveness about Paul's belief that Christ is the end of all things. The doctrine of the last things is dissociated here from the idea of judgement. In Colossians and Ephesians, from which these quotations have been taken, there is little about the last judgement. Paul thinks rather of the time when Christ will be all in all. The two ideas are not inconsistent, and Paul never gave up his belief in a last judgement, although his emphasis was shifting.

This belief that Christ will be the end of things is evidence of the very high conception which Paul had of his Person. In the epistle to the Romans it is said of God that all things are unto him. "For of him, and through him, and unto him, are all things" (Rom. 11.36). But in Colossians and Ephesians it is Christ unto whom "all things are".

The statement that all things are unto God or Christ is not easy to interpret. It does not mean that all things will lose their identity in Christ, nor does it imply that all things will be redeemed. It means that at the last nothing will exist except that which is redeemed and is in Christ. When the last enemy, death, is destroyed, God and Christ will be all in all,[1] and everything which exists will exist by virtue of Christ's redeeming work.

Paul's belief that Christ will be the end has little direct background in Jewish thought. In Second Isaiah God is called the First and the Last,[2] and sayings of the third century after Christ claim that the world was created *for* or *to* certain distinguished leaders. According to Sanh. 98b. "Rab (d. 247) said: 'The world was created only for David.' Samuel (d. 254) said: 'for Moses'. R. Johanan (d. 279) said: 'for Messiah'."[3] These sayings may well represent ideas which were current before the third century, but they do not carry the same deep content as the Pauline sayings. They may mean no more than that David, Moses, or the Messiah is the turning-point in human history.[4]

---

[1] 1 Cor. 15.26 ff.   [2] Isa. 41.4; 43.10,11; 44.6; 48.12.

[3] Cf. Strack-Billerbeck, *Kommentar zum NT*, III, p. 626. The preposition which is translated "for" or "to" is l^e.

[4] The idea of Moses as a turning-point in history is found in the Assumption of Moses, according to which Moses lived 2,500 years after the creation (Ass. Mos. 1.1) and the time from Moses' death to the appearing of God as redeemer will be 2,500 years (Ass. Mos. 10.2). Cf. Strack-Billerbeck, op. cit., IV, pp. 994-5.

Paul may have been influenced by Stoic terminology. Marcus Aurelius says of nature "Unto thee are all things",[1] and this may reflect earlier Stoic teaching with which Paul was acquainted. But Paul's belief that Christ will be the end grew out of his own thought and experience. More than anything else which he says about the cosmic work of Christ it bears the stamp of originality.

The only other writing of the New Testament in which Christ is called the end is in the Apocalypse, in which Jesus says: "I am the Alpha and the Omega, the first and the last, the beginning and the end" (Rev. 22.13). These titles are given also to God in Rev. 1.8 and 21.6. The title "first and last" comes from Isaiah, according to whom God says "I am the first and I am the last. And beside me there is no God" (Isa. 44.6). The words "Alpha and Omega" are merely another way of saying "first and last". The words "beginning and end" may have meant no more to the writer than "Alpha and Omega" and "first and last". It is possible, however, that since the author was writing to churches in Asia Minor, he may have been using a formula which was a legacy of Paul's doctrine that Christ is the end. This doctrine was expounded in the letters to the churches of Colossae and Ephesus, both of which are in Asia Minor. Although this may explain the presence in the Apocalypse of the formula "the beginning and the end", there is no evidence that the author probed as deeply in his thought as did Paul.

Other Aspects of Creative Activity
The New Creation

In the Old Testament there are prophecies that God will make a new creation. "For, behold, I create new heavens and a new earth:

[1] Meditations, IV, 23. Lebreton, *History of the Doctrine of the Trinity*, I, p. 301, contrasts the teaching of Paul about Christ with that of the Stoic Chrysippus about the Logos. He writes: "For Chrysippus everything comes from the Logos by physical dissociation and degeneration, everything returns to the Logos by the progressive absorption of individual beings in the total being. Here, on the other hand, everything comes from Christ by a free act of creation which in no way diminishes his greatness; everything tends towards Christ, not to be absorbed and lost in him, but to be united in him, and to live in him."

and the former things shall not be remembered, nor come into mind" (Isa. 65.17; cf. Isa. 66.22). The prophecy is taken up by pseudepigraphical writings, and used to describe the blessings of the Messianic age. The climax of God's purposes will be a new beginning, when heaven and earth will be transformed and a new and eternal age will be inaugurated.

Paul uses these ideas in his epistles. "If any man is in Christ, he is a new creature" (2 Cor. 5.17; cf. Gal. 6.15). Christians are men and women who "have put on the new man, which is being renewed unto knowledge after the image of him that created him" (Col. 3.10).

Paul, following the teaching of Christ, believed that the new creation was already taking place. It was not complete, and many struggles had to be fought, but new creatures were already in existence.

Paul does not, however, describe Christ as the creator of the new heaven and the new earth. The creation occurs "in Christ" but he is not said to be its agent.

This belief in the new creation is implicit in the Fourth Gospel. After the resurrection, when Jesus breathed the Spirit into his disciples, he was creating them anew. As God breathed life into the nostrils of man at the creation of the world, so Christ breathed eternal life into his followers (John 20.22).

A kindred idea is that of the new birth. Unless a man can be born again of water and the Spirit, he cannot enter into the kingdom of God (John 3.5; cf. 1 Pet. 1.3).

The clearest description of a new creation is to be found in the Apocalypse. A glittering account of the formation of a new heaven and a new earth is given in the last chapters of the book. When Christ, the Lamb, is with him, God will bring the new Jerusalem. In the Apocalypse the new heaven and the new earth lie in the future. There is no hint of the Pauline belief that the new creation has already begun.

These other aspects of creative activity, Christ sustaining the universe, Christ as the end of all things, and the new creation, show the variety of ways in which the New Testament writers, and especially Paul, expounded the divine power of Christ and his relationship to the Father. They support the view that Paul knew that the functions which he ascribed to Christ were divine and not human, and that he was attempting to elaborate his belief in Christ's divinity. The same may be said in a more limited way of the Fourth Evangelist and the author of the Epistle to the Hebrews.

CHAPTER 9

JESUS AND SALVATION

The idea of salvation has a central place in Christian thought and worship. It runs through the scriptures like a thread which holds together the complex design. Both Old and New Testaments affirm the intention of the Almighty to save his people, and in the New Testament Jesus himself is described as "saviour". The questions which have been asked about judgement and creation will now be asked about salvation. Are certain kinds of saving acts regarded in Jewish thought as the work of God alone? And are such acts attributed in the New Testament to Jesus Christ?

The Israelite and Judaistic Background

Salvation is a deliverance from one condition to another. The aim of this discussion is to discover if the Jews believed that there were some conditions *from* which only God could save men, and some conditions *to* which only God could save them. The Old Testament and later Jewish teaching about salvation will be examined in two sections: salvation from exile, oppression, or death, to a longer and fuller life on earth; salvation from death and sin to eternal life and to communion with God.

Salvation from exile, oppression, or death, to a longer and fuller life on earth

There are many incidents recorded in which a man saves another from physical danger. For example, Reuben delivered Joseph out of the hand of his brothers (Gen. 37.21). The congregation of the Israelites was instructed to deliver a manslaughterer from his avenger (Num. 35.25). A man could also rescue others from injustice, as Jeremiah presupposed when he said to the king of Judah: "Execute ye judgement and righteousness, and deliver the spoiled out of the hand of the oppressor" (Jer. 22.3).

Human beings also saved the nation. Joshua and several of the judges are said to have saved the people in battle,[1] and two of them, Othniel and Ehud, are given the title "saviour".[2] David is said to have saved the people,[3] and in a later work, the First Book of the Maccabees, Eleazar is described as giving himself to save the people,[4] and Judas is called "he who saves Israel".[5]

In spite of these examples it is usually God who is described as the saviour both of the individual and of the nation. He saves the needy (Job 5.15) and the afflicted (Ps. 18.27). It is to him that the Psalmist prays for deliverance from "workers of iniquity" and "bloodthirsty men" (Ps. 59.2). It was God who delivered the people from the Egyptians (Ex. 14.30), the Philistines (1 Sam. 14.23), and the Assyrians (2 Chron. 32.22).

Some of the prophets assert that God alone has power to save. Jeremiah describes the powerlessness of other gods (Jer. 2.28; cf. Jer. 11.12), and affirms that God is the source of salvation:

> Truly in vain is the help that is looked for from the hills, the tumult on the mountains: truly in the Lord our God is the salvation of Israel (Jer. 3.23).

The Second Isaiah stresses the uniqueness of God's work as saviour:

> I, even I, am the Lord; and beside me there is no saviour (Isa. 43.11).
>
> . . . and there is no god else beside me; a just God and a saviour; there is none beside me (Isa. 45.21).

Even the Messianic passages of the Old Testament refrain from describing the Messiah as a saviour. The Second Psalm, for example, speaks of an anointed king who will receive the nations for an inheritance, but never claims that he will save or deliver the people. Isa. 9.1–6 tells of a child who is born to rule over the people, but does not call him a saviour. Even the ruler of Isa. 11.1–10, who will slay the wicked and inaugurate an era of miraculous peace, is not hailed as a saviour. The usual words which describe salvation

---

[1] Josh. 10.6; Judges 2.16,18; 3.9,15,31; 6.14–15; 8.22; 13.5.
[2] Judges 3.9,15. "Saviour" translates the participle *moshiyaʿ*, which could also be translated "he who saves".
[3] 1 Sam. 9.16; 10.27.   [4] 1 Macc. 6.44.   [5] 1 Macc. 9.21.

and deliverance[1] are not used of him. Jeremiah prophesies that in the days of the Messianic king "Judah shall be saved, and Israel shall dwell safely" (Jer. 23.6), but the use of the passive verb "shall be saved" suggests that Yahweh and not the Messiah will save the people.

An exception is Mic. 5.6b, in which a Messianic prince is described as a deliverer:

> And he shall deliver us from the Assyrian, when he cometh into our land, and when he treadeth within our border.

There are prophecies of a Messianic prince in later writings, in which he is regarded as a saviour. The Book of Jubilees foretells the coming of a prince of the tribe of Judah, of whom it says: "In thee shall be found the salvation of Israel" (Jub. 31.19). And the seventeenth and eighteenth Psalms of Solomon speak of a Messiah who will overthrow the enemies of the nation and gather a holy people together. This means that he performs the task of salvation.

It is clear from the above evidence that the Jews did believe that human beings could save men from exile, oppression, and death, and that the Messiah could be regarded as a deliverer. At the same time some writers, especially when speaking of the deliverance of the nation, stress the fact that God is the saviour. And the majority of references to a Messiah tell of his work as a ruler rather than as a saviour.

Salvation from death and sin to eternal life and to communion with God

A belief in eternal life developed comparatively late in Jewish thought. The dead were supposed either to perish or to eke out a shadowy existence in Sheol. Even Job. 19.25 does not reveal more than the hope of a momentary existence after death. But in the forty-ninth and seventy-third Psalms a hope of eternal life is expressed. According to the forty-ninth Psalm this life will be attained by redemption from the power of Sheol:

> None of them can by any means redeem his brother,
> Nor give to God a ransom for him:
> (For the redemption of their soul is costly,

[1] *y-sh-'*, which is generally translated "save", and *n-ts-l*, which is generally translated "deliver".

And must be let alone for ever:)
That he should still live alway,
That he should not see corruption (Ps. 49.7–9).

But God will redeem my soul from the power of Sheol:
For he shall receive me (Ps. 49.15).

The Psalmist says that redemption from Sheol to eternal life is the work of God alone,[1] and in Dan. 12.2,3, where there is a prophecy of a resurrection, there is no suggestion that it is achieved by a human agent. The same emphasis on the divine initiative is found in some of the pseudepigraphical writings. In 1 Enoch 83–90 it is God himself who intervenes to save the righteous, and to set up a new Jerusalem. In the first sixteen Psalms of Solomon it is God who will raise the righteous to eternal life. In the seventeenth and eighteenth of these psalms, in which the Messiah is said to defeat the nation's enemies and to gather the people together, there is no indication that he inaugurates an everlasting kingdom or raises the righteous dead.[2]

There are two writings in which a Messianic deliverer is described who leads men from death to eternal life. They are the Similitudes of Enoch and the Testaments of the Twelve Patriarchs. The Son of Man in the Similitudes of Enoch is not explicitly said to save, but his work is integral to the salvation of the righteous from death to eternal life. He will be the judge of the world, the champion and ruler of the righteous. He has "preserved the lot of the righteous" (1 Enoch 48.7). And he will choose out the righteous on the day of salvation:

And he shall choose the righteous and holy from among them:
For the day has drawn nigh that they should be saved (1 Enoch 51.2).

The other example of a deliverer from death to eternal life is not strictly a Messiah but a Priest. He is described in the Testament of Levi as a Priest who will "give to the saints to eat from the tree of life" (Test. Levi 18.11). He will open Paradise for the righteous (Test. Levi. 18.10; Test. Dan. 5.12). Here is no mere military champion, but a saviour who will give men eternal life.

Although the main trend in Jewish thought seems to have been

---

[1] Cf. Ps. 73.23–6.   [2] Cf. R. H. Charles, *Eschatology*, pp. 270–2.

that God would save men from death to eternal life, the Similitudes of Enoch and the Testaments of the Twelve Patriarchs suggest that the task would be performed by the Son of Man or the Priest.

A related theme is that of salvation from sin to eternal life and to communion with God. In the Old Testament itself salvation from sin results in communion with God rather than eternal life. This is the theme of Psalm 51.11,12,14:

> Cast me not away from thy presence;
> And take not thy holy spirit from me.
> Restore unto me the joy of thy salvation:
> And uphold me with a free spirit. . . .
> Deliver me from bloodguiltiness, O God, thou God of my salvation.[1]

Not only individuals but also the nation can be saved by God from sin:

> For with the Lord there is mercy,
> And with him is plenteous redemption.
> And he shall redeem Israel
> From all his iniquities (Ps. 130.7,8).[2]

In Jeremiah's prophecy of the New Covenant (Jer. 31.34) the new nation will be one in which each individual has the privilege of communion with God. Jeremiah says that God's willingness to pass over men's sins leads to their individual knowledge of him. This passage reminds us that forgiveness is essential to salvation from sin. And forgiveness is the prerogative of God.

The Suffering Servant of Second Isaiah is closely connected with salvation from sin. It is disputed whether the Servant refers to an individual or to the nation or a part of the nation. In any case, however, the Servant makes possible the forgiveness of sin. "With his stripes we are healed" (Isa. 53.5). "By his knowledge shall my righteous servant justify many: and he shall bear their iniquities" (Isa. 53.11). The usual Hebrew words for "save" and "deliver" are not used to describe the Servant's work, and he is not said himself to forgive the sins of men. At most he makes forgiveness possible by his vicarious suffering. Yet in the idea of the Suffering Servant is the possibility of the development of a

---

[1] Cf. Ps. 39.8; 79.9.   [2] Cf. Ezek. 36.29; 37.23.

belief in a deliverer who would save men from sin by his self-sacrifice. This theme, however, is not developed in Jewish discussions and expositions of the Servant Songs.[1]

Three passages in non-canonical writings suggest that someone other than God may be instrumental in saving men from sin. The first is 1 Enoch 10.11,20-2, in which it is said that the angel Michael will cleanse the earth from all sin. The other passage is from the Testament of Levi 18.10-12, in which it is said that the coming Priest will bind Beliar, and give his children power to tread upon evil spirits. A third passage is from the Testament of Dan in which it is prophesied that the Priest will deliver the captives taken by Beliar (Test. Dan. 5.11).

Whether these passages actually say that someone other than God can save men from sins, is open to dispute. One thing they do not say is that anyone other than God can forgive sins. There is little enough evidence that men or angels were able to save men from sins. There is no evidence that they were able to forgive sins.[2] And since forgiveness is necessary for salvation from sins, the complete process can be achieved only by God.

Another part of the process of salvation which is a uniquely divine prerogative is the act of raising the dead. In none of the passages discussed is it said that a man or an angel will actually raise the dead to everlasting life. Although the Messiah is expected by some writers to deliver men from death to life, the actual process of resurrection is performed by God alone.[3]

The evidence which has been reviewed leads to certain conclusions which are of importance for understanding the Christian attitude to Jesus Christ and salvation.

First, physical salvation from exile, death, or oppression, to a longer and fuller life is usually said to be the work of God, but is sometimes said to be effected by human saviours.

Secondly, salvation from death and sin to everlasting life and to

[1] Cf. S. Mowinckel, *He that Cometh*, pp. 330-3, and M. D. Hooker, *Jesus and the Servant*, pp. 53-6.

[2] Cf. Strack-Billerbeck, *Kommentar*, I, pp. 495 f.

[3] Cf. Strack-Billerbeck, op. cit., I, pp. 523-4, and S. Mowinckel, op. cit., p. 337.

communion with God is nearly always said to be the work of God, but there are one or two possible exceptions to the rule.

Thirdly, two parts in the process of this second kind of salvation are forgiveness and resurrection, both of which were regarded in Jewish thought as the unique prerogative of God.

If any man was supposed to save people from death and sin and to give them eternal life, he would be thought by many Jews to possess uniquely divine functions. If he was supposed to forgive sins and to raise the dead to eternal life, it would almost certainly be assumed that he was exercising functions which were hitherto regarded as God's alone.

The Hellenistic and Pagan Background

The title "saviour" was a favourite one in the Eastern Mediterranean both before and after the time of Christ. It was given to many gods and goddesses, including the traditional deities Zeus, Apollo, Artemis, Athena, the healing god Asclepius, and the deities of the mystery cults, Hermes, Serapis, and Isis. Heroes, especially the founders of cities, were hailed as saviours. The title was given to Philip of Macedon, the Ptolemies of Egypt, and the Seleucids of Syria. Julius Caesar and Augustus received the title, and it was often used in the context of Caesar-worship.[1] In Hellenistic circles, if a man was called "saviour", it was not a difficult step to call him "god" as well. In the mystery religions the cultic deity was connected with the process of salvation from death and sin to life. When Jesus was claimed to perform this kind of salvation, and was given the title "saviour", many people in the Hellenistic world would suppose that he was regarded as God.

The Synoptic Gospels

The word "save" (σώζειν) is used in the synoptic gospels to describe healing. When he had healed a man with a withered hand, Jesus said:

Is it lawful on the sabbath day to do good, or to do harm? to save a life, or to kill? (Mark 3.4).

[1] Cf. P. Wendland in *ZNTW*, V (1904), pp. 336–9.

When Jairus wanted his daughter to be healed, he asked "that thou come and lay thy hands on her, that she may be saved (σωθῇ),[1] and live" (Mark 5.23, cf. Luke 8.50).

A more important use of the word "save" is to describe salvation from sin. Jesus called himself the Son of Man, who had "come to seek and to save that which was lost" (Luke 19.10). When Zacchaeus promised to restore what he had wrongfully taken from others, Jesus said: "To-day is salvation come to this house" (Luke 19.9). When Jesus granted forgiveness to a sinful woman, he said: "Thy faith hath saved thee" (Luke 7.50). It is this kind of salvation to which Matthew refers in his account of the birth of Jesus:

> And thou shalt call his name Jesus; for it is he that shall save his people from their sins (Matt. 1.21).

Jesus claimed for himself the power to grant forgiveness. He forgave the sinful woman (Luke 7.48). And in the story of the paralytic (Mark 2.1–12) the act of healing occurs after Jesus has pronounced forgiveness. Jesus affirms that "the Son of man hath power on earth to forgive sins" (Mark 2.10). The granting of forgiveness is part of the process of salvation from sins, and in Jewish thought it was regarded as the prerogative of God. When he said that he had power to forgive sins, Jesus was making a high claim for himself.

Jesus spoke also of deliverance from death, but did not explicitly claim that he was the agent of this kind of salvation. According to Mark 13.13 he said: "He that endureth to the end, the same shall be saved." This does not make it clear that Jesus himself will save. There is a similar ambiguity about Mark 8.35:

> For whosoever would save his life shall lose it; and whosoever shall lose his life for my sake and the gospel's shall save it.

This saying does not mean that an individual has power to save his own life. But it does not make it clear whether Jesus or God the Father will be the agent of salvation. It could be argued, however, from the context of both these sayings that Jesus is the saviour.

[1] Here the Revised Version translates "be made whole".

The thirteenth chapter of Mark is concerned with the coming of Christ as judge, and Mark 8.35 ff reaches its climax in the future coming of the Son of Man. If, however, the thirteenth chapter of Mark is not a unity,[1] an argument from the context can have little weight. In any case, Jesus does not claim to save from death as clearly as he claims to save from sins and to forgive.

There is no evidence in the synoptic gospels that Jesus was expected to raise the dead to eternal life. There is an incident in which he brings a young man to life again (Luke 7.11–17),[2] but this is salvation from death to a longer life on earth. And when he tells the disciples of John the Baptist to report to their master that "the dead are raised up" (Luke 7.22=Matt. 11.5), he is referring to incidents like the raising of the young man.

The condition into which men can be saved is described in the synoptic gospels as "life" (ζωή) or "eternal life" (ζωή αἰώνιος). This life is characteristic of the "age to come" which was expected in Judaism. It is a life which is not limited by death and is connected with the "world to come" and the coming of the Son of Man. But in so far as the Kingdom of God has already come through the ministry of Jesus, there is a sense in which eternal life is present as well as future.

According to the teaching of Jesus eternal life can be obtained by sacrificing worldly riches and following him. To the man who asked "What shall I do that I may inherit eternal life?" (Mark 10.17), his final answer was:

> One thing thou lackest: go, sell whatsoever thou hast, and give to the poor, and thou shalt have treasure in heaven: and come, follow me (Mark 10.21).

Those who leave house and family for his sake and the gospel's sake will have "in the world to come eternal life" (Mark 10.30). But these sayings, while they link Jesus with salvation to eternal life, do not actually say that he gives men such life. In the story of the Sheep and the Goats Jesus says that the Son of Man will call on the righteous to inherit the kingdom prepared for them

---

[1] For a discussion of the unity of Mark 13 see Vincent Taylor, St Mark, pp. 636–44.

[2] The story of Jairus' daughter (Mark 5.21–4,35–43) may be a case of healing, rather than of raising from the dead. See Taylor, op. cit., pp. 285 ff.

(Matt. 25.34), and this kingdom is one in which they will receive eternal life (Matt. 25.46). This does suggest that it is the Son of Man who will save the righteous to life.

Jesus is never called "saviour" in the synoptic gospels, although the very name Jesus suggests the idea of a saviour.[1] But there is no evidence that he himself encouraged men to give him the title. He did, however, claim to save men from sins, and to have power to forgive them. There is not such strong evidence that he claimed to save men from death to eternal life, but there are indications of such a claim in the story of the Sheep and the Goats. He never claimed to bring about a resurrection from death to eternal life. According to the synoptic gospels, however, Jesus said enough about his saving powers to support men's belief in his divinity.

The Acts of the Apostles

In the Acts of the Apostles the words "save" and "salvation" describe physical healing (Acts 4.9; 14.9), rescue from drowning (Acts 27.20,31), physical nourishment (Acts 27.34), and the deliverance of the Hebrews from Egypt (Acts 7.25). These are examples of salvation from physical dangers and limitations to a longer and fuller life on earth.

More often the words describe salvation from sin and death to eternal life. At Pentecost Peter quotes the words of Joel:

And it shall be, that whosoever shall call on the name of the Lord shall be saved (Acts 2.21).

In the speech of Acts 4 he says:

And in none other is there salvation: for neither is there any other name under heaven, that is given among men, wherein we must be saved (4.12).

And to the Apostolic Council in Jerusalem he says:

But we believe that we shall be saved through the grace of the Lord Jesus (Acts 15.11).

[1] The Hebrew form of the name was *Jeshua'*, meaning "He whose salvation is Yahweh", or "God's salvation"; see Vincent Taylor, *Names of Jesus*, p. 5.

Twice in the Acts Jesus is given the title "saviour" (Acts 5.31; 13.23), and in 5.31 it is as saviour that he gives remission of sins:

Him did God exalt with his right hand to be a prince and a saviour, for to give repentance to Israel, and remission of sins.

The date of the speeches in Acts has been much disputed, and we cannot be certain that they contain an accurate report of early Christian preaching. But since the statements about the part of Jesus in the work of salvation are in agreement with his own claims for himself in the synoptic gospels, it is reasonable to assume that the Acts is giving a faithful account of the early Church's beliefs about the subject. Jesus saves men from sin to life. He claimed no less for himself, and the Acts perpetuates this teaching.

The speeches of Acts make one advance on the synoptic gospels. They give Jesus the title "saviour". It is quite credible that such a step should have been taken early in the history of the Christian Church. Since Jesus himself had claimed to save men, it was a natural development to give him the title "saviour".

Paul

Paul uses the title "saviour" twice of Jesus, both examples being in his later epistles. One example refers to the coming again of Christ:

For our citizenship is in heaven; from whence also we wait for a saviour, the Lord Jesus Christ (Phil. 3.20).

The other describes him as the saviour of "the Body", that is, the Church:

For the husband is the head of the wife, as Christ also is the head of the church, being himself the saviour of the body (Eph. 5.23).

Since Paul then goes on to speak of Christ's sanctifying and cleansing of the Church (Eph. 5.26), he is in this passage regarding Christ as a saviour from sin.

Jesus is never the subject of the verb "save" in Paul's epistles, but there is no doubt that Paul regarded him as the agent of salvation, not only because he used the title "saviour" but also because he expressed the idea in other language. Christ is the redeemer, who "redeemed us from the curse of the law" (Gal. 3.13).[1] He is the deliverer, who "gave himself for our sins, that he might deliver[2] us out of this present evil world" (Gal. 1.4). He has set men free from the bondage of the law (Gal. 5.1). He has reconciled men to God (Eph. 2.16), and it is through him that a man can be delivered[3] from "the body of this death" (Rom. 7.24,25). These are all ways of saying that Christ saves men from sin and death.[4] He delivers men too from the "wrath to come" (1 Thess. 1.10). And although he is not said to dispense forgiveness,[5] in him we have the forgiveness of sins (Eph. 1.7; Col. 1.14).

The condition into which Christ saves men is both present and future. Those whom Christ has set free, are able to "live by the Spirit" (Gal. 5.25). Theirs is the "law of the Spirit of life" (Rom. 8.2). But a further salvation awaits them. Jesus will deliver them from the wrath to come (1 Thess. 1.10). Paul does not explicitly say that Christ will raise men from dead. It is God who will raise them (2 Cor. 1.9; 4.14). But it is "in Christ" that all will be made alive (1 Cor. 15.22), and Paul says of Christ that "the last Adam became a life-giving spirit" (1 Cor. 15.45). These last two statements are part of Paul's exposition of the meaning of resurrection. They are evidence that in fact Paul believed that Christ would raise up the dead.

Paul ascribes to Christ the kind of saving power which was generally supposed in Judaism to be uniquely divine. In the epistles Christ is a saviour, redeemer, and deliverer from sin and death. He saves men to a life which is in the Spirit. He is not actually said to forgive, but forgiveness is obtained "in him". And his part in the final salvation is described in a way that implies that he would raise up the dead.

[1] In 1 Cor. 1.30 Christ is called "redemption" and according to Rom. 3.24 redemption is "in Christ". Gal. 4.5 may also mean that Christ himself redeems.

[2] The verb is ἐξαιρεῖν.

[3] The verb here and in 1 Thess. 1.10 is ῥύεσθαι.

[4] Christ is never said to justify men. "It is God that justifieth" (Rom. 8.33, cf. Rom. 3.30). But justification is "in Christ" (Gal. 2.17).

[5] According to Col. 3.13 "the Lord forgave you". But it is uncertain whether "the Lord" refers to God the Father or to Jesus Christ.

The Epistle to the Hebrews

The title "saviour" never appears in the Epistle to the Hebrews, but the verb σώζειν (save) occurs twice. In Heb. 5.7 it refers to the part which God played in the resurrection of Christ, and in Heb. 7.25 it describes the saving work of Christ himself:

> Wherefore also he is able to save to the uttermost them that draw near unto God through him, seeing he ever liveth to make intercession for them.

Jesus is called "author of salvation" (ἀρχηγὸς τῆς σωτηρίας) (Heb. 2.10), and "cause of eternal salvation" (αἴτιος σωτηρίας αἰωνίου) (Heb. 5.9). He will appear when salvation is consummated:

> so Christ . . . shall appear a second time, apart from sin, to them that wait for him, unto salvation (Heb. 9.28).

He is not said to forgive sins, but his sacrificial death makes forgiveness possible (Heb. 9.22–8). It is not suggested that he will raise men from the dead.

Although the author of this epistle does not say much about Christ's saving work, he believed that Christ was the author and cause of salvation and could "save to the uttermost them that draw near unto God through him". He believed, in fact, that Christ could save men from sin and death to eternal life.

The Johannine Writings

Both the Fourth Gospel and the First Epistle of John call Jesus the "saviour of the world" (John 4.42; 1 John 4.14). The chief purpose of the incarnation was the salvation of men:

> I came not to judge the world, but to save the world (John 12.47).

> For God sent not the Son into the world to judge the world; but that the world should be saved through him (John 3.17).

This salvation is from death, since Christ came "that whosoever believeth on him should not perish" (John 3.16). It is also a salvation from sin. Men are the bondservants of sin (John 8.34–5), but "If therefore the Son shall make you free, ye shall be free indeed" (John 8.36).

In the First Epistle Jesus is said to forgive sins:

If we confess our sins, he is faithful and righteous to forgive us our sins, and to cleanse us from all unrighteousness (1 John 1.9).[1]

In the Gospel Jesus, after his resurrection, gives his disciples authority to forgive sins:

Receive ye the Holy Spirit: whose soever sins ye forgive, they are forgiven unto them; whose soever sins ye retain, they are retained (John 20.22–3).

This is a greater authority than that which is committed to Peter and the disciples in the sayings recorded in the Gospel according to St Matthew. There Jesus gives authority to "bind and loose" (Matt. 16.19; 18.18), which probably refers to the right to define what is lawful and unlawful.[2] In John 20.23 Jesus transmits the right to forgive, a right which was regarded as divine. Because they were abiding in Christ, and had received the Holy Spirit, the disciples were able to exercise a function which was generally regarded as God's alone.

Salvation brings men eternal life. This can be a present possession:

He that heareth my word, and believeth him that sent me, hath eternal life (John 5.24; cf. John 6.54; 1 John 5.11–12).

But salvation is also concerned with the future. In the gospel Jesus is said to have power to raise men from the dead. In John 11.25 he says:

I am the resurrection and the life: he that believeth on me, though he die, yet shall he live: and whosoever liveth and believeth on me shall never die.

This saying is found in the story of the raising of Lazarus. But Lazarus was raised to a longer life on earth, and this saying refers to a life which will have no end. It refers to the resurrection at the last day. Jesus says that he will carry out this final resurrection:

For the hour cometh, in which all that are in the tombs shall hear his voice, and shall come forth; they that have done good, unto the resurrection of life; and they that have done ill, unto the resurrection of judgement (John 5.28–9).

[1] For the last clause compare 1 John 1.7: "The blood of Jesus his Son cleanseth us from all sin."

[2] See A. H. McNeile, *St Matthew*, p. 243.

For this is the will of my Father, that every one that beholdeth the Son, and believeth on him, should have eternal life; and I will raise him up at the last day (John 6.40).

He that eateth my flesh and drinketh my blood hath eternal life; and I will raise him up at the last day (John 6.54; cf. also 6.39).

Nowhere else in the New Testament is Christ's part in the final resurrection described as clearly and as positively as in the Fourth Gospel. The Johannine writings emphasize all those aspects of Christ's saving work which imply that he is performing God's unique functions. They teach that Jesus liberates men from sin and death to eternal life, that he forgives sins, and that he will raise men up at the last day.

Other New Testament Writings

In the Pastoral Epistles only God and Christ are said to save men. The Second Epistle to Timothy speaks of God "who saved us" (2 Tim. 1.9), and the First Epistle (1 Tim. 1.15) declares: "Christ Jesus came into the world to save sinners." In these epistles the title "saviour" is used often of Christ, and the impression is given that it is a title which has gained general recognition in the Church. It is used of both God and Christ,[1] and in the Epistle to Titus, whenever God is called "saviour", Christ also is called "saviour".[2] He is described as one who saves men from death to life:

. . . our Saviour Christ Jesus, who abolished death, and brought life and incorruption to light through the gospel (2 Tim. 1.10).

And he saves men from sin:

. . . our great God and Saviour Jesus Christ; who gave himself for us, that he might redeem us from all iniquity, and purify unto himself a people for his own possession, zealous of good works (Titus 2.13–14; cf. 1 Tim. 1.15).

The Second Epistle of Peter gives the title "saviour" to Jesus Christ five times (2 Pet. 1.1,11; 2.20; 3.2,18). It seems to be accepted as a regular title of Jesus. But in the other writings there is

[1] Of God in 1 Tim. 1.1; 2.3; 4.10; Titus 1.3; 2.10; 3.4. Of Christ in 2 Tim. 1.10; Titus 1.4; 2.13; 3.6.

[2] Titus 1.3 and 4; 2.10 and 13; 3.4 and 6.

no clear link between Christ and salvation,[1] except in the Apocalypse, where salvation is ascribed to "the Lamb" (Rev. 7.10).

Conclusion

In Jewish thought great stress was laid on God's work as saviour both of the nation and of individuals. While human beings performed certain saving acts, such as military victory and the relief of the oppressed, they were hardly ever said to save men from sin to eternal life. And forgiveness of sins and the resurrection of the dead were regarded as the unique functions of God.

In the New Testament Jesus is said not only to save men from death and sin to eternal life but also to forgive sins and to bring about the final resurrection of the dead. He himself, according to the synoptic gospels, forgave sins and claimed to save men from sins. It is likely also that he taught that he himself would bring men to eternal life. The New Testament writings continued to ascribe these functions to him, and the Fourth Gospel also affirmed that he would raise men up at the last day.

[1] James says that the implanted word can save (1.21), and the First Epistle of Peter says that the water of baptism saves (3.21). James assumes that a Christian can save others from death (Jas. 5.20) and Jude exhorts Christians to save others from the fire of judgement (Jude 23). The other writers of the New Testament, however, were careful not to use such expressions.

CHAPTER 10

FATHER AND SON

The belief in the divinity of Christ raised the problem of his relation to God. If he could be called God and Lord, if he could act as judge, creator, and saviour, if he could be the object of prayer and worship, and be ascribed divine titles, what was his relation to the God whom he himself worshipped and to whom men had access through him? This is the core of the trinitarian problem.

When Christ was regarded as one who came from God to men, he could be interpreted in terms of the extension of the divine personality. His divinity could be explained by likening him to Wisdom or the Word, or by ascribing to him the uniquely divine functions. When, however, he was regarded as one who represented men before God and prayed to God, a different kind of interpretation was required. In an earlier chapter a distinction was made between extension and interaction of the divine personality.[1] Wisdom and Word are concepts which were used to describe the extension of the divine personality. But they were not adequate to account for the way in which Christ and God had dealings one with another, and acted upon each other.

The idea which was used in later accounts of the doctrine of the Trinity to interpret the interaction of the divine personality was that of Father and Son. It is found in the New Testament and on occasions the mode of its presentation shows that the writers were consciously attempting to answer a problem. The Father-Son motif is not the only one which expresses the relationship. The most important Pauline statement about the matter (Phil. 2.6 ff) does not include the word "Son". In the Epistle to the Hebrews the title "High Priest" is used to describe the interaction between God and Christ. But the Father-Son idea was ultimately the most

[1] See pp. 38–40.

171

influential in Christian thought. Of all the titles which describe Jesus' interaction with God, "Son of God" is best fitted to express the idea of Jesus' divinity. Most of the titles of Jesus are used to show how he comes from God, but not to describe his interaction with God. As Son of Man he comes to save and serve and judge mankind. As Christ he is anointed to rule over men. As Lord he has dominion over the created universe. All these titles describe the relation of Jesus to the world, but "Son of God" describes his relationship with God. The title "High Priest", which is used with great effect in the Epistle to the Hebrews, shows how Jesus appears before God to make intercession for men, but does not imply that Jesus himself is God. It is a title of interaction but not of divinity. "Son of God" suggests both the divinity of Jesus and the existence of a family relationship within the Godhead.

In this chapter the New Testament interpretation of the relationship between Father and Son will be examined, but reference will first be made to the pagan and Hebrew background.

The Gentile World

The use of the title "Father" in the Gentile world has already been discussed.[1] It is found in many cults, in Indian religion, in traditional Greek religion, in the mystery religions which enjoyed great popularity at the beginning of the Christian era, and in philosophy. Complementary to this belief that God is Father is the belief that there are sons of God. In Greek mythology children were said to have been born of the union of gods and goddesses, and some of the gods had children by union with mortals. For example, Heracles was the son of Zeus and Alcmene, Achilles was the son of Peleus and the goddess Thetis, Aeneas was the son of Anchises and the goddess Aphrodite. Such men were naturally called sons of the gods.

In the countries of the Middle East a tradition had grown up that the king was the son of the gods. In Babylonia he was regarded as a son of the gods by adoption, and not as physically their child. In Egypt, however, the king was believed to be a descendant of the

[1] See pp. 42–3.

god by birth. This belief was linked with the belief that the Pharaoh was the god himself. In the Hellenistic and Roman Empires the deification of the ruler was often connected with the belief that he was a son of the gods. Alexander the Great was described as the son of the Egyptian god Ammon. The Ptolemies of Egypt were given titles such as "son of Isis and Osiris", "begotten of the gods", "son of the sun", "god of the god and goddess". The Roman Emperor Augustus and his successors were called *divi filius* (son of god), and temples were built in their honour, first in the East and later in the West.

In the polytheistic climate of the ancient world a man who was hailed as son of god was also treated as a god. If he belonged to the divine family, he was a god. Other men than kings and heroes were acknowledged as divine. For example Apollonius of Tyana was called a son of Zeus. Indeed in the mystery religions the idea was promulgated that all initiates were sons of god. In the Hermetic writings it is said that a man can be born again in the same way as Hermes was born again so that he becomes "god, a son of god". In Stoic philosophy the idea is found that all men are the offspring of deity. Cleanthes says in his hymn to Zeus, "For we are thy offspring".

The title "Son of God" was used in such a way in the near East that it immediately suggested that its bearer was a divine being and often a god. When Christians used it of their saviour it would suggest to many Gentile ears that he was regarded as a god.

Hebrew Thought

The Father-Son motif in Christianity has its origins in Hebrew not in Gentile thought. Although the motif was intelligible to Gentiles, it is to the Old Testament that we must turn for an understanding of its origin in Christianity. The Hebrew use of the title "Father" for God has been discussed in an earlier chapter.[1] The title "Son of God" is also found in Hebrew writings. It is used in a variety of ways in the Old Testament. In Gen. 6.2 and Job. 1.6; 2.1; 38.7 it describes angels, members of the heavenly host. More often, however, it refers to the Hebrew nation. Moses was commanded

[1] See pp. 43–4.

173

to convey to Pharaoh God's message: "Israel is my son, my first-born" (Ex. 4.22). According to Hos. 11.1 God says: "When Israel was a child, then I loved him, and called my son out of Egypt." In other passages the people are described in the plural as "sons". The English translation is usually "children" but the Hebrew literally means "sons". So in Isa. 1.2 God says: "I have nourished and brought up sons, and they have rebelled against me." And in Jub. 1.24 God says, "And I will be to them a father and they shall be my sons."

The plural use "sons" implies that each individual is a son of God, and not only the nation collectively. According to some writers it is a condition which is given to the righteous. Thus in Ps. Sol. 13.8: "He will admonish the righteous as a son of his love, and will educate him as a firstborn." The Son of Sirach writes:

Be as a father unto the fatherless,
And instead of a husband unto their mother:
So shalt thou be as a son of the Most High,
And he shall love thee more than thy mother doth (Ecclus. 4.10).

The title "Son of God" was also used of the king. God says of David: "I will be his father, and he shall be my son" (2 Sam. 7.14). As in Babylonian religion, the king was thought to become God's son when he ascended the throne. This idea is found in Ps. 89.26–7:

He shall cry unto me, Thou art my father,
My God and the rock of my salvation.
I also will make him my firstborn,
The highest of the kings of the earth.[1]

It is uncertain whether the title "Son of God" was used of the Messiah before the time of Jesus. In a few rabbinic sayings after the time of Christ the Messiah is said to be "Son of God", but there is no sure evidence of the identification before the time of Christ.[2] The description of the Messiah as παῖς in 4 Ezra probably refers to the Servant rather than the Son of God.[3]

[1] Cf. Ps. 2.7: "Thou art my son; this day have I begotten thee."
[2] Strack-Billerbeck, *Kommentar zum NT*, III, pp. 15–22; Dalman, *Words of Jesus*, pp. 268–89.
[3] Cf. 4 Ezra 7.28; 13.32, 37, 52; 14.9. *Filius meus* in the Latin translation probably renders the Greek παῖς. Cf. Mowinckel, *He that Cometh*, p. 294.

1 Enoch 105.2, in which God speaks of "I and my Son", is probably a later interpolation. Strack-Billerbeck, however, point out that the title "Son of God" is given to the Messiah in rabbinic literature when passages like Ps. 2.7 are cited. According to the evangelists (Mark 14.62 and parallels) the High Priest identified the Christ with the "Son of the Blessed".[1] There is therefore some evidence that the Christ and the Son of God were identified before the New Testament was written.

The use of the title "Son of God" in the Old Testament does not imply divinity. Sometimes when it refers to angels it implies a supernatural status, but when it refers to the nation or the king or the individual it means that they are chosen of God and have a close connection with him. The title itself when used of Jesus did not raise the problem of the unity of God. It was, however, a title which could be used to attempt to answer that problem. In the New Testament it was claimed by Jesus for himself and applied by others to him. It is used in such a way as to explain the relationship between Jesus and his Father.

The Sayings of Jesus

In his own sayings Jesus claims to be different from other men. He describes himself as the Son of Man who will come in the clouds to judge. He claims to exercise the divine prerogative of forgiveness, and, with some reluctance, he admits that he is the Christ. But it is through the title "Son of God" that he expresses most clearly his relationship to God. There are four passages in which he admits his Sonship.

1. Of that day or that hour knoweth no one, not even the angels in heaven, neither the Son, but the Father (Mark 13.32).

Dalman and Bultmann think that in its original form this was a Jewish saying,[2] and that "neither the Son, but the Father" is a

[1] Cullmann, *Christologie*, p. 280, thinks that the connection could have already been made because of the close link between the thought of the King and the expectation of the Messiah. Cf. Dodd, *Interpretation of the Fourth Gospel*, p. 253.

[2] Dalman, op. cit., p. 194; Bultmann, *Geschichte der synoptischen Tradition*, p. 130.

Christian addition. But Schmiedel is right in arguing that this is one of the "foundation pillars"[1] on which the genuine teaching of Jesus can be based. The evangelist would not have recorded a saying in which Jesus' knowledge was limited, unless he had believed that saying to be genuine.

> 2. He had yet one, a beloved son: he sent him last unto them, saying, They will reverence my son. But those husbandmen said among themselves, This is the heir; come, let us kill him, and the inheritance shall be ours (Mark 12.6, 7).

These words come from the parable of the Labourers in the Vineyard, and refer to the death of Jesus. Bultmann says that it is not a genuine parable of Jesus because of its allegorical form, and because of its contents.[2] There is no reason, however, why Jesus should not have couched his teaching in allegorical form, and the nature of the contents suggests that the parable was taught before his death, because the manner of the son's death is not described. Moreover, it is consistent with Jesus' reticence about his Sonship that he should have referred to it by the allusive method of allegory.

> 3. Again the high priest asked him, and saith unto him, Art thou the Christ, the Son of the Blessed? And Jesus said, I am: and ye shall see the Son of man sitting at the right hand of power, and coming with the clouds of heaven (Mark 14.61,2).

In Matthew Jesus' reply is worded differently:

> Thou hast said: nevertheless I say unto you, Henceforth ye shall see the Son of man sitting at the right hand of power, and coming on the clouds of heaven (Matt. 26.64).

In Luke both question and answer are different from Mark's and Matthew's versions:

> If thou art the Christ, tell us. But he said unto them, If I tell you, ye will not believe: and if I ask you, ye will not answer. But from henceforth shall the Son of man be seated at the right hand of the power of God. And they all said, Art thou then the Son of God? And he said unto them, Ye say that I am (Luke 22.67–70).

[1] *Encyclopaedia Biblica*, p. 1881.   [2] Op. cit., p. 191.

Although the Greek idiom εἶπας, "Thou hast said" (Matt. 26.64), was an equivalent of "Yes", there is no evidence that the Aramaic equivalent had the same implication. The phrasing of Matt. 26.64 suggests that Jesus means that he is Son of Man rather than Son of God. He does not deny his divine Sonship outright but immediately shifts the emphasis to another title. His reluctance to answer outright may have been caused by the question about his Messiahship and not by that about his Sonship. But in Luke's account the two questions are separated. In both his answers Jesus refuses to be direct, but in the answer to the question about Sonship he does not shift the emphasis to another title.[1]

Because it is difficult to see why Matthew or Luke should have wanted to alter the Markan version, it is probable that the original version of Jesus' reply is found in Matthew or Luke and he said "Thou hast said". This does not constitute a denial of Sonship but a refusal to affirm it before the High Priest. Jesus did not refuse to affirm his Sonship before others. It was the eagerness of his judges to trap him which led him to give a non-committal answer.

> 4. All things have been delivered unto me of my Father: and no one knoweth who the Son is, save the Father; and who the Father is, save the Son, and he to whomsoever the Son willeth to reveal him (Luke 10.22 = Matt. 11.27).

The authenticity of the saying has been questioned. Its resemblance to the style of the Fourth Gospel has been noticed, but this does not disprove its originality, for some of the Johannine sayings may well have had a basis in fact. Bousset points out that there is a parallel in Hermetic writings, which suggests that the saying has been influenced by external ideas.[2] The Hermetic saying is: "I know thee, Hermes, and thou (knowest) me. I am thou, and thou art I."[3] Since the gospel saying contains no mention of an identification between Father and Son, and since the only verbal parallel with the Hermetic saying is the word "know", the comparison gives little support to a theory of dependence on Hermetic ideas.

Even if the clause "no one knoweth who the Son is, save the

[1] Cullmann, op. cit., pp. 119–21.   [2] Bousset, *Kyrios Christos*, p. 48 f.
[3] Papyrus, Lond. cxxii.50.

Father", which is omitted by some of the Fathers, is an interpolation,[1] the rest of the saying speaks of Jesus as one who has a unique and intimate knowledge of the Father.

The title "Son of God" occurs on other occasions in the synoptic gospels but not on the lips of Jesus himself. He is hailed as Son of God by demoniacs (Mark 3.11; 5.7). In the temptation Satan asks him to prove by miracles that he is the Son of God (Matt. 4, 3, 6= Luke 4.3, 9). At the baptism of Jesus a voice from heaven is heard saying: "Thou are my beloved son" (Mark 1.11). And at the transfiguration the voice says: "This is my beloved son" (Mark 9.7). In Matthew's version of Peter's confession at Caesarea Philippi, Peter says: "Thou art the Christ, the Son of the living God" (Matt. 16.16). Matthew also records the words of those who mocked Jesus when he was on the cross: "If thou art the Son of God, come down from the cross"; and the cry: "He trusteth on God; let him deliver him now, if he desireth him: for he said, I am the Son of God" (Matt. 27.40, 43). At the crucifixion the centurion says: "Truly this man was a son of God" (Mark 15.39) but from his pagan point of view "son of God" may have meant no more than "a divine being" like the demi-gods or heroes.[2]

Although the sayings of Jesus about his Sonship are few, some of them have a sure place in the tradition. His words about Sonship do not imply equality with the Father. There were things which the Son did not know (Mark 13.32). But as Son he had a unique relationship with the Father (Matt. 11.27= Luke 10.22). And at important moments in his life, baptism and transfiguration, he was specially conscious of his Sonship.

The uniqueness of his Sonship is demonstrated by the way in which he talks of others as "sons of God". The peacemakers will be called sons of God (Matt. 5.9), and those who love their enemies and pray for their persecutors will be sons of their Father (Matt. 5.44–5; cf. Luke 6.35). Jesus teaches that men can become God's sons, but Jesus himself is already God's Son.

[1] Such is the view of T. W. Manson, *Sayings of Jesus*, p. 80.

[2] According to Luke 23.47, the centurion said: "Certainly this was a righteous man."

The Sonship of Jesus has been thought by some scholars to have been regarded at first as an adopted Sonship. There is no evidence for or against this in the sayings of Jesus. The case for adoptionism is based on events in the life of Jesus such as his baptism and birth and resurrection, and will be discussed in the next section.

Some of Jesus' sayings suggest his subordination to the Father. In answer to the man who addressed him as "Good Master", he said, "Why callest thou me good? None is good save one, even God" (Mark 10.18). When this is considered together with the statement which limits Jesus' knowledge (Mark 13.32), and the statement which he made in Garden of Gethsemane, in which he binds himself to his Father's will ("Not what I will, but what thou wilt", Mark 14.36), it is clear that in his earthly ministry he spoke and behaved as one who was subordinate to the Father. Although he claimed a unique relationship to the Father, he had a duty of obedience, and shared human limitations of knowledge.

His sayings about his resurrection and the coming of the Son of Man do not show whether he believed he would retain any status of subordination in the future. As Son of Man he would perform the divine function of judgement and be seated at the right hand of power (Mark 14.62). If any form of subordination is suggested by the phrase "right hand of power", it is of the slightest nature.

The Early Church

There are few references to Jesus as Son of God in the Acts of the Apostles.

1. The Western text reads: I believe that Jesus Christ is the Son of God (8.37).

These are the words of the Ethiopian eunuch who was baptized by Philip.

2. And straightway in the synagogues he proclaimed Jesus, that he is the Son of God (9.20).

This is a description of Paul's preaching immediately after his conversion.

3. Thou art my Son, this day have I begotten thee (13.33).

This quotation from Ps. 2.7 occurs in Paul's speech at Antioch in Pisidia.

The language of Acts suggests that "Jesus Christ is the Son of God" was an early form of Christian creed. Cullmann argues that "the divine Sonship of Jesus Christ and His elevation to the dignity of *Kyrios*, as consequence of His death and resurrection, are the two essential elements in the majority of the confessions of the first century."[1] Cullmann supports his view by referring to Acts 8.37, quoted above, and also to the following:

> Having then a great High Priest, who hath passed through the heavens, Jesus the Son of God, let us hold fast our confession (Heb. 4.14).
>
> Whosoever shall confess that Jesus is the Son of God, God abideth in him, and he in God (1 John 4.15).
>
> ... concerning his Son, who was born of the seed of David according to the flesh (Rom. 1.3).

Cullmann admits that affirmation of the divine Sonship is lacking in some of the Christian confessions (e.g. 1 Cor. 15.3 ff; 1 Pet. 3.18 ff; 1 Tim. 3.16; 2 Tim. 4.1). Moreover, three of the confessions of Sonship come from those writings which lay great stress on Sonship, Paul, John, and Hebrews. The only confession which does not come from them is Acts 8.37 which is found only in the Western Text.[2]

We should therefore speak with caution about the popularity of this title in the early Church, for it seems to have been used chiefly by those writers who made a sustained attempt to think out the relationship between Christ and God.

This does not mean that the confession did not exist. In his

---

[1] Cullmann, *Earliest Christian Confessions*, p. 57.

[2] Cullmann believes that his argument is supported by 2 Tim. 2.8 and Phil. 2.6 ff. These passages, however, can be discounted because they do not contain the title "Son of God". They are evidence for the writers' awareness of Jesus' divine Sonship. In Phil. 2.6 ff Jesus is said to have been "in the form of God", and in 2 Tim. 2.8 he is said to be "of the seed of David". But if they were referring to credal formulae of Sonship, surely the title "Son of God" would be included.

Christologie, arguing from the occurrence of the confession at the baptism of the eunuch by Philip (Acts 8.36–8), Cullmann claims that the confession of Jesus as Son of God was used at baptism. He points out that Jesus' own consciousness of Sonship can be traced to his baptism in Jordan.[1]

The title is absent from many of the shorter New Testament writings. It does not occur at all in the Pastoral Epistles, James, 1 Peter, or Jude. It is used twice in Revelation, once of Jesus (Rev. 2.18) and once of the faithful believer (Rev. 21.7). 2 Pet. 1.17 records the words of God at the transfiguration: "This is my beloved Son." The title seems to have won wider acceptance when it was used as a tool for thought, as a means of expressing the answer to a problem, the problem of Christ's relationship to God.

It has been argued that the first Christians believed that Christ was adopted as Son of God at some particular point in time. Johannes Weiss contends that this kind of Christology is found in Peter's speech in Acts 2.36, where God is said to have made Jesus "both Lord and Christ" at the resurrection.[2] Although this is strictly an exaltation to Lordship and Messiahship rather than Sonship, it does mean that Jesus entered into a new status after his resurrection. Moreover, in his speech in Acts 13.32–3 Paul claims that the resurrection of Jesus fulfils the words of Ps. 2.7: "Thou art my son; this day have I begotten thee."

Weiss also stresses the early Church's belief in the humanity of of Christ. Peter described Jesus as "a man approved of God unto you by mighty works and wonders and signs" (Acts 2.22). The power which Jesus exercised was God's. The importance of his work lay not in the status which God had granted him but in the fact that God was with him. This attitude to Jesus is seen not only in the Acts of the Apostles but also in the synoptic gospels. After describing the healing of a man who was sick of the palsy Matthew comments (Matt. 9.8): "But when the multitudes saw it, they were afraid, and glorified God, which had given such power unto men." The power was God's and the healer was a man.

Four incidents in the synoptic gospels militate against Weiss's

[1] *Christologie*, p. 297.
[2] J. Weiss, *History of Primitive Christianity*, I, pp. 118 ff. Cf. II, p. 476.

thesis. The first is Peter's own confession that Jesus is the Christ (Mark 8.29). This confession was made long before the resurrection, and conflicts with the view that Jesus was made Christ at his resurrection. The second incident is the transfiguration, when Jesus was revealed in supernatural glory to his disciples, and the heavenly voice pronounced the words "This is my beloved Son" (Mark 9.7). These words imply either that Jesus was already the Son of God, or that he became Son of God at the transfiguration. A third passage is the story of Jesus' trial before the High Priest, in which, according to Mark, he admits he is the "Son of the Blessed" (Mark 14.61–2). And the fourth and most famous stumbling-block to Weiss's interpretation is the story of the baptism of Jesus, in which the heavenly voice says: "Thou art my beloved Son" (Mark 1.11). All these passages suggest that Jesus was either Christ or Son of God before his resurrection.

Weiss attempts to answer this difficulty. The first three passages are described as declarations about the future of Jesus, and not descriptions of his present status.

> Even the confession of Peter implied in the older tradition only an ardent faith in Jesus's glorious future: at the Transfiguration the veil was lifted for a moment and the disciples had a glimpse of what was to be; and although in the presence of the high priest Jesus acknowledged himself to be the Son of God, it was only in the sense that hereafter or henceforth—from now on, in the immediate future—he would occupy the appropriate position. The sequence of ideas is perfectly consistent; Jesus, a man, chosen by God, equipped with higher powers and revelations and destined for Messiahship, but only after his death exalted to be the Son of God and installed in his royal office as Messiah.[1]

The fourth passage, which is from the baptismal story, is explained differently. Weiss believes that there was a development in Christology. It was felt necessary to relate the baptism to Jesus' divine Sonship. The kerygma of Acts speaks of the anointing of Jesus with the Holy Spirit—a clear reference to his baptism (Acts 10.38; 4.27). The synoptic gospels record that the divine voice called him "my Son", and the Western text of Luke goes even further and ascribes to God the words of Ps. 2.7, "This day have

[1] Op. cit., I, p. 122.

I begotten thee." The evidence suggests that Christians had changed their minds about the time of adoption. At first they had believed that it coincided with Jesus' elevation to the right hand of God. Later they dated it back to his baptism.

Weiss endeavours to reconcile the two opinions. He makes a distinction between the anointing and the coronation of Jesus. At his baptism he was anointed. After his resurrection he was crowned. This time-lag between anointing and coronation had a precedent in the histories of Saul and David who were anointed some time before their actual succession to the throne. (1 Sam. 10.1 f, 16.13).[1]

Weiss's arguments must now be met point by point. First, the dating of the adoption to the exaltation is based on only two passages in Acts. In Acts 2.36 Peter says that Jesus was made Lord and Christ after his exaltation. Nothing is said about his Sonship in Acts 2, but the quotation of Ps. 2.7 in Acts 13.33 implies that Jesus was made Son of God at his resurrection, and although it speaks of a begetting, this may be a vivid way of describing an adoption. Weiss has shown that the Christology of Acts implies a change of status after the resurrection. He has not shown, however, that it is a prominent doctrine in the primitive Church. Out of all the speeches in Acts there are only two brief passages which provide evidence of adoptionism.

Secondly, Weiss's explanation of the incidents in the synoptic gospels is open to question. At the transfiguration the divine voice said: "This is my beloved Son." Weiss suggests that the words were prophetic of a future glory. But they could equally well refer to an adoption which took place at that moment or a relationship which was already in existence.

The same is true of the words of God at the baptism of Jesus. With the exception of the Western reading of Luke 3.22 there is no clear statement that Jesus began to be Son of God at his baptism. The priority of the Western reading has not been established. Streeter argues that it has disappeared from many versions of Luke because of assimilation to the other gospels.[2] It is equally likely,

---

[1] Ibid., p. 122.

[2] B. H. Streeter, *The Four Gospels*, pp. 143, 188, 276; cf. Harnack, *History of Dogma*, I, p. 191. Lagrange, *Critique Textuelle*, p. 171, suggests that Justin,

however, that the Western reading was inserted into the text later, in an area where adoptionism was prevalent. If the version in Mark is original, the idea that adoption took place at Jesus' baptism is not ruled out but is not clearly present.

Thirdly, the passages in Acts which speak of the anointing of Christ (Acts 4.27; 10.38) do not by themselves support adoptionism. According to these passages Jesus became "Messiah" when he was anointed with the Spirit. It is quite possible that he was already Son of God before he undertook the office of Messiah.

There are only three passages in Acts and the synoptic gospels which provide clear evidence for adoptionism (Luke 3.22, Western Text; Acts 2.36; 13.33), and one of these (Luke 3.22) is a disputed reading. Other passages in Mark could be interpreted as adoptionist, but could equally well be interpreted in other ways. We cannot conclude from this array of evidence that adoptionism was the earliest form of Christology, or that the authors of these passages understood their Christological implications. The authors of the synoptic gospels and Acts believed that the baptism and resurrection of Jesus were the fulfilment of certain sayings of the Old Testament, but they did not try to work out a detailed account of the origin of Christ's Sonship.

Another argument, which has been used in favour of the view that adoptionism was the earliest form of Christology, is concerned with the order of the earliest gospel. Mark begins his story with the baptism of Jesus, and says nothing about his birth, infancy, and youth. It may be contended that Mark implies that Jesus became God's Son when he was baptized. In the preface to the Gospel, however, the title "Son of God" is used absolutely, as though it had always applied to Jesus.

It would be even more rash to argue that Luke and Matthew were pushing adoptionism a stage further back, when they intro-

---

who gives the Western variant in his *Dialogue with Trypho* lxxxviii.8, may have been responsible for the quotation from Ps. 2.7. C. S. C. Williams, *Alterations to the Text of the Synoptic Gospels and Acts*, p. 47, points out that the variant is not supported by several important Western authorities, including the Syriac versions, one of the Old African manuscripts, and Irenaeus and Cyprian.

duced the story of the Virgin Birth of Jesus (Matt. 1.20; Luke 1.35). The infancy narratives teach that Jesus was Son of God not by adoption but by birth. A child who was born of a woman through the overshadowing of the Spirit was not an adopted child. If he had been adopted by God, he would have had a natural father as well as his father by adoption. But although the Christology of the infancy narratives excludes a literal adoptionism, it does not imply the pre-existence of Christ, but would be consistent with the view that Christ first came into existence when he was born of Mary.

The Christology of the early Church was not fully worked out. The verses which have been discussed could have led to a belief in adoptionism. They could equally well have led, as they did, to the traditional Christology. They were not intended as a detailed statement of doctrine, nor were they formulated in order to defend the Church against heresies. They do not show that the early Church had a particular kind of Christology, but rather that it was feeling its way to a more clearly formulated account of the person of Christ.

The Pauline Epistles

By stressing both the humanity and divinity of Christ Paul raises the problem of Christ's relationship to the Father. According to Paul, the earthly Jesus was inferior to the Father. He was sent into the world by God who "spared not his own Son, but freely gave him up for us all" (Rom. 8.32). When he came to earth he "emptied himself, taking the form of a servant" (Phil. 2.7). This inferiority applies not only to the earthly Christ. The exalted Christ is Lord, but the Father is God. Paul often speaks of "the God and Father of our Lord Jesus Christ" and "God the Father and the Lord Jesus Christ".[1] There is "one God" and "one Lord".[2] Statements like this suggest that, however exalted Jesus may be, he is not God.

[1] Rom. 1.7; 1 Cor. 1.3; 2 Cor. 1.2; Gal. 1.3; Phil. 1.2; Col. 1.3; 1 Thess. 1.1; 2 Thess. 1.2; Philem. 3; Eph. 1.2.
[2] 1 Cor. 8.6; Eph. 4.6.

On the other hand Paul speaks of Christ as "God over all" (Rom. 9.5), and describes him as judge and creator.[1] He is the image of the invisible God (Col. 1.15), and men call upon him as Lord as they call upon God as Lord (1 Cor. 12.3). These contrasting views of Christ present a problem to us. But did they present a problem to Paul? It is often supposed that the New Testament writers were unaware of the existence of problems posed by their own writings. Speaking of Paul's attitude to the questions, "Could monotheism be preserved?" and "Could justice be done to the humanity of Christ?", R. S. Franks says: "Paul himself saw no problems. The charismatic character of his theology prevented them arising in his mind."[2] But can Paul really have been ignorant of the difficulty raised by his attitude to Christ? Even though he may not have clearly formulated the problem, he would perceive its existence. Indeed some of his statements make a contribution to its solution.

There is little evidence that Paul accepted an adoptionist Christology. One interpretation of Rom. 1.3 ff would lead to an adoptionist position. This passage describes Christ as "*declared* to be the Son of God with power, according to the spirit of holiness, by the resurrection of the dead". The first word may be translated "declared", "appointed", or "separated". If it means "appointed", an adoptionist interpretation could be given to the passage. The third translation, "separated", however, is the most likely, since in Rom. 1.1 Paul uses ἀφορίζειν to mean "separate", and ὁρισθέντος, occurring in close proximity, probably has the same meaning. Paul is saying that by the resurrection Christ was separated from the rest of men in order to be "Son of God with power". Before the resurrection, it is implied, he had become "Son of God in humiliation". This passage describes a change from humiliation to power but not an adoption into Sonship.

Paul often writes as if Christ had a subordinate position to the Father. It was natural for him to describe the earthly Christ as subordinate, for the earthly Christ was "Son of God in humiliation" and had "emptied himself". As a man he prayed to God, and

---

[1] Col. 1.16; 1 Thess. 5.2 ff; 2 Thess. 2.1–12.
[2] R. S. Franks, *The Doctrine of the Trinity*, p. 37.

was obedient to God. Paul does not confine this subordinate status, however, to the earthly Jesus but extends it to the risen Lord. The resurrection itself was the act not of Christ but of the Father. "God raised him from the dead."[1] Again, when Paul writes of "the God and Father of our Lord Jesus Christ" he is not thinking merely of the earthly Jesus. The Father is *God* and the risen Christ is the *Lord*. The most striking passage which shows the eternal subordination of Jesus to the Father is 1 Cor. 15.24–8:

> Then cometh the end, when he (Christ) shall deliver up the Kingdom to God, even the Father; when he shall have abolished all rule and all authority and power. For he must reign, till he hath put all his enemies under his feet. The last enemy that shall be abolished is death. For, He put all things in subjection under his feet. But when he saith, All things are put in subjection, it is evident that he is excepted who did subject all things unto him. And when all things have been subjected unto him, then shall the Son also himself be subjected to him that did subject all things unto him, that God may be all in all.

These words describe a Lordship of temporary duration. When all the enemies of God have been overthrown, the Lord Christ will hand over his kingdom to the Father. Here Paul seems to be teaching a subordinationism which is not limited to the earthly life of Christ but which is ultimate and absolute. The final status of the Son is one of subjection to God. And in this passage God is not Father, Son, and Holy Spirit, but Father only.

In his later epistles Paul does not include any statements which make the subordination so explicit. But the idea of Christ's subordination to the Father continues to be present. In Colossians, although Christ is described as creator and all the fullness of God is said to dwell in him (1.16, 19; 2.9), Christ is distinguished from God. The Colossians are told: "Your life is hid with Christ in God" (3.3). And God is described as "the Father of our Lord Jesus Christ" (1.3).

The most sustained effort in Paul's writings to explain the relationship of Christ to the Father is Phil. 2.5–11. This passage states that Christ was in the form of God and counted it not a prize

---

[1] Rom. 4.24; 8.11; 10.9; 1 Cor. 6.14; 15.15; 2 Cor. 4.14; Gal. 1.1; Col. 2.12; 1 Thess. 1.10; Eph. 1.20.

to be on equality with God. Christ is not actually called God but is said to be of divine rank and nature. He is set alongside God in the order of things. A voluntary humiliation ("he emptied himself") is necessary before he assumes the form of man. This emphasis on Christ's own agency in his incarnation shows that Christ is no puppet in the hands of the Father. The incarnation was Christ's own act as well as the Father's. When he had emptied himself he was clearly subordinate to the Father. He was "obedient even unto death" (2.8). The action of the Father was needed to raise him from this humiliation. God "highly exalted him" (2.9). In his position of exaltation he received "the name which is above every name" (2.10). From the context it is shown that this name is "Lord". For the name is given to him "that in the name of Jesus every knee should bow . . . and that every tongue should confess that Jesus Christ is Lord, to the glory of God the Father" (2.10, 11).

The title "Lord" carries with it implications of divinity, but Christ is not called God. The Father is God, and the last word is for him. Everything is intended for his glory. Honour given to Christ is ultimately honour given to God the Father.

This passage contains Paul's nearest approach to a solution of the problem of Christ's relationship to the Father. The subordinationism is less marked than in 1 Corinthians. It is clearly mentioned only in the account of the humiliation. It is not explicitly said that either the pre-existent or the exalted Christ was subject to the Father. The emphasis is on the divinity of Christ rather than his subordination. Before his incarnation he was in the form of God, on an equality with God. After his exaltation he was given the name Lord and received that obeisance from all creatures which according to Isa. 45.23 was to be given to God. Yet he is not actually called God.[1]

In Rom. 9.5 Paul called Jesus God spontaneously. It is not characteristic of his reflective writing that he should give this title

---

[1] It has been argued in another chapter (p. 87) that Paul may have written this hymn in Philippians himself. In any case he must have accepted its teaching, and it represents his view of the relationship between Father and Son.

to Jesus. The reason for his reticence is the difficulty of providing an adequate explanation of Christ's relationship to the Father. This reticence is preserved even in Phil. 2.5 ff. Paul states that Christ belongs to the same order of being as God the Father, but he implies that in the end God the Father is supreme. Within the order of Godhead the Father has a priority over the Son.

The Epistle to the Hebrews

The author of this epistle was conscious that Christ was God, but often he speaks as though Christ were subordinate to God. On the one hand he says of Christ: "Thy throne, O God, is for ever and ever" (1.8) and describes him as creator, the effulgence of God's glory and the one who "upholds all things by the word of his power" (1.2, 3). On the other hand Jesus is the High Priest who makes intercession for men to God (chs. 3—10 *passim*).

There are two main categories through which the writer explains the relationship of Christ to the Father. They are the Father-Son category and the God-Priest category.

The title "Father" is used only twice of God in the epistle. It occurs in 12.9 and 1.5, the latter being a quotation from 2 Sam. 7.14. But "Son" is used eleven times of Christ (1.2,5 (twice), 8; 3.6; 4.14; 5.5,8; 6.6; 7.28; 10.29). Also in 7.3 it is said that Melchizedek was "made like unto the Son of God". And in 12.7,8 believers are likened to sons of God: "God dealeth with you as with sons." A list of references, however, does not do justice to the importance of the Father-Son concept for Hebrews. The main theme of the section 1.1—3.6 is Jesus' superiority to the angels and Moses because he is the Son of God. As Son he is the climax of God's revelation. God had formerly spoken in the prophets. He has "at the end of these days spoken unto us in his Son" (1.1,2). This Son is an agent in creation, the one "through whom also he made the worlds". He is "heir of all things". He possesses the attributes which were ascribed in Judaism to Wisdom, for he is "the effulgence of his glory, and the very impress of his substance". After his purification of sins, he sat down at the right hand of God. As Son of God he is addressed as God: "Thy throne, O God, is for ever and ever" (1.8). He has laid the foundation of the

earth (1.10), and is himself eternal (1.12). He was made a little
lower than the angels (2.7) but is now exalted so that all things are
put in subjection under his feet. By his death and suffering he acts
as author of men's salvation and brings "many sons to glory"
(2.10). Whereas Moses was a servant in God's house Jesus is a son
who is over the house (3.5,6).

These opening chapters of the epistle show Jesus as the eternal
Son of God, the creator, saviour, and Lord. They depict him as
one who can be addressed not only as Son of God but also as God.

Yet this Son of God had become man, and was subject to human
infirmities. "Though he was a Son, he learned obedience by the
things which he suffered" (5.8). He was crucified and trodden
under foot by men. He was tempted, though he was "without
sin" (4.15), and he can succour those who are tempted (2.18). As a
man he prayed and cried to God. He offered up "prayers and
supplications with strong crying and tears unto him that was able
to save him from death" (5.7).

Here then, as in Paul, there is a contrast between the eternal Son
of God and the humiliated, tempted, suffering, dying son of God.
The idea of Son explains this contrast between power and humiliation. As the Son he stands on the godward side of reality. He is
Lord and Creator, the effulgence of God's glory. As a Son also he
is different from the Father and learns obedience to him.

There are two passages in the Epistle to the Hebrews which
could be given an adoptionist interpretation. The first is Heb. 1.5
in which there is a quotation of Ps. 2.7:

> Thou art my Son,
> This day have I begotten thee.

The author is chiefly interested in the first part of the verse,
"Thou art my Son". He is providing evidence for the Sonship of
Jesus and is not concerned with proving the time at which that
Sonship was obtained. Although the verse could be used to support
adoptionism, the author of Hebrews uses it for a different purpose.

The second of these passages is Heb. 1.5 which is based on 2
Sam. 7.14:

> I will be to him a Father,
> And he shall be to me a Son.

Here again the emphasis is on the Sonship of Christ and not on the fact that the Sonship is to begin at a particular time.

Adoptionism is quite out of harmony with the teaching of this epistle. The very chapter in which these quotations are made describes Jesus as the eternal Son of God, who laid the foundations of the earth and whose throne is for ever and ever.

From chapter three onwards the category of High Priest is used together with that of Son. As High Priest Jesus shared the temptations and infirmities of men. He was a priest of different status from the Levitical priests, for he was a priest after the order of Melchizedek. Yet he had priority over Melchizedek, for Melchizedek's nature was modelled upon that of the Son of God. Melchizedek is described as "having neither beginning of days nor end of life, but made like unto the Son of God" (Heb. 7.3).

Christ, the High Priest, was eternal and after his exaltation was made perfect (2.10; 5.9; 7.28). He appears before God in the heavenly sanctuary and makes intercession for men (7.25; 9.24). Now in so far as he is an intercessor he is subordinate to the Father. It is consistent with this outlook, that although Jesus is expected to come again as saviour (9.28), it is God and not Jesus who is Judge. Jesus' position is that of mediator. The writer says:

> Ye are come . . . to God the Judge of all, and to the spirits of just men made perfect, and to Jesus the mediator of a new covenant (12.23,24).

The Epistle to the Hebrews, like Paul, sets Christ within the divine eternal order of being but assumes that Christ is secondary or subordinate to the Father. How far the writer was aware that there was a problem we cannot be sure. But his arguments about the Melchizedek priesthood and his emphasis on the exalted status of the Son of God suggest that he was feeling after a solution of that problem which is basic for the doctrine of the Trinity.

The Johannine Writings

The Johannine writings contain a fuller discussion of the relationship between Father and Son than any other part of the New Testament. The paradox of the relationship is expressed in John 1.1: "The Word was with God, and the Word was God." Throughout the Johannine writings, however, the most prominent title of Christ is "Son" and the most prominent title of God is "Father". Vincent Taylor estimates that the title "Father" occurs 121 times in the Fourth Gospel and 16 times in the Johannine Epistles as against 123 times in the rest of the New Testament.[1] Nearly half the instances of the word in the New Testament come from the Johannine writings. The title "Son" occurs 28 times in the Fourth Gospel and 24 times in the Johannine Epistles as against 67 times in the rest of the New Testament.[2] This title has a distinctive place in the Fourth Gospel, and the Father-Son relationship is the dominant category for a description of the relation between Christ and his Father.

John seems to have been more conscious of the problem than other writers were. There is no formal discussion of it. Comments are introduced incidentally. But, especially in the Farewell Discourses, the comments are expanded in such a way that it is clear that the evangelist had given much thought to the question.

On the one hand Jesus is described as the Word which took part in the creation, which was God and was with God. He is judge and saviour, and Thomas addresses him as God. He claims titles such as Resurrection and Life, Good Shepherd, Bread of Life, all of which imply an exalted status. On the other hand there are sayings which imply that he is subordinate to the Father:

The Father is greater than I (John 14.28).

For as the Father hath life in himself, even so gave he to the Son also to have life in himself (John 5.26).

The Son can do nothing of himself, but what he seeth the Father doing (John 5.19).

My teaching is not mine, but his that sent me (John 7.16).

The evangelist often implies that the words of Jesus have an eternal significance, and do not apply solely to his incarnate life. When he describes himself as the vine, and his Father as the husbandman, he is ascribing the initiative to the Father (John 15.1 ff). This section refers not only to the relationship between the incarnate Jesus and his disciples but also to the relationship which

[1] Vincent Taylor, *The Person of Christ*, p. 150. [2] Ibid., p. 147.

the risen Jesus had with them. And the other sayings which have been quoted probably refer to the eternal status of Jesus.

One of John's ways of stating the paradox is to emphasize the unity of Father and Son. When these statements appear in close proximity to statements about the inferiority of Christ to the Father, they show that the evangelist was aware of the problem. An example of the interweaving of these two strands of thought is John 10.29,30:

> My Father, which hath given them unto me, is greater than all; and no one is able to snatch them out of the Father's hand. I and the Father are one.

The first part of this passage shows the supremacy of the Father. The second part shows the unity of Father and Son. Another example of the way the two kinds of thought meet is John 17.22:

> And the glory which thou hast given me I have given unto them; that they may be one, even as we are one.

The glory is given by the Father. But the unity of Father and Son is an acknowledged fact which provides a model for the unity of the Church.

The risen Jesus as well as the earthly Jesus speaks as one who depends on the Father. In John 20.21 Jesus says to his disciples, "As the Father hath sent me, even so send I you." He returned to the disciples with authority, and continues to work as judge. He is in the rank of Godhead. When a man approaches God he approaches Father and Son. The destiny of the believer is to be in the Son and the Father. "If that which ye heard from the beginning abide in you, ye also shall abide in the Son, and in the Father" (1 John 2.24). And both the Father and the Son abide in the believer. "If a man love me, he will keep my word: and my Father will love him, and we will come unto him, and make our abode with him" (John 14.23).

A pattern is emerging in the Johannine thought. The eternal Word shared the glory of God before the world existed (17.5). He took part in the creation of the world and was incarnate as Jesus Christ. When he rose from the dead he received the glory which was with him before the creation of the world (17.5). He abides with those who believe in him, and he will do for ever. He is judge.

He is saviour. He is the bread of life, the good shepherd. He is even called God both at the beginning and the end of the Gospel. On the other hand he has been sent by the Father. He was sent by the Father even after the resurrection. The Father gives him authority to save and to judge. He is begotten of the Father and is in the bosom of the Father.

The evangelist was aware of the problem of Christ's relationship to the Father, and the nature of his statements shows that he was attempting a solution. The close attention that is given to the relationship between Father and Son, the emphasis on the Son's dependence combined with the emphasis on his authority, and the explicit and deliberate statements that he is God are proof enough that the writer was not only aware of the problem but was answering it.

The above discussion has shown that the New Testament never deliberately explained Christ in terms of adoptionism. We should agree with Rawlinson who says that if the Gentile Christians had been left to themselves, it is possible that the divinity of Christ might have been explained in an adoptionist sense. But, says Rawlinson, "The Gentile Christians were not left to themselves."[1] Their faith was expounded by Paul and John and the writer of the Epistle to the Hebrews.

The other New Testament writers did not work out the implications of their statements about Christ. They were not adoptionists.

The view which was adopted by Paul, John, and Hebrews is not even subordinationism. None of these writers implies that. As the Son of God he obeys his Father, he is sent to earth by his Father and raised from the dead by his Father. Even in his exaltation he is secondary to the Father because he is a Son. It is misleading to call this subordinationism, for Christ is set in the order of Godhead. Some of the leading theologians of the Christian Church have admitted that within the order of Godhead Christ is secondary to the Father. Thus Augustine claims that the Father has a meta-physical priority,[2] and Calvin claims that the Father has a primacy

---

[1] A. E. J. Rawlinson, *New Testament Doctrine of the Christ*, p. 269.

[2] *De Trinitate*, XV.47. Cf. L. Hodgson, *The Doctrine of the Trinity*, pp. 142–75.

of order.[1] Paul, John, and the writer of Hebrews have not worked out the problem in detail or with subtle refinement, but they are in essential agreement with later thought when they admit that the Father has priority but both Father and Son are God.

[1] *Institutes*, I, xiii.18–26. Cf. Hodgson, op. cit., pp. 171–3.

PART III

The Divinity of the Spirit

CHAPTER 11

THE NATURE OF THE SPIRIT AND HIS RELATION TO CHRIST

The doctrine of the Holy Spirit has long been a Cinderella of theology. It has suffered from much neglect, and has always been one of the most difficult doctrines to discuss. In the New Testament, although there are many statements about the Spirit's activity, the views of the writers are not easy to summarize or express in systematic form. The Church eventually formulated a definite statement of its views about the Spirit. The Nicene Creed says that the Spirit is worshipped together with the Father and the Son, and the Athanasian Creed repeats the views of many of the Fathers when it says: "So the Father is God: and the Son is God: and the Holy Spirit is God." The doctrine of the Spirit, however, did not occupy the major part of the attention of theologians, and the controversies of theology centred round the Person of Christ. If Christianity had been a binitarian religion, teaching that God consisted of two persons, Father and Son, its doctrinal conflicts would not have been very different from what they were. The Spirit seems to have been included in the doctrine of God almost as an afterthought about which men had no strong feelings, either favourable or hostile.

In spite of the neglect of the doctrine, the theologians of the early Church felt constrained to include the Spirit as a third person of the Godhead. The reason for this was partly their awareness that the Church was a temple of the Spirit, and that the Spirit worked through its institutions. But the chief reason was their faithfulness to the biblical tradition. Although the New Testament does not contain a developed doctrine of the Spirit, its account of the Spirit's nature and activity is such that no subsequent theologian could neglect the Spirit in his account of the nature of God.

In the first part of this chapter the nature of the Spirit in the New Testament will be discussed. Was the Spirit a person or an impersonal force? In the second part of the chapter the evidence of the New Testament for the relation of the Spirit to Christ will be examined. Then in the next chapter the evidence for the belief that the Spirit is God will be considered.

The Person of the Spirit

In our survey of the Old Testament attitude to the Spirit it was concluded that the Spirit was often described in language which suggested that he was a person closely related to God, and was capable of speaking to men, of driving them to action and prophecy, and of feeling emotions. Although in many places he was described in such a way that he could have been regarded as an impersonal power, the underlying assumption was that he was a conscious agent.[1]

This belief was accepted in the New Testament. There is abundant evidence that the Spirit was regarded as a personal being, who was capable of experiences of grief and approval, who could forbid and be lied to, who could guide and inspire.

When Jesus warned his disciples about the tribulation which awaited them, he said: "But whatsoever shall be given you in that hour, that speak ye: for it is not ye that speak, but the Holy Spirit" (Mark 13.11). It was not a mere mindless force which he promised would direct them.

In his discussion of the Spirit in the Acts of the Apostles, E. F. Scott says: "In one or two passages of Acts it (the Spirit) seems to be regarded as a personal agency. Philip is caught away by it, as Elijah had been; it speaks to Peter; Ananias lies to the Spirit. More often it is conceived impersonally as a divine energy which is at the same time a sort of substance."[2]

This is a misleading statement. In the Acts there are sixty-two references to the Spirit. In eighteen of these the Spirit is described in terms which suggest that he is a person, who speaks, forbids, thinks good, appoints, sends, bears witness, snatches, prevents, is

[1] See pp. 30-1.   [2] *The Spirit in the New Testament*, p. 87.

deceived, tempted, and resisted.[1] Most of the other references describe how men are filled with the Spirit and act through or in the Spirit,[2] and although these references do not of themselves imply that the Spirit is a person, they do not contradict the impression given by the other passages.

Paul also speaks of the Spirit as if he were a person. The Spirit is grieved, bears witness, cries, leads, and makes intercession.[3] There are many other references which do not directly imply but are consistent with the belief that the Spirit is personal.

According to the Johannine writings the Spirit bears witness, speaks, teaches, conducts as a guide.[4] He is described as παράκλητος, which may be translated "Comforter" or "Advocate", both of which are personal titles.[5] The evangelist gives the title παράκλητος to Jesus as well as the Spirit,[6] and there is no reason to doubt that both Paracletes were regarded as personal.

Similar language implying that the Spirit is personal is found in other parts of the New Testament. According to the First Epistle of Peter, the Spirit testifies (1.11). According to the First Epistle of Timothy, he speaks (4.1). The author of Hebrews says that the Spirit speaks and bears witness in the writings of the Old Testament (3.7). And several times in the Apocalypse the Spirit is said to speak (2.7,11,17,29; 3.6,13,22; 14.13).

If these examples had been few in number, they could have been dismissed as metaphorical. But since they come from different

---

[1] The Spirit speaks (1.16; 8.29; 10.19; 11.12; 13.2; 28.25), forbids (16.6), thinks good (15.28), appoints (20.28), sends (13.4), bears witness (5.32; 20.23), snatches (8.39), prevents (16.7), is lied to (5.3), tempted (5.9), and resisted (7.51; cf. 6.10).

[2] E.g. men are filled with the Spirit (2.4; 4.8; 9.17; 13.9), act through the Spirit (21.4), and in the Spirit (19.21).

[3] Rom. 8.14,16; 8.26; Gal. 4.6; Eph. 4.30.

[4] John 14.26; 15.26; 16.13; 1 John 5.7.

[5] C. K. Barrett, JTS, N.S., I, p. 14, argues that Paraclete in the Fourth Gospel refers to the Spirit of Christian paraclesis or exhortation. If he is right, the nearest English equivalent to παράκλητος would be "exhorter", which is just as much a personal title as "Comforter" or "Advocate", although it sounds slightly incongruous.

[6] When Jesus calls the Spirit ἄλλος παράκλητος (John 14.16) he is referring to the Spirit, and implies that he himself is παράκλητος. Cf. 1 John 2.1.

authors, and are comparatively numerous, they cannot lightly be pushed aside. A Spirit which makes intercession, can be grieved and register approval, is a personal being. And the Paraclete of the Fourth Gospel, guiding and instructing men, and sharing some of the functions of the Christ, cannot be explained as an impersonal force.

Not every description of the Spirit implies that he is personal. Some passages suggest that he is a dynamic force which is poured upon men, and which fills them and dwells in them. Indeed most of the references to the Spirit would be consistent with this idea. For example the prophecies about baptism with the Spirit do not refer to "*the* Spirit" but to "Spirit".[1] This omission of the definite article and the comparison with water baptism suggest that the Spirit is a fluid-like effluence rather than a person. In the second chapter of the Acts the disciples are said to have been filled with the Holy Spirit. The event is regarded as a fulfilment of Joel's prophecy that God would "pour out of his Spirit upon all flesh". The partitive genitive "of my Spirit"[2] would be more appropriate to an impersonal essence than to a person. Other phrases like "fervent in spirit", "being borne in the Holy Spirit", and the repeated Pauline phase "in the Spirit" are claimed to support the view that the Spirit is a power or effluence rather than a person.[3] In the Fourth Gospel when Jesus says to the disciples "Receive ye Holy Spirit",[4] there is no definite article before the word πνεῦμα (Spirit). At a crucial point in the gospel story it is not made clear what is the Spirit's nature. The phrase "partakers of Holy Spirit", which occurs in the Epistle to the Hebrews, suggests something impersonal.[5]

In the epistles the number of definitely personal references to the Spirit is small compared with the large number of references which

---

[1] Mark 1.8; Matt. 3.11; Luke 3.16.

[2] ἀπὸ τοῦ πνεύματός μου (Acts 2.18).

[3] Cf. Acts 15.29 (Western text); 18.25; Rom. 9.1; 12.11; 14.17; 15.16; 1 Cor. 6.11; 12.3,9,13; 14.16, etc.

[4] λάβετε πνεῦμα ἅγιον (John 20.22).

[5] μετόχους . . . πνεύματος ἁγίου (Heb. 6.4; cf. Heb. 3.14, μέτοχοι τοῦ Χριστοῦ where the definite article is used).

can be otherwise interpreted. And the same is true of the Acts and the synoptic gospels.

Bultmann makes a distinction between the animistic and the dynamic interpretations of the Spirit.[1] According to the animistic interpretation the Spirit is an independent, personal power, which can fall like a demon upon a man, and take possession of him. According to the dynamic interpretation the Spirit is an impersonal power which, like a fluid, fills a man. Bultmann thinks that the word "Spirit" is used in both senses in the Acts and the Pauline Epistles. The animistic sense is characteristic of the Old Testament. The dynamic sense is characteristic of Hellenistic thought.

The strength of Bultmann's argument is undeniable. There is, of course, a background to the dynamic interpretation in Hebrew as well as Hellenistic thought. But Bultmann rightly makes a contrast between the two attitudes to the Spirit.

A comment of a general nature needs to be made about Bultmann's distinction. The dynamic descriptions of the Spirit do not actually imply that the Spirit is impersonal. They would be consistent with the belief that the Spirit is personal. On the other hand the references which imply that the Spirit is a person are in conflict with the belief that the Spirit is impersonal. The only view which can account for all the references and preserve a general consistency is the view that the Spirit is personal.

It would be wrong, of course, to assume that the New Testament is always consistent. The writers were not trained in logic and were not attempting to construct a system of thought. Consistency was not their primary aim. Nevertheless, they did not deliberately court inconsistency. Where paradoxes were unavoidable, they accepted them, but when they could be avoided, they did not invent them. Since there is no inconsistency between the personal descriptions of the Spirit and those which are not necessarily personal, there is no strong case for believing that the New Testament writers embraced at one and the same time two conflicting doctrines of the Spirit.

This assumption that the writers were consistent in their

---

[1] *Theology of the New Testament*, I, pp. 155–7.

attitude to the person of the Spirit is confirmed by an examination of certain passages, in which the Spirit is described both animistically and dynamically. In Acts 2.4 the Spirit is described first dynamically: "And they were all filled with Holy Spirit", and then animistically: "They began to speak with other tongues as the Spirit gave them utterance." The first reference could be either personal or impersonal. The second can only be personal. In this narrative account of Pentecost the author is not trying to bring out a paradox in his conception of the Spirit. There is no good reason for detecting an inconsistency here. The author treated the Spirit as a personal being who, because he was divine, could fill many different men at the same time.

Another passage in which animistic and dynamic descriptions accompany each other is Acts 11.12–16. In Acts 11.16 is a reference to baptism with the Holy Spirit, which could be interpreted in a dynamic sense. But in verse 12 Peter says "And the Spirit bade me go with them", which indicates the personal nature of the Spirit.

In Acts 13.2–9, the two different attitudes appear in close proximity. In verse 9 Saul is said to have been filled with the Holy Spirit, but in verse 2 the Holy Spirit speaks, and in verse 4 "sends out" Barnabas and Saul.

The author was not conscious of any inconsistency when he included in the same passage descriptions of the Spirit in both animistic and dynamic senses. He was able to do this because the dynamic references were consistent with the passages in which the Spirit was said to behave like a person. This is true not only of the Acts of the Apostles but also of the writings of Paul and John and the sayings of Jesus himself. The more the Christians meditated about the Spirit, and the more they experienced his activity in their own lives and in the life of the community, the more they were conscious of his personal nature.

The Spirit and the Christ

The Messiah was not often connected with the Spirit in Old Testament prophecy. Isaiah, however, prophesied the coming of a ruler on whom the sevenfold spirit would rest (11.2), and Deutero-Isaiah said that the Spirit of the Lord would be upon one who was anointed to preach the good tidings to the meek (61.1). But these passages are isolated. The Spirit's activity in the Messiah is a very minor theme in the Old Testament.

A connection is made between the Spirit and the Servant in Isa. 42.1. Yahweh says of the Servant: "I have put my spirit upon him." The Servant, however, is not clearly connected with the Messiah until the New Testament.[1]

Although the relation between the Spirit and the Messiah was not a leading motif in the Old Testament, material was there for further development. A step forward was made by John the Baptist, who, according to the synoptic evangelists, prophesied the coming of one who would baptize with the Holy Spirit.[2] The authenticity of this prophecy has often been questioned. T. W. Manson argues that John the Baptist prophesied the coming of a prophet who would baptize with the fire of judgement.[3] Hence the reference to "baptism with fire" in Matthew and Luke. Because they believed that his prophecy was fulfilled when Christ sent the Spirit to the Church, the early Christians added the words "with Holy Spirit" to the prophecy of "baptism with fire". Mark omitted the word "fire" but retained the reference to the Holy Spirit.

Manson supports his theory by quoting Acts 19.1–6 in which the disciples of John say that they have not heard whether there is a Holy Spirit. If the disciples of John did not know of Spirit-baptism, Manson argues, it cannot have been mentioned in the teaching of their master.

Büchsel, however, claims that a prophecy of a baptism with the Spirit was actually uttered by John.[4] The Baptist, says Büchsel, prophesied a baptism of both judgement and salvation. The Coming One will be a burner of chaff as well as a gatherer of wheat. The burning of chaff corresponds to the baptism with fire. The gathering of wheat corresponds to the baptism with Holy Spirit.

Acts 19 does not present an insuperable obstacle to Büchsel's

---

[1] See pp. 159–60. [2] Mark 1.8; Matt. 3.11; Luke 3.16.
[3] *Sayings of Jesus*, pp. 40–1.
[4] *Der Geist Gottes im Neuen Testament*, pp. 141–4.

interpretation. The disciples of John said that they had not heard whether there was a Holy Spirit. This may mean that they did not know whether John's prophecy about the Spirit had been fulfilled. It does not imply that John made no prophecy about baptism with the Spirit.[1]

Büchsel's account of John's teaching is convincing. The Baptist, like the great prophets, spoke not only of judgement but of restoration.[2] He incorporated into his teaching the well-known prophecy of Joel about the outpouring of the Spirit. When "the Coming One" arrived, there would be a day of reward as well as condemnation.

If Büchsel is right, we can understand the development of early Christian thought. John's teaching enabled the apostles to understand and explain their experience at Pentecost.[3]

When Jesus began his ministry, John had already uttered his prophecies which connected the Spirit with a "Coming One". He did not link the Spirit, however, with the Messiah, but expected that the "Coming One" would be Elijah, whose return had been foretold by Malachi. Jesus corrected this part of John's teaching and claimed that John was the Elijah, while he himself was the Messiah.[4] It is surprising, however, that the recorded sayings of

[1] Acts 19.2 reads: 'Αλλ' οὐδ' εἰ πνεῦμα ἅγιόν ἐστιν ἠκούσαμεν. The Revised Version translates: "Nay, we did not so much as hear whether the Holy Ghost was given." This is probably a faithful paraphrase, but a more literal translation is found in the margin: "Nay, we did not so much as hear whether there is a Holy Ghost."

[2] C. K. Barrett, *The Holy Spirit and the Gospel Tradition*, p. 126, suggests that the earliest form of the saying referred to baptism by wind and fire (πνεύματι καὶ πυρί). In that case the saying would refer only to judgement and not to restoration.

[3] There is evidence that the link between the Spirit and the Messiah was made before the time of John the Baptist. The Damascus Document says: "And he (God) caused them to know by his anointed his Holy Spirit and a revelation of truth" (Damasc. Doc. II, cf. Millar Burrows, *The Dead Sea Scrolls*, p. 350). Although this document belongs to the tenth or eleventh century A.D., it reflects the teaching of the Qumran sect which seems to have flourished in the first century B.C. Possibly the Baptist was influenced by the teaching of the Qumran sect.

[4] Mark 9.13: "But I say unto you, that Elijah is come, and they have also

Jesus about the Spirit are very few in number. Since the prophecies about the Spirit were in the air at the beginning of Jesus' ministry, he might have been expected to have spoken at greater length about the matter. If he had done so, the evangelists would have seized the opportunity to perpetuate his teaching. Their comparative silence suggests that Jesus had very little to say about the Spirit. A number of scholars go further and argue that the synoptic references to the Spirit are not genuine utterances of Jesus, but were introduced into the gospel tradition in order to support the Church's doctrine. It will be necessary therefore to examine the few references to the Spirit which occur in the sayings of Jesus. We should remember that most of the scholars who question the genuineness of Jesus' teaching upon this theme, also question the genuineness of the Baptist's teaching. As reasons have already been given for accepting the synoptic record of John's teaching, it will be assumed that Jesus was acquainted with John's prophecies.

1. Of the seven passages in which Jesus is said to have spoken about the Spirit, the first is Mark 3.29, which has parallels in Matt. 12.31 and Luke 12.10. The Markan version is:

> But whosoever shall blaspheme against the Holy Spirit hath never forgiveness, but is guilty of an eternal sin.

This saying occurs in the account of a controversy in which the scribes accused Jesus of casting out demons by Beelzebul, the prince of demons. Branscomb describes this saying as a "product of the apostolic age",[1] a view which is held by many scholars.[2] He suggests that the saying is an answer to a charge which was levelled not against Jesus during his ministry but against his followers after Pentecost.

---

done unto him whatsoever they listed, even as it is written of him." This saying identifies John the Baptist with Elijah. Matthew makes the meaning clearer when he comments: "Then understood the disciples that he spake unto them of John the Baptist" (Matt. 17.13).

[1] Branscomb, *St Mark*, p. 74.

[2] Cf. C. K. Barrett, op. cit., pp. 103–7.

The saying, however, has the note of authenticity. It is the kind of reply which the situation demanded. Jesus was accused of employing the chief of demons to work his miracles. He answered that he was working through the power of the Holy Spirit of God. To accuse the Holy Spirit of being Beelzebul was the gravest possible sin.

The attack on the authenticity of the saying has not succeeded. Attempts which have been made to show its dependence on a knowledge of the Septuagint have not been convincing.[1] The saying is perfectly credible, and is likely to have been spoken by Jesus in controversy with his critics.

The Q version of this saying is generally assumed to have less claim to authenticity than the Markan version. Luke 12.10 reads:

> And every one who shall speak a word against the Son of man, it shall be forgiven him: but unto him that blasphemeth against the Holy Spirit it shall not be forgiven.

The practice of some scholars is to take it for granted that of two similar sayings only one can be original. This is an unwarrantable

---

[1] C. K. Barrett, ibid., pp. 104–5, attempts to prove that the saying has been formed under the influence of the Septuagint. He argues that there are several traces in the gospels of the Greek version of Isaiah 63. The nearest parallel in the Old Testament to "blasphemy against the Spirit" is Isa. 63.10, "they grieved his holy spirit". In this passage the prophet is speaking of the deliverance of the Israelites from Egypt. In 63.14a, according to the Massoretic text, he says: "The Spirit of the Lord caused them to rest." The LXX reads: "The Spirit descended from the Lord and led them." Barrett claims that there are close parallels between the language of the LXX at this point and the language of the baptismal narratives in the synoptic gospels. Both the prophecy and the baptismal narrative use the verb καταβαίνειν to describe the descent of the Spirit. Both use the verb ἀνοίγειν to describe the opening of the heavens (see Isa. 64.1).

Barrett has not shown, however, that there is a close connection between the LXX of Isaiah 63 and Mark 3.28–30. The verbal connection is not there. There is only the link between two ideas, "grieving the Spirit", and "blaspheming against the Spirit". Moreover, the parallels between Isaiah 63 and the baptismal narratives are not very great. It is not a striking coincidence that the words καταβαίνειν and ἀνοίγειν occur in both. It is striking that while Isaiah 63 uses ὁδηγεῖν to describe the Spirit's leading, Matt. 4.1 uses ἀνάγειν, and Luke 4.1 uses ἄγειν.

assumption. Public speakers repeat themselves, and sometimes repeat themselves inexactly. They utter sayings which are similar but not identical. Jesus would do the same, and it is not surprising that sayings have survived which are similar but not exactly alike. This particular saying may have been influenced by the theological and apologetic need of the Church, but is probably authentic, since it subordinates the Son of Man to the Spirit, and such an idea would not have been invented by Jesus' disciples.

J. Wellhausen and others have suggested that "Son of Man" is a misrepresentation of the Aramaic *bar nasha* which may be translated "man". The saying, they argue, means that blasphemies against men would be forgiven, but not blasphemies against the Holy Spirit.[1]

C. K. Barrett supports the interpretation of Origen who argued that heathens blasphemed in their ignorance against the Son of Man, but Christians blasphemed knowingly against the Spirit. The latter blasphemy was beyond forgiveness.[2]

Since, however, the term "Son of Man" usually stands for the coming Messiah in the teaching of Jesus, it is better to accept the view that "Son of Man" in this saying refers to Jesus. Blasphemy against the Christ is being compared with blasphemy against the Spirit. The saying's offensiveness to an orthodox Christian is proof of its authenticity.

2. Mark 13.11 (cf. Matt. 10.20; Luke 12.12; 21.15).

> But whatsoever shall be given you in that hour, that speak ye: for it is not ye that speak but the Holy Spirit.

This saying has often been rejected as unauthentic. One reason for the scepticism which has been felt about it is that it occurs in the Markan Apocalypse. Yet even if the apocalypse as a whole is not a trustworthy account of the teaching of Jesus, it may well include a number of genuine sayings.[3]

Another reason for rejecting this saying has been given by E. F. Scott, who claims that "it contemplates conditions which did

---

[1] J. Wellhausen, *Einleitung*, 2nd ed., pp. 66 f.
[2] C. K. Barrett, op. cit., p. 106.
[3] Cf. V. Taylor, *The Gospel according to St Mark*, pp. 636–44.

not arise until a later time".[1] But why should not Jesus have made provision against future dangers? He knew that his disciples would find themselves in perilous situations, in which their courage and their wits would be tested. Mark 13.11 records how he assured them that in such moments their speech would be guided by the Holy Spirit. The saying has a thoroughly genuine ring.

Of the two parallels to the saying in the Gospel according to St Luke, the version in Luke 21.15 is slightly different from the Markan form. It reads: "I will give you a mouth and wisdom." C. K. Barrett argues that this is the original form of the saying. The version of Luke 21.15 cannot be secondary as Luke would not remove the references to the Holy Spirit. Barrett concludes that the Markan form of the saying arose during the persecutions which befell the Church.[2]

Taylor differs from Barrett on the ground that Luke's version "has a distinctly Johannine ring and appears to reflect the doctrine of the Exalted Christ".[3] This argument is not very strong, as it is quite possible that Luke's style could occasionally have a Johannine ring, without having been influenced by John.

Barrett's argument fails to convince, not for Taylor's reasons, but because he assumes that Jesus could not have uttered both Mark 13.11 and Luke 21.15. Luke, however, believed that it was possible for Jesus to utter two similar sayings, since he has recorded both the saying of Luke 12.12 which is similar to Mark 13.11, and that of Luke 21.15. Indeed if 12.12 were an expansion of 21.15, it is hardly likely that Luke would include 21.15. As it would be quite possible for the two sayings both to have been spoken by Jesus, there is no reason to reject either of them.

3. Luke 11.13.

> If ye then, being evil, know how to give good gifts unto your children, how much more shall your heavenly Father give the Holy Spirit to them that ask him?

This saying has a parallel in Matt. 7.11 in which the words "good gifts" appear instead of the words "the Holy Spirit". Most

---

[1] Op. cit., p. 73.　　　[2] Op. cit., pp. 131 f.　　　[3] Op. cit., p. 509.

scholars assume that only one of these sayings is genuine.[1] If that assumption is correct, the Matthaean form is original, as Luke would introduce the reference to the Spirit for doctrinal reasons. The possibility that Jesus uttered two similar sayings has been too easily discounted. The case for this saying's authenticity, however, is not as good as in the two previous sayings. An alteration from Matt. 7.11 could have been made by a simple verbal change. Hence little weight can be attached to Luke 11.13 as an authentic record of the teaching of Jesus.

4. Matt. 12.28.

> If I by the Spirit of God cast out demons, then is the kingdom of God come upon you.

Luke 11.20 reads "If I by the finger of God. . . ." Although Luke has a fondness for archaisms like "the finger of God", it is unlikely that he would have omitted a reference to the Spirit. Since each of these sayings occurs in the same context, it is improbable that both are original sayings of Jesus. Luke seems to have preserved the original form of the saying, which did not include the word "Spirit".

5. Luke 4.18.

According to Luke, Jesus read from Isaiah 61 when he preached in the synagogue at Nazareth. The passage which he read begins with the words: "The Spirit of the Lord is upon me". Jesus said that this prophecy had been fulfilled that very day. If this is a genuine narrative and Jesus really applied these words to himself, the saying is of supreme importance for an understanding of his teaching about the Spirit. Creed and many others claim that the details of the preaching have been improvised by the evangelist. They think that Luke has made a colourful substitute for Mark's briefer account of Jesus' preaching in 1.15.[2] On the other hand,

---

[1] E.g. Büchsel, *Der Geist Gottes*, p. 189; C. K. Barrett, op. cit., pp. 126–7; T. W. Manson, op. cit., p. 82; E. F. Scott, op. cit., p. 73–4; J. M. Creed, *The Gospel according to St Luke*, p. 158.

[2] J. M. Creed, op. cit., p. 66.

Vincent Taylor points out that in Mark's account of Jesus' visit to Nazareth there is an abrupt transition from the people's astonishment at Jesus' work to their indignation against him. Taylor asks: "Is a sermon like that described in Luke 4.23–7 presupposed?"[1] Indeed Jesus may well have preached such a sermon, for he was greatly influenced by the later chapters of Isaiah. He interpreted his own work in terms of the Suffering Servant.[2] And he echoed these words of Isa. 61.1 in Luke 7.22 (= Matt. 11.5), when he said: "The poor have good tidings preached to them." There is a strong case for supposing that Jesus quoted Isaiah 61 as a prophecy about himself.

6. Mark 12.36 (cf. Matt. 22.43).

The words "David himself said in the Holy Spirit" introduce a quotation from Ps. 110.1. Jesus himself is said to have made the quotation. It was quite natural for a Jew of Jesus' time to speak of the Psalms in this way. The Jews believed that the scriptures were written under the guidance of the Holy Spirit. There is no reason for doubting the authenticity of the saying.

7. Mark 14.38 (cf. Matt. 26.41).

The spirit indeed is willing, but the flesh is weak.

Wellhausen and others have rejected this saying because they claim that the contrast between flesh and spirit is Pauline.[3] The contrast existed, however, before the time of Paul, for it is found in the Old Testament.[4] In any case, whether the saying is genuine or not, it is about the spirit of men, not the Holy Spirit. Jesus is speaking of the weakness of his disciples, who had not the tenacity to keep awake.

Of the seven sayings about the Spirit which have been discussed two are probably unauthentic (Luke 11.13 and Matt. 12.28), and one is irrelevant. The other four have strong claim to authenticity, and

[1] Op. cit., p. 298 (cf. Mark 6.1–6a).
[2] The view that Jesus identified himself with the Servant is challenged by J. Knox, *The Death of Christ.* Cf. M. D. Hooker, *Jesus and the Servant.*
[3] J. Wellhausen, *Das Evangelium Marci*, p. 120.
[4] Cf. Isa. 31.3.

provide a small but important quantity of information about Jesus' attitude to the Spirit. He regarded the Spirit as a person who was able to speak through men, and against whom blasphemy could be committed. The Spirit was God's Spirit and guided men in the composition of the scriptures. The most important of all these sayings is the quotation from Isa. 61.1, in which Jesus claimed that the Spirit had anointed him. The blessing of the Spirit was the guarantee of his Messianic office.

Although these sayings may be regarded as genuine, it is surprising that the evangelists have not recorded any more of Jesus' teaching about the Spirit. With their experience of the Spirit's activity in the Church, they might have been expected to have included a great number of Jesus' words upon this theme. Is their silence a sign that Jesus had very little to say about the Spirit? Several explanations have been suggested.

E. F. Scott thinks that in Jesus' day the doctrine of the Spirit had fallen into the background, and that Jesus "never harked back to archaic models". The idea of the Spirit, he believes, was not congenial to Jesus, since he felt that it removed God to a distance. The "gusts of religious emotion", which were associated with the Spirit, were "foreign to Jesus".[1] Scott's argument is open to objection. Since John the Baptist taught about the Spirit, as we have argued, and since the Jews expected that in the future the Spirit would be given—which cannot be denied—Jesus could not have regarded the idea of the Spirit as "an archaic model". It was not an obsolete idea but the object of vivid expectation.

Vincent Taylor claims that not all Jesus' sayings about the Spirit have been preserved. Because there was no dispute about the doctrine in the early Church, the sayings were not needed for controversy, and because the Church was daily aware of the presence of the Spirit, the sayings were not required to strengthen the faith of the community.[2]

Taylor lays too much emphasis on the importance of controversy in the formation of the tradition. Doctrine was evangelical as well

---

[1] Op. cit., pp. 77–80.
[2] *The Doctrine of the Holy Spirit*, pp. 53–4.

as polemical. Christians desired others to share their experiences and would have treasured Jesus' teaching about the Spirit, not in order to refute their critics, but in order to attract others into the Church.

C. K. Barrett believes that the eschatological thought of Jesus is the key which unlocks the mystery. Jesus did not prophesy the existence of a Spirit-filled community, because he did not foresee an interval between his resurrection and the Parousia. If he did not expect an interim period between the two events, there was no place for teaching about the Spirit.[1]

Barrett's theory involves some highly doubtful assumptions. The first is that Jesus expected an immediate Parousia. He himself confessed ignorance of the day of the Lord, and although he may not have expected a long interval between his death and the Parousia, it is an arbitrary assumption that he did not expect an interim period. Secondly, Barrett supposes that neither John the Baptist nor Jesus said anything about the Spirit. There are good reasons, however, for believing that the evangelists have preserved genuine records of the teaching of both the Baptist and Jesus about the Spirit. It is not, as Barrett supposes, the complete absence but rather the meagreness of the teaching which has to be explained.

The most satisfactory answer to the problem is that of R. N. Flew, who argues that "there are few sayings about the Spirit, because Jesus saw that a richer and profounder understanding of the Spirit was needed than any which His disciples with their lack of insight could glean from the Old Testament; and this reinterpretation of the Spirit's work, could only be lived out in His own ministry".[2] Jesus' comparative silence was caused not by a lack of interest in the doctrine but by a consciousness that the future of the doctrine depended on his work rather than his teaching. He himself gave hints about the importance of the Spirit's work in his own life. But he was content to let the disciples discover the power of the Spirit in their own experience, for that was the only way in which they could really learn about it. After Pentecost they understood that Jesus had made possible the outpouring of the

[1] Op. cit., p. 160.   [2] *Jesus and His Church*, 2nd ed., p. 51.

Spirit, and Paul found that the ethic which Jesus had handed down was a spiritual ethic which superseded the legalism of the Jews, and that his sacrificial death had established a new, spiritual covenant.

The work of the Spirit in the expanding Church is the main theme of the Acts of the Apostles, and although the author's doctrine of the Spirit is not as rich and profound as Paul's, he is not silent about the Spirit's relation to Christ. John the Baptist's prophecy was fulfilled at Pentecost, and in his speech in Acts 2 Peter claimed that the exalted Christ had poured out the Spirit upon the apostles. It was Peter too who recalled how Jesus had been anointed with the Holy Spirit, presumably at his baptism (Acts 10.38). There is no suggestion in Acts that Christ was identified with the Spirit. In Acts 16.7 the "Spirit of Jesus" is mentioned, and there are references to the "Spirit of the Lord"[1], but "the Lord" may mean either God or Jesus.

In the Pauline epistles the Spirit and Christ are closely associated. In some passages Paul writes as if they were almost identical. It is this part of Paul's teaching which will be considered first.

The most famous of the passages in which Paul appears to identify the Spirit with Christ is 2 Cor. 3.17–18:

> Now the Lord is the Spirit: and where the Spirit of the Lord is, there is liberty. But we all, with unveiled face reflecting as a mirror the glory of the Lord, are transformed into the same image from glory to glory, even as from the Lord the Spirit.

These words cannot be understood apart from their context. Paul has been writing of the contrast between the old covenant which was ratified in the wilderness, and the new covenant, which was established by Christ. Moses was the minister of the old covenant, and when he came down from the mountain, his face shone, but the glory which was on his face gradually faded away. Not one man alone, but all the members of the Church are ministers of the new covenant. They possess a glory which is not fading but growing. When Moses came down from the mountain, he put a veil over his face, in order that the children of Israel might not be able to see the glory which was passing away. And when the old covenant is read, that veil remains. Under the new covenant,

[1] Acts 5.9; 8.39.

however, the veil has been removed. "But whensoever a man shall turn to the Lord", writes Paul, "the veil is taken away" (3.16).[1]

The crucial question is whether "the Lord" in 2 Cor. 3.17 refers to Christ or to Yahweh. Scholars have supported both interpretations. Bousset, Gunkel, Dodd, and Strachan argue that the sentence "Now the Lord is the Spirit" identifies Christ with the Spirit.[2] E. F. Scott and Rawlinson claim that "the Lord" in 2 Cor. 3.17 refers to Yahweh in Ex. 34.34, to which Paul alludes in the preceding verse.[3] Scott contends that "the Lord is the Spirit" is a condensed way of saying: "The Lord represents the rule of the Spirit."

The context supports the link with Yahweh and with the quotation from Exodus. But since Old Testament quotations which were originally about Yahweh are sometimes transferred by Paul to Christ,[4] it is possible that in 2 Cor. 3 he meant "Christ" by "the Lord". Moreover, in this epistle there is no clear instance of the application of the title "Lord" to God the Father. Elsewhere in the epistle the "Lord" is Christ.[5] These considerations support the view that Christ and the Spirit are being identified.

If, however, Paul had deliberately intended to identify them, he would have made the process of his thought plainer. In fact the argument at this stage has nothing to do with Christ. Although Christ is mentioned in the chapter, the contrast in this section is between the dispensation of the law and the dispensation of the Spirit. Paul claims that the Lord whom Moses confronted was the Spirit to whom the new covenant belongs.

[1] This verse recalls Ex. 34.34: "But when Moses went in before the Lord to speak with him, he took the veil off, until he came out."

[2] Bousset, *Kyrios Christos*, 1st ed., p. 126; Gunkel, *Die Wirkungen des Heiligen Geistes*, p. 90; Dodd, *Apostolic Preaching*, p. 47; Strachan, *Second Epistle to the Corinthians*, p. 88.

[3] E. F. Scott, op. cit., p. 181; cf. Rawlinson, *New Testament Doctrine of the Christ*, p. 155.

[4] See pp. 89–90, 102.

[5] Possible exceptions are 6.17, and 12.1,8. It is important to notice, however, that almost immediately after this crucial passage in 2 Cor. 3, there is a clear reference to the Lordship of Christ in 2 Cor. 4.5: "For we preach not ourselves, but Christ Jesus as Lord."

The identification of Christ with the Spirit was not in the foreground of Paul's thought. If he had been asked, perhaps he would have admitted that the Lord whom Exodus mentions was the Christ, just as he believed that the Lord in Joel 2.32 and the Lord in Isa. 45.23 ff was the Christ. If he had made this admission it would have followed that 2 Cor. 3.17 was identifying not only Yahweh but also Christ with the Spirit. Paul, however, did not draw out the implications of his statement. At the most it may be argued that while he did not consciously identify Christ with the Spirit, the implication of his thought might lead to such an identification.

There are several instances in Paul's writings of similar functions being ascribed to Christ and the Spirit. One of these functions is intercession. According to Rom. 8.26b "the Spirit himself maketh intercession for us with groanings which cannot be uttered". In the same chapter (Rom. 8.34) Paul writes: "It is Christ Jesus . . . who also maketh intercession for us." The proximity of these two verses suggests that Paul was speaking of the same person in both. A closer examination of the passages shows that the idea of the Spirit's intercession has a different origin from that of Christ's intercession. Paul is not ascribing one and the same activity first to the Spirit and then to Christ. He is describing two different activities, one of which belongs to the Spirit and the other to Christ. The first verse describes prayer which is directed by the Spirit. Even when a man's prayer is unintelligible, consisting of apparently incoherent cries and groans, it is the Spirit who is making intercession "with groanings which cannot be uttered". The second verse, however, refers to the pleas which the heavenly Christ makes for the forgiveness of sinful man. These prayers are not made by human beings as are the Spirit's intercessions. They are made by Christ to the Father. "It is Christ Jesus that died, yea rather, that was raised from the dead, who is at the right hand of God, who also maketh intercession for us." The idea has its origin in Isa. 53.12c where the Servant is said to have "made intercession for the transgressors". In the New Testament it is appropriated not only by Paul but also by the author of Hebrews who affirms that "he ever liveth to make intercession for them", and by John who describes Christ as "an advocate with the Father".[1]

Since the references to intercession in Romans 8 refer to two different kinds of intercession, they do not prove that Paul identified Christ with the Spirit.

Other significant parallels are those in which both Christ and the Spirit are said to "dwell in" or to "be in" the members of the Church. The most important illustration of this type of thought is Rom. 8.9 ff:

> But ye are not in the flesh, but in the spirit, if so be that the Spirit of God dwelleth in you. But if any man hath not the Spirit of Christ, he is none of his. And if Christ is in you, the body is dead because of sin; but the spirit is life because of righteousness. But if the Spirit of him that raised up Jesus from the dead dwelleth in you, he that raised up Christ Jesus from the dead shall quicken also your mortal bodies through his Spirit that dwelleth in you.

The Spirit of God and the Spirit of Christ are identical in this passage. The relation of the Spirit to Christ is not so clear. The Spirit "dwelleth in you", and Christ "is in you". It does not follow, however, that the Spirit and the Christ are the same person. Paul does not write about "him that raised up the Spirit from the dead". Even if the functions of Christ and the Spirit overlap, it does not follow that the two persons are identical.

Another important connection between Christ and the Spirit is found in the way in which Paul describes the life of the Christian. It is a life which is both "in Christ" and "in the Spirit". The instances in which these and similar phrases occur are very numerous. The first phrase, "in Christ", is used to describe almost all aspects of the Christian life. Converts are "baptized into Christ" or "buried with him in baptism".[2] In their new condition they "all are one man in Christ Jesus".[3] The Christians' life is "hid with Christ in God".[4] They rejoice "in the Lord".[5] They "speak in Christ".[6] They command and exhort each other "in

---

[1] Heb. 7.25; 9.24; 1 John 2.1. [2] Rom. 6.3,4; Gal. 3.27; Col. 2.12.
[3] Gal. 3.28.   [4] Col. 3.3.   [5] Phil. 3.1; 4.4.
[6] 2 Cor. 2.17; 12.19.

Christ"[1]. Their rulers are "over them in the Lord"[2]. As a community they are "one body in Christ"[3]. When their earthly lives end, they will be called "the dead in Christ" or "they which are fallen asleep in Christ".[4]

The phrase "in the Spirit", which translates either ἐν(τῷ) πνεύματι or (τῷ) πνεύματι is used in similar fashion. It is in the Spirit that men walk and live.[5] In the Spirit they make confession of their faith and speak the mysteries of God.[6] And into one Spirit they are baptized.[7]

In spite of these resemblances, the phrases "in Christ" and "in the Spirit" are not interchangeable in the writings of Paul. Christians are not exhorted to "put on the Spirit", or "to conform to the image of the Spirit". But they are called upon to "put on Christ" and "conform to his image". As L. S. Thornton points out, Romans 6 would be "intolerably obscured" if "Spirit of Christ" were substituted for "Christ".[8] It would indeed be impossible for Paul to speak of "dying with the Spirit" or of the resurrection of the Spirit from the dead.

Thornton has attempted to clarify the difference between "Christ" and "the Spirit". "The indwelling of the Spirit", he writes, "involves the indwelling of Christ; consequently the indwelling of Christ is inseparable from the quickening. But the Spirit is never regarded as the *content* of the quickened life. He is the agent of revelation, who brings the content of truth to the Spirit of man; and by consequence we have the mind of Christ."[9]

This distinction between content and agent is artificial. If Christians walk by the Spirit, if their conduct is the fruit of the Spirit, if their Church and their individual bodies are temples of the Spirit, then the Spirit is the content of the quickened life. The indwelling Christ and the indwelling Spirit can each be regarded both as content and as agents. Thornton shows that he is in

---

[1] 2 Thess. 3.12; 1 Thess. 4.1.   [2] 1 Thess. 5.12.
[3] Rom. 12.5; cf. 1 Cor. 12.20; Eph. 4.12.
[4] 1 Thess. 4.16; 1 Cor. 15.18.   [5] 2 Cor. 12.18; Gal. 5.16,25.
[6] 1 Cor. 12.3; 14.2.   [7] 1 Cor. 12.13.
[8] L. S. Thornton, *The Incarnate Lord*, p. 323.   [9] Ibid., p. 324.

difficulties, because he appeals to the Fourth Gospel as a justification of his interpretation of Paul:

> In St Paul's teaching the parallelism and identification between Christ and His Spirit are so close, that by looking at this side only we might suppose them to be simply identical in all respects, and so conclude that the Two must be taken to be One. If, however, we note the marked differences of Pauline language in describing the functions respectively of Christ and His Spirit, and if we then turn to the teaching of St John about the Paraclete, it will become clear that this simple identification cannot stand. The identification is best understood as that of a mutual interpenetration with divergence of functions.[1]

Thornton rightly says that there is some difference of function. But this difference is largely dependent on the fact of the incarnate life, death, and resurrection of Christ. Since the Spirit did not die and rise, men cannot die and rise with the Spirit. Paul's language about the Spirit can be understood only when we realize that he had not truly isolated the Spirit as a distinct person. Although the problem of Christ was a real one for him, the problem of the Spirit's relationship to the Father or the Son was not. The reason for this is to be found in the distinction which was made in an earlier chapter between extension and interaction of personality.[2] Wisdom, Word, and Spirit were regarded in Judaism as an extension of the personality of God, but there was little evidence that they responded to God in a full and reciprocal personal relationship. The Spirit in Paul is very much on a par with these Judaistic concepts. The Spirit of God leads men and drives them, but there is little suggestion that the Spirit responds to God. Even when Paul describes the Spirit as making intercession, the Spirit does this through the mouth of man, when he enables a man to pray. The heavenly intercession of Christ involves a much greater degree of reciprocal activity than the Spirit's intercession. While, however, there is little evidence in Paul's epistles for interaction between Father and Spirit, there is ample evidence in Paul for interaction between Father and Son. Not only was the Son a heavenly intercessor, but he had received a kingdom from his Father and would surrender it to him again. Even before his incar-

[1] Ibid., p. 360.   [2] See pp. 38–40.

nation he chose not to remain on an equality with God, but emptied himself, abandoning the riches of his divine existence for the poverty of a human life. Here indeed is no mere extension of the Father's personality but a being with a will of his own, who makes his own choices, and interacts in love with his Father.

The Johannine writings achieve a greater clarity than Paul in their exposition of the relationship between the Spirit and Christ. The Spirit is not identified with Christ. Both in the words of Jesus and in the general plan of the writings the Spirit is a distinct being. "And I will pray the Father," says Jesus, "and he shall give you another Paraclete, that he may be with you for ever, even the Spirit of truth."[1] The first Paraclete was Jesus, the second the Spirit. It is this Spirit which descended upon Jesus at his baptism, and without which a man cannot enter into the Kingdom of God.[2] Although Jesus was a bearer of the Spirit, the rest of mankind was unable to receive the Spirit until Jesus had been glorified.[3] The Spirit was finally given to the disciples by the risen Christ himself.[4] The function of the Spirit was to glorify Christ, and to reveal the truth about him. "He shall glorify me," says Jesus, "for he shall take of mine, and shall declare it unto you."[5] The Spirit guides into all truth.[6]

It is possible that when Jesus says "I go away, and I come unto you",[7] he is speaking of the coming of the Spirit. But since he speaks in the same chapter of the difference between himself and "another Paraclete", it is more likely that "I come unto you" refers to his own resurrection.

The Spirit is said in John to abide *with* Christians and to be *in* them.[8] On the other hand it is never suggested that Christians abide *in* the Spirit as they abide in Christ and the Father. The distinction

---

[1] John 14.16–17.

[2] The baptism of Jesus is presupposed in John 1.32–4. In John 3.5 Jesus says: "Except a man be born of water and the Spirit, he cannot enter into the kingdom of God."

[3] "For the Spirit was not yet given; because Jesus was not yet glorified" (John 7.39b).

[4] John 20.22.   [5] John 16.14.   [6] John 16.13.

[7] John 14.28.   [8] John 14.17.

which Thornton makes about the teaching of Paul is much truer of the Fourth Gospel. The Spirit is the agent which leads men to a knowledge of Christ and to communion with him. Christ is the one in whom the Christian lives.

The Epistles of John have little to say about the Spirit, but when he is mentioned he is distinguished from Christ. The Spirit bears witness to Christ and enables men to confess Christ.[1] There is no indication that the Spirit is identical with Christ.

The Johannine writings make a strict distinction between Christ and the Spirit. Although their doctrine of the Spirit is not as rich and full as Paul's, the relation of the Spirit to both Father and Son is made clearer than it is by Paul. This is partly because one of the Johannine writings is a gospel. The author of the gospel, whose thoughts were centred upon the incarnate life of Christ, was bound to make the distinction between Christ and the Spirit. Paul, however, when he wrote his epistles, was chiefly thinking of the risen Christ, the Christ of his own and the Church's experience. For this reason he did not make as clear a distinction between Christ and the Spirit as did the Fourth Evangelist. Paul's life was both in Christ and in the Spirit; the Spirit dwelt in him and Christ dwelt in him. He was not concerned about the metaphysical relation between the two, and made no consistent effort to distinguish between their persons and activities.

The doctrine of the Spirit is not as prominent in the rest of the New Testament as in John and Paul. In so far as it appears, it does not give warrant for the belief that the Spirit was Christ. The only evidence for such a view is found in the Epistle to the Hebrews, in which Christians are called "partakers of Christ" and "partakers of the Holy Spirit",[2] but this evidence is discounted by the general tendency of the epistle to regard the Spirit as other than Christ. Those who put Jesus to death not only trod under foot the Son of God but did despite to the Spirit of grace, who in the context must be different from the Son of God. And when Jesus offered himself up he acted through "eternal spirit".[3]

The New Testament supports the view that the Spirit was not

---

[1] 1 John 4.2; 5.8.   [2] Heb. 3.14; 6.4; cf. 3.1.   [3] Heb. 10.29; 9.14.

identified with Christ, but was regarded as personal, although, as
we have seen, many of the references are consistent with the view
that he was an impersonal force. The Spirit did not respond to the
Father in the same way as did the Son. Only Paul speaks of the
Spirit's making intercession. And even this passage is best interpreted as a description of the guidance given by the Spirit to men's
own prayers and intercessions, rather than as part of a dialogue
between the Spirit and the Father.

CHAPTER 12

THE SPIRIT AND GOD

According to the Athanasian Creed the Holy Spirit is fully God and shares without qualification the divinity of Father and Son. The Spirit, like Father and Son, is both God and Lord, uncreated, incomprehensible, eternal, and almighty. We shall consider whether there is any trace of this doctrine in the New Testament. The problem will be approached in the same way as the problem of Christ's divinity. First, we shall ask whether the Spirit was ever called God in the New Testament. Secondly, we shall consider whether the Spirit received worship and prayer. And thirdly, we shall examine the part which the Spirit played in the execution of the unique functions of deity.

Was the Spirit called God?

Only a few passages can be used to support the view that the Spirit was called God in the New Testament, and the evidence of these passages is of doubtful value. Three passages will be examined separately.

1. 1 Cor. 6.19–20:

> Or know ye not that your body is a temple of the Holy Spirit which is in you, which ye have from God? and ye are not your own; for ye were bought with a price: glorify God therefore in your body.

Augustine claims that this passage implies that the Holy Spirit is God.[1] Taking the words "in your body" as an adjectival phrase dependent on the word "God", he translates the last clause as "Glorify therefore the God in your body". Augustine argues that since the body is called "a temple of the Holy Spirit which is in you", "the God in your body" must be the Holy Spirit.

[1] Augustine, *De Trinitate*, I.13.

224

Augustine's interpretation is mistaken and is due to the absence of the definite article in Latin. The Greek is:

δοξάσατε δὴ τὸν θεὸν ἐν τῷ σώματι ὑμῶν

and the Latin translation which Augustine gives is:

Glorificate ergo Deum in corpore vestro.

Since however the definite article τόν is not repeated before the phrase ἐν τῷ σώματι ὑμῶν, the phrase is adverbial and not adjectival. The Greek means "Glorify therefore God with your body" or "in your body", and the preposition ἐν is used either instrumentally or locally.

Another early reading, of which Augustine does not seem to be aware, would support his belief that the Spirit in this passage is identified with God. Marcion and Tertullian read: *Glorificate et portate Deum in corpore vestro* (Glorify and carry God in your body).[1] This would imply that God is identical with "the Holy Spirit which is in you". The textual evidence shows, however, that the reading of Marcion and Tertullian has arisen from scribal errors.[2]

In 1 Cor. 6.19–20 Paul does not identify the Holy Spirit with God. The Corinthians are being exhorted to glorify God with their body which is a temple of the Spirit. The distinction which Paul makes between the Spirit and God is shown in verse 19 when he speaks of "the Holy Spirit which is in you, which ye have from God." God is the giver and the Spirit is his gift.

2. 2 Cor. 3.17–18.

Now the Lord is the Spirit: and where the Spirit of the Lord is, there is liberty. But we all, with unveiled face reflecting as a mirror the glory of the Lord, are transformed into the same image from glory to glory, even as from the Lord the Spirit.

It has already been argued that "the Lord" in this passage stands for "Yahweh".[3] Paul is interpreting a reference to Ex.

---

[1] This reading is also supported by the Old Latin *g* and the Vulgate.
[2] See Lietzmann, *I Korintherbrief*, p. 29, for a full account.
[3] See pp. 215–17

34.34 in which it is stated that "Moses went in before the Lord".
He says that the Lord before whom Moses went is the Spirit. So
much has already been argued. A further question remains. Did
Paul think that the Lord and the Spirit were identical? Lietzmann
argues that Paul means that he, who is Lord as person, is Spirit as
substance.[1] This interpretation would be correct if the Greek had
read ὁ δὲ κύριος πνεῦμά ἐστιν (The Lord is Spirit). Since the
Greek has τὸ πνεῦμα instead of πνεῦμα, Lietzmann's explanation is unsatisfactory.

The passage can be understood only if we consider the context.
Paul is contrasting the old covenant with the new. He is contrasting
the law of the letter with the law of the Spirit. The Old Testament
says that when Moses turned to the Lord he took the veil off his
face. Paul argues that the Lord whom Moses confronted represents
the dispensation of the Spirit. Although Moses inaugurated a
covenant of the letter, the Lord whom he confronted stood for the
realm of the Spirit. When a man turns to the Lord, Paul argues, the
veil is done away and the man finds the liberty of life in the Spirit
in contrast to the bondage of life under the law.

Paul's emphasis is on the fact that Moses had contact with the
realm of the Spirit. There is no sustained attempt to explain the
precise relationship between the Lord, Yahweh, and the Spirit.
But it cannot be denied that Paul actually says that "the Lord *is the*
Spirit". He is not content to say that the Lord is the giver of the
Spirit, or that the Lord is Spirit (omitting the definite article).

Are we then to say that Paul is deliberately identifying the Holy
Spirit with Yahweh? There is no other evidence for this point of
view in Paul's writings, and even the immediate context militates
against the identification. When he writes "The Lord is the Spirit:
and where the Spirit of the Lord is, there is liberty", the apparent
identification is followed by the phrase "Spirit of the Lord" which
suggests that Spirit and Lord are different. Paul's point is that the
Lord is represented by the Spirit in his relationship with men. As
far as men are concerned, the Lord confronts them as the Spirit.
Nevertheless, the language which Paul uses shows the direction in
which his thought is moving. He does not intend to identify the

[1] *II Korintherbrief*, pp. 113–15.

Spirit with Yahweh, but, having written "The Lord is the Spirit", he does not alter his words but qualifies them by a reference to "the Spirit of the Lord". His mind was not yet prepared for the acknowledgement that the Spirit was God. His thought about the Spirit was moving in the same direction as his thought about Christ, but it had not advanced so far. Although he acknowledged in Rom. 9.5 that Christ was God, he never gave such honour to the Spirit.

3. John 4.24:

> God is Spirit: and they that worship him, must worship in spirit and truth.

If the Greek πνεῦμα is translated "a Spirit", it is possible that God is being identified with the Spirit. Such a translation, however, is misleading. In this verse πνεῦμα is used in an adjectival sense.[1] God belongs to the realm of Spirit. Hence the worship which is appropriate to him is worship offered in spirit.

Of the three passages which have been discussed only one, 2 Cor. 3.17–18, suggests that the Spirit may have been explicitly identified with God. And Paul's statement is followed by such a modification that he cannot be said to have accepted the identification consciously.

Was the Spirit an object of worship and prayer?

There is only one verse in the New Testament which can be interpreted as meaning that the Spirit was worshipped. The Greek of Phil. 3.3 is:

ἡμεῖς γάρ ἐσμεν ἡ περιτομή, οἱ πνεύματι θεοῦ λατρεύοντες, καὶ καυχώμενοι ἐν Χριστῷ Ἰησοῦ, καὶ οὐκ ἐν σαρκὶ πεποιθότες.

The Revised Version translation is:

> For we are the circumcision, who worship by the Spirit of God, and glory in Christ Jesus, and have no confidence in the flesh.

The crucial phrase is οἱ πνεύματι θεοῦ λατρεύοντες, which may be translated (with the R.V.) "who worship by the Spirit of

[1] Cf. C. H. Dodd, *Interpretation of the Fourth Gospel*, p. 225; Bultmann, *Ev. Joh.*, p. 141.

God" or, alternatively, "who worship the Spirit of God", since the verb λατρεύειν is followed by an object in the dative case. If πνεύματι θεοῦ is the object of λατρεύειν, the verse is evidence for the worship of the Holy Spirit. Modern commentators do not seriously consider the possibility of πνεύματι θεοῦ being the object of the verb, but in earlier times the verse was sometimes accepted as evidence for the practice of worship of the Spirit. Such an interpretation is given by Augustine.[1] In support of the view that πνεύματι θεοῦ is object is the parallelism which would result between the Spirit and Christ. There is a symmetry about the clause "who worship the Spirit of God and glory in Jesus Christ". Augustine's interpretation, however, is not convincing because Paul is stressing the fact that Christian worship and service is offered through the Spirit and not through mere observance of the law. Hence the Revised Version translation is to be preferred: "who worship by the Spirit of God".

An alternative reading θεῷ for θεοῦ is given by some authorities. Then the translation would be "who worship God in Spirit". The evidence for θεοῦ, however, is much stronger than for θεῷ. It is indeed possible that neither θεοῦ nor θεῷ appeared in the original text, for neither occurs in the Chester-Beatty Papyrus. Then the clause would be translated "who worship by the Spirit".

There is no evidence in the New Testament that the Spirit was worshipped or received prayer. Even in the documents of the first five centuries the evidence is exceedingly rare. L. Hodgson claims that no hymns or prayers were addressed to the Spirit before the tenth century.[2] There is, however, clear evidence that the Spirit was worshipped in conjunction with Father and Son. Worship was offered not only through the Spirit but also to the Spirit. According to the Nicene Creed, the Spirit is worshipped and glorified together with the Father and the Son. And Basil of

---

[1] *De Trinitate*, I.13.

[2] *The Doctrine of the Trinity*, p. 232. "Now it is true, so far as I know, there is extant no instance of hymns or prayers addressed to the Holy Spirit that is certainly earlier than the tenth century. It is also true that the standard form of Christian worship is worship offered by the Christian to the Father in union with the Son through the Spirit."

Caesarea claims that in the third century Origen used a form of
the Gloria in which the Spirit was placed on the same level as
Father and Son.[1]

There is evidence which is even earlier. According to the
"Ascension of Isaiah" both Christ and the Holy Spirit are objects
of worship (Asc. Isa. 9.36):

> And I saw the Lord and the second angel, and they were standing. And the
> second whom I saw was on the left of my Lord. And I asked: "Who is
> this?" and he said unto me "Worship him, for he is the angel of the Holy
> Spirit, who speaketh in thee and the rest of the righteous.

Since the angel of the Holy Spirit is equivalent to the Holy
Spirit, this passage is clear evidence that the Spirit was worshipped
at the time when the words were written.

The date of the work is uncertain. The section from which this
passage comes is called "The Vision of Isaiah". It has been dated
at the latest to the end of the second century, and may have been
in circulation much earlier.[2]

[1] *De Spiritu Sancto*, 73. H. B. Swete, *The Holy Spirit in the Ancient Church*,
pp. 312 f, quotes Niceta of Remesiana, who, in *De Spiritu Sancto*, 5–19,
written in the second half of the fourth century, writes: "It is idle to refuse
to Him (sc. the Holy Spirit) the name of God or the worship due to God,
when you cannot deny that He has the power of God. I will therefore adore
Father, Son and Holy Spirit with one and the same religious worship, not
separately, as the heathen worship their 'gods many', but as One God."

[2] R. H. Charles in his edition of the *Ascension of Isaiah* claims that the
section known as the *Vision of Isaiah* (Asc. Isa. 6—40.40) was known to
Ignatius. According to Asc. Isa. 11.16 the virgin birth of Jesus escaped the
notice of "all the heavens and all the princes and all the gods of this world".
In his epistle to the Ephesians 19, Ignatius says that the virgin birth escaped the
notice of the prince of this world. Charles (pp. xlv and 77) claims that Ignatius
was dependent on the *Ascension of Isaiah*. He writes (p. 77): "Throughout
10.8—40.19 the concealment of the real nature of Christ is the entire theme,
and as a subordinate factor of this the concealment of Mary's virginity. In the
Epistle of Ignatius, on the other hand, the subject is introduced abruptly and
obviously forms part of a received doctrine, such as is presented in our text."
Charles' argument is not convincing. The doctrine that the virgin birth
escaped the notice of the powers of evil need not have been put forward first
in the *Vision of Isaiah*. It may have been formulated considerably earlier.
Ignatius refers to the doctrine in general terms and is not linguistically
dependent on the *Vision of Isaiah*. Indeed, since the *Vision of Isaiah* contains

Another piece of evidence is to be found in third-century Acts of Thomas, 27;

> Come, Holy Spirit, and cleanse their reins and their heart, and give them the added seal, in the name of the Father and Son and Holy Spirit.[1]

This verse is the conclusion of an invocation in which the Holy Spirit is addressed by different titles. The first invocation is to the "holy name of Christ". Then follow eight invocations to the Holy Spirit, who is addressed as "power of the Most High . . . gift of the Most High . . . compassionate mother . . . communion of the male . . . she that revealeth the hidden mysteries . . . mother of the seven houses . . . elder of the five members . . . Holy Spirit".

This kind of invocation can be classed as prayer.[2] A definite request is made of the Holy Spirit. The Acts of Thomas show that prayer was made to the Spirit in the third century. Nevertheless since the Ascension of Isaiah and the Acts of Thomas do not belong to the main stream of Christian literature, they cannot be used as proof of the generally accepted character of prayer and worship.

The practice of offering prayer and worship to the Spirit did not grow quickly. There is no trace of it in the Scriptures and it did not occur often until the Middle Ages. Even then it was much less frequent than prayer and worship offered to the Father and the Son.

Was the Spirit believed to perform the unique functions of Deity?

In earlier chapters it has been shown how the functions of judgement, creation, and salvation were ascribed to Christ. These were

---

teaching which savours of Docetism (11.17), it is unlikely that Ignatius would have accepted a doctrine on the evidence of this writing.

Although Charles has not succeeded in proving that the *Vision of Isaiah* was already written in Ignatius' time at the beginning of the second century, he has shown that it was known to the writer of the *Actus Petri Vercellenses*, which were written either at the end of the second century or at the beginning of the third (pp. xliv and 77). He has also shown that there are echoes of the *Vision of Isaiah* in the second century Protoevangel of James (see Charles, pp. 75–6). It is clear then that the *Vision of Isaiah* was written before the end of the second century.

[1] See M. R. James, *The Apocryphal New Testament*, p. 376.
[2] See p. 97.

regarded by Jews as unique functions of God. We shall now consider whether the Spirit was thought to perform these functions.

There is only one passage in which the Spirit is described as a judge. This is John 16.8–11:

> And he (the Paraclete), when he is come, will convict the world in respect of sin, and of righteousness, and of judgement: of sin, because they believe not on me; of righteousness, because I go to the Father, and ye behold me no more; of judgement, because the prince of this world hath been judged.

The precise meaning of this passage is obscure and has been the theme of much discussion.[1] One thing, however, is perfectly clear. The Spirit passes judgement. It is a judgement against the world and reassures the Christian that he is right in resisting the world's ways. It cannot be said on the basis of this passage that the Spirit was seriously regarded as the supreme judge at judgement day, for first, the judgement which, according to John, the Spirit passes, will take place continually in this present age, and, secondly, it is not certain precisely what function the Spirit was supposed to play in the court of judgement. Moreover there is no hint elsewhere in the Johannine writings or in the rest of the New Testament that the Spirit is regarded as judge. It is clear that in John 16.8–11, the doctrine is only in embryo.

The second function is that of creation. Although in later Christian hymns the Holy Spirit is hailed as creator, the biblical support for the idea is not very strong. According to Gen. 1.2 the Spirit of God moved upon the face of the waters at the beginning of the creation. Another Old Testament reference is Ps. 33.6:

> By the word of the Lord were the heavens made;
> And all the host of them by the *ruah* ("Spirit" or "breath") of his mouth.

Apart from these two verses there is no statement in either the Old or New Testament which supports the idea that the Spirit was active in the creation of the world.

The Spirit is often connected, however, in the Old Testament with the new creation. The Jews expected a new age which would be marked by an outpouring of the Spirit and a renewal of the lives of men. This idea was already beginning to be developed in

[1] Cf., especially, Lightfoot, *St John*, ad. loc.

the writings of Ezekiel, who prophesied that God would give his people a new heart and a new spirit (36.26–7):

A new heart also will I give you, and a new spirit will I put within you: and I will take away the stony heart out of your flesh, and I will give you an heart of flesh. And I will put my spirit within you . . .

In chapter thirty-seven, Ezekiel describes a vision of dead bones which are clothed with life. In the Revised Version the English word "spirit" is not used, but the Hebrew *ruah* which may be translated "spirit" occurs several times and is translated as "breath" or "wind" (Ezek. 37.9):

Then said he unto me, Prophesy unto the wind (*ruah*), prophesy, son of man, and say to the wind (*ruah*), Thus saith the Lord God: Come from the four winds (*ruhoth*), O breath (*ruah*), and breathe upon these slain, that they may live.

The dead Israel, according to Ezekiel, will be revived when the *ruah* is breathed upon the slain. The Spirit brings in the new life.

A similar idea lies behind Isa. 44.3:

I will pour my spirit upon thy seed, and my blessing upon thine offspring.

And according to Joel 2.28, the Lord promises: "I will pour out my spirit upon all flesh."

Although the Jewish writers linked the new creation with the Spirit, it is almost always God who creates and not the Spirit. The only exception is Ezekiel 37, in which *ruah* is invoked to breathe upon the slain that they may live.

The connection between the Spirit and the new creation is not as clear in the New Testament as in the Old. In no passage of the New Testament is the Spirit described as agent in the new creation. Paul speaks of a "new creation" or "new creature", but does not mention the Spirit in the same context.[1] Although he links the Spirit with baptism and the Christian life,[2] and regards the "new

---

[1] 2 Cor. 5.17: "Wherefore if any man is in Christ, there is a new κτίσις." Gal. 6.15: "For neither is circumcision anything nor uncircumcision, but there is a new κτίσις." The word κτίσις may be translated "creation" or "creature". In either case Paul is writing about a new creation.

[2] For baptism see 1 Cor. 6.11; 12.13. For the new life see Rom. 8.2 ff; 1 Cor. 12.4 ff; Gal. 5.16 ff.

covenant" as spiritual,[1] he does not connect the Spirit with the idea of the new creation.

In the Fourth Gospel the Spirit is active in both the new creation and the new birth. The description of Christ's meeting with his disciples after the resurrection is deliberately constructed to show that a new creation is taking place (John 20.22):

> And when he had said this, he breathed on them, and saith unto them, Receive ye the Holy Spirit.

It is not the Spirit, however, but the Father and the Son who are agents on this occasion. The Spirit is the gift which the Father and the Son bestow upon the disciples.

Akin to the idea of the new creation is that of the new birth, which John links with the Spirit. Men must be born, he says, of water and the Spirit before they can enter into the Kingdom of God (John 3.5). But he does not suggest that the Spirit is the agent who brings about this new birth.

There is no evidence elsewhere in the New Testament that the Spirit was agent in the new creation or the new birth. The reference in Titus 3.5 to "the washing of regeneration and renewing of the Holy Spirit", and the great conclusion of the Apocalypse with its account of the new heaven and the new earth say nothing of the agency of the Spirit.[2] In the other passages of the New Testament in which a new birth is described there is no indication that the Spirit was active. According to 1 Pet. 1.3 it was "the God and Father of our Lord Jesus Christ, who according to his great mercy begat us again unto a living hope by the resurrection of Jesus Christ from the dead". It is "the Father of lights" of whom it is written in Jas. 1.18 that "of his own will he brought us forth by the word of truth, that we should be a kind of firstfruits of his creatures".

The connection of the Spirit with the divine functions of judgement and creation has been examined. The third function which was discussed in the section about Christ's divinity was the function of

---

[1] Cf. 2 Cor. 3.6: who also made us sufficient as ministers of a new covenant; not of the letter, but of the spirit.

[2] Revelation 21 and 22.

salvation. This is not said to be performed by the Spirit in the New Testament. The Spirit is never called "saviour" and never said to save.

The evidence which has been considered in this chapter leads to conclusions which are mainly negative. Apart from John's statement about the work of the Spirit in judgement, there is no indication that the Spirit was believed to perform the uniquely divine functions. There is no evidence that the Spirit was the object of prayer and worship. And the only passage which supports the belief that the Spirit was regarded as God is 2 Cor. 3.17–18. The support which this solitary passage gives is weak, for immediately Paul has said that the Lord is the Spirit he speaks of the Spirit of the Lord, which suggests that there is a distinction between Lord and Spirit.

In the New Testament there is no development of the doctrine of the Spirit parallel to the development which has been traced in Christology. In later times the Spirit was the object of prayer and worship, and was explicitly said to be God. But this did not occur in New Testament times.

The doctrine of the Spirit did not develop as quickly as the doctrine of Christ, and worship was not given to the Spirit as soon as to Christ. The reason for this difference is that Christ had been incarnate. There was no problem about whether he was a person or not. For most people, and especially for Jews, it is easier to worship a person than an idea. Although the Spirit was described by many of the New Testament writers as a person, the personal nature of Christ was much easier to understand than the personal nature of the Spirit. The belief that Christ was a person was more firmly accepted than the belief that the Spirit was a person. For this reason the worship of Christ arose long before the worship of the Spirit, and men were calling upon Christ as God long before they called upon the Spirit as God.

PART IV

The Rise of the Trinitarian Problem

CHAPTER 13

THE THREEFOLD FORMULAE

In the New Testament are many formulae which mention Father, Son, and Spirit. In this chapter we shall consider whether the use of these triadic formulae is evidence that a doctrine of the Trinity was being formulated in New Testament times, and we shall also consider at what stage in the history of the Church these formulae appeared.

Widely diverging opinions have been held about both the doctrinal implications and the date of origin of the formulae. Many traditional writers have taken them as evidence for the antiquity of the doctrine of the Trinity. Many modern writers assume that the formulae in no way suggest the existence of a doctrine of the Trinity. Some writers think that trinitarian formulae originated with Jesus himself, basing their view on the words ascribed to the risen Jesus in Matt. 28.19. Others, like Cullmann,[1] argue that originally there were formulae which referred to Jesus, later there arose bi-partite formulae which referred to Father and Son, and as a further development the triadic formulae came into existence.

Before a judgement can be made about these conflicting theories, the New Testament texts must be examined. They will be divided into three groups. The first group will contain only one passage, Matt. 28.19. This passage is treated separately because of the great amount of discussion which it has raised, and because more than any other saying of the New Testament it suggests the growth of a trinitarian doctrine. The second group will contain Pauline sayings, and will include sayings from Ephesians but not from the Pastoral Epistles. The third group will contain non-Pauline sayings.

[1] Cullmann, *Earliest Christian Confessions*, pp. 35 ff.

Matthew 28.19

πορευθέντες οὖν μαθητεύσατε πάντα τὰ ἔθνη, βαπτίζοντες αὐτοὺς εἰς τὸ ὄνομα τοῦ πατρὸς καὶ τοῦ υἱοῦ καὶ τοῦ ἁγίου πνεύματος.

Go ye therefore, and make disciples of all the nations, baptizing them into the name of the Father and of the Son and of the Holy Spirit.

According to Matthew these words were spoken by Jesus to his disciples after his resurrection. The authenticity of the saying has been questioned on textual, literary, and historical grounds. Many scholars suppose that the saying reflects the teaching of the Church of the late first century and is not an utterance of Jesus himself.

The textual arguments against the saying's authenticity will be considered first. There is no need to go very fully into the problem as it has already been discussed exhaustively. F. C. Conybeare has attempted to show that the earliest form of the text was:

Go and make disciples of all the nations in my name.[1]

Eusebius often writes as if he were aware of such a version, although he makes reference also to the threefold formula. Conybeare argues that the threefold formula is quoted by Eusebius only in his later works, but this is disputed by Chase,[2] who thinks that he continued to write as if there were a single formula even after he had begun to refer to the threefold formula. Conybeare comes to the conclusion that the original form of the saying was the single formula, but his case is not strong. There is no evidence in any of the manuscripts or versions which supports him, and there are several ways of accounting for the reference to a single formula in Eusebius. Chase, for example, suggests that Eusebius is conflating Matt. 28.19 with Mark 16.17 ("In my name shall they cast out demons").[3] Lebreton[4] claims that he is conflating Matt. 28.19 with Luke 24.47 ("that repentance and remission of sins should be

---

[1] F. C. Conybeare, *ZNTW*, II (1901), pp. 275–88. P. 281—Eusebius appears to have found in the codices of Caesarea the following form of text: πορευθέντες μαθητεύσατε πάντα τὰ ἔθνη ἐν τῷ ὀνόματί μου, διδάσκοντες αὐτοὺς τηρεῖν πάντα ὅσα ἐνετειλάμην ὑμῖν.

[2] F. H. Chase, *JTS*, VI, pp. 483 ff.

[3] Ibid., pp. 489–92.

[4] *History of the Dogma of the Trinity*, I, p. 438.

preached in his name unto all the nations"). Crehan argues that he is giving a short summary of what the candidate for baptism was required to do.[1] It is also possible that Eusebius was conflating Matt. 28.19 with the passages in Acts where baptism is said to be in the name of Jesus. Whichever may be the correct explanation the textual arguments against the authenticity of Matt. 28.19 are not convincing.

The arguments of "literary" and "historical" criticism against the authenticity of Matt. 28.19 are stronger than the textual arguments. From the point of view of "literary" criticism, the verse has no synoptic or other parallels. The passage which most resembles it is Mark 16.15–18 in which there is no mention of the threefold name. There is in fact no evidence apart from Matt. 28.19 that Jesus used the threefold formula.

The case against the historicity of the saying rests mainly on historical criticism.[2] In the Acts of the Apostles baptism was in the name of Jesus Christ and not in the threefold name. Would the Acts record baptism in the one name, critics ask, if Jesus had commanded baptism in the threefold name? Moreover Paul speaks of being baptized into Christ or into Christ Jesus, phrases which are closer to Acts than to Matthew. It is strange that there should have been no reference to the threefold formula if it had been uttered by Christ himself.

Crehan attempts to explain this silence about the threefold formula by arguing that it was used by the person who was baptizing, while the single formula refers to the confession which was made by the candidate for baptism. "The command to baptize", he writes, "authorized the disciples to use the Trinitarian formula in the act of baptizing, while the language of Acts refers to the part taken in the rite by the candidate."[3] He supports his argument by pointing out that whereas the active voice of βαπτίζειν is used in Matt. 28.19, the passive voice is used wherever baptism in or into the name of Jesus Christ is mentioned

[1] J. Crehan, *Early Christian Baptism and the Creed*, p. 25.
[2] Cf. W. F. Flemington, *New Testament Doctrine of Baptism*, pp. 107–9, and H. G. Marsh, *Origin and Significance of Baptism*, p. 115.
[3] Crehan, op. cit., p. 76.

in the Acts of the Apostles and the Pauline Epistles. The words "baptizing in the name", etc., he argues, show that the name was pronounced by the person who was performing the rite, and the passive form "be baptized in the name", etc., refers to the part played by the person who was being baptized.[1] There is no strong evidence in support of Crehan's theory. It is not at all clear even from the writings of the first four centuries that a threefold formula was used only by the baptizer while a confession of the Lord Jesus was made by the person who was receiving baptism. Moreover, the earliest evidence outside the scriptures for the use of a threefold formula at baptism is Justin's Apology.[2] Support is found in Irenaeus, the Apostolic Constitutions, and various apocryphal writings.[3] Such support indicates that the threefold formula was used at baptism but does not prove that it was used universally. It is the support which we should expect to be accorded to a practice which had started several decades after Jesus' earthly ministry. Stronger support would have been given to a practice instituted by Jesus himself.

Crehan has not explained why the threefold formula is never connected with baptism in the New Testament except in Matt. 28.19. He has put forward an explanation only of the difference between "baptism in the name of the Father, Son, and Spirit" and "being baptized into the name of Christ". If the threefold formula was used by the person who conducted the rite, it is strange that it should not have been repeated in the New Testament or the writings of the Apostolic Fathers.

The conclusion to which this discussion leads is that the three-fold formula is part of the original text of Matt. 28.19 but unlikely to have been uttered by Jesus himself. It is probably a formula which was developed in the early Church and was later ascribed to Jesus. A formula of this nature may have been in use for some time before it was included in the gospel tradition. As it must have been included in the tradition by about A.D. 80 it is likely that it was being used ten or twenty years earlier. It cannot, however, be

---

[1] Ibid., pp. 76, 88.　　　　　　[2] *Apol.*, i.61

[3] Irenaeus, *Epideixis* 3; *Const. Apol.*, iii.16. For details of evidence see Crehan, op. cit., pp. 79–84.

brought forward as evidence about the teaching either of Jesus or
of the earliest Jerusalem church.

Pauline Sayings

But we are bound to give thanks to God alway for you, brethren beloved
of the Lord, for that God chose you from the beginning unto salvation in
sanctification of the Spirit and belief of the truth: whereunto he called you
through our gospel, to the obtaining of the glory of our Lord Jesus Christ
(2 Thess. 2.13–14).

These verses are evidence that God, Christ, and the Spirit were
to the forefront of Paul's mind. They do not, however, show that
he was aware of a problem of the Trinity. But it is not surprising,
when we consider such a passage as this, that the problem of the
Trinity was discussed in later years.

Now there are diversities of gifts, but the same Spirit.
And there are diversities of ministrations, and the same Lord.
And there are diversities of workings, but the same God, who worketh all
things in all (1 Cor. 12.4–6).

The triadic pattern of this section is obvious. Weiss[1] contends
that Paul had in mind a formula such as that which is found in
2 Cor. 13.14. In 1 Cor. 12 and the following chapters Paul writes
of the work of the Spirit. In his experience, the Spirit, the Lord,
and God are operative in the Christian life. They give unity to the
diverse gifts and activities of individual Christians. As in 2 Thess.
2.13–14, there is no doctrine of the Trinity but there is material
for the development of a doctrine. A further step in the direction
of a doctrine, however, is taken in 1 Corinthians, in so far as Paul
lays great emphasis on the work of the Spirit.

The grace of the Lord Jesus Christ, and the love of God, and the communion of the Holy Spirit, be with you all (2 Cor. 13.14).

As Weiss points out, this may be a formula of the Church, which
Paul has taken over. It is equally probable, however, that Paul
expanded a formula which he used elsewhere—"The grace of the

[1] *I Korintherbrief*, ad. loc.

Lord Jesus (Christ) be with you",[1] and that this expression was made as a result of his own religious experience.

It has been argued that this saying is not a step in the direction of a trinitarian confession but a way of expressing God's act of salvation.[2] The formula tells us that God had sent his Son, had given the Spirit, and would finally save the faithful. Although this view is right in its claim that the formula expresses God's act of salvation, it is mistaken in its assumption that the formula is not a step in the direction of a trinitarian confession. It was the product of thoughts which were leading towards a trinitarian doctrine, and its frequent use in the Church would speed the growth of such doctrine.

The three passages which have just been mentioned bear the clear impress of the threefold formula. Many other sayings of Paul, however, reveal on closer examination the influence of a threefold pattern. Some of these will now be mentioned.

> Now that no man is justified by the law in the sight of God is evident . . . Christ redeemed us from the curse of the law . . . that we might receive the promise of the Spirit through faith (Gal. 3.11–14).

> And because ye are sons, God sent forth the Spirit of his Son into our hearts, crying, Abba, Father (Gal. 4.6).

> Now he that stablisheth us with you in Christ, and anointed us, is God; who also sealed us, and gave us the earnest of the Spirit in our hearts (2 Cor. 1.21–2).

> Being made manifest that ye are an epistle of Christ, ministered by us, written not with ink, but with the Spirit of the living God (2 Cor. 3.3).

> For the kingdom of God is not eating and drinking, but righteousness and peace and joy in the Holy Spirit. For he that herein serveth Christ is well-pleasing to God, and approved of men (Rom. 14.17–18).

> That I should be a minister of Christ Jesus unto the Gentiles, ministering the gospel of God, that the offering up of the Gentiles might be made acceptable, being sanctified by the Holy Spirit (Rom. 15.16).

> Now I beseech you, brethren, by our Lord Jesus Christ, and by the love of the Spirit, that ye strive together with me in your prayers to God for me (Rom. 15.30).

[1] Rom. 16.20,24; 1 Cor. 16.23; 1 Thess. 5.28; 2 Thess. 3.18.
[2] H. Lietzmann, *An die Korinther* (ed. Kümmel), p. 214.

For we are the circumcision, who worship by the Spirit of God, and glory in Christ Jesus (Phil. 3.3).

. . . since the day ye heard and knew the grace of God in truth; even as ye learned of Epaphras our beloved fellow-servant, who is a faithful minister of Christ on our behalf, who also declared unto us your love in the Spirit (Col. 1.6–8).

For through him we both have our access in one Spirit unto the Father (Eph. 2.18).

Christ Jesus . . . in whom each several building, fitly framed together, groweth into a holy temple in the Lord; in whom ye also are builded together for a habitation of God in the Spirit (Eph. 2.20–2).

For this cause I bow my knees unto the Father, from whom every family in heaven and on earth is named, that he would grant you, according to the riches of his glory, that ye may be strengthened with power through his Spirit in the inward man; that Christ may dwell in your hearts through faith (Eph. 3.14–16).

Other passages have been brought forward as evidence of the presence of the threefold pattern in the thought of Paul, but they do not carry as much weight as those which have been quoted, and sometimes the threefold pattern is so greatly hidden by other more prominent ideas that it cannot be said to have been consciously present in Paul's mind.

The passages, however, which have been quoted, show that Paul frequently linked together Father, Son, and Spirit. There were other groups of three in his thought, such as, for example, faith, hope, and love, but the triad which he mentions most often is that which is the basis of the doctrine of the Trinity.

Non-Pauline Passages

There are no tripartite formulae as such in the Fourth Gospel, but the threefold pattern is more prominent there than in any other part of the New Testament. A discussion of the threefold pattern in the Fourth Gospel will be found in the next chapter. In the remainder of this chapter attention will be confined to other writings.

According to the foreknowledge of God the Father, in sanctification of the Spirit, unto obedience and sprinkling of the blood of Jesus Christ (1 Pet. 1.2).

This passage has several phrases which are reminiscent of 2 Thess. 2.13–14. It also has the same threefold structure. But the verbal similarity is not great enough to warrant any theory of the dependence of either of the passages on the other.

Selwyn has suggested that 1 Pet. 1.2 may have been influenced by Matt. 28.19. "This would be not unnatural", he writes, "if the Matthaean passage were first written as the concluding section of a collection of *verba Christi*."[1] The baptismal nature of the Matthaean formula, Selwyn says, would have made it specially appropriate for the writer of 1 Peter.[2] Selwyn's theory has little solid support. The Matthaean and Petrine passages agree only in their reference to the Father. While Peter speaks of Jesus Christ, Matthew speaks of the Son. While Peter speaks of the sanctifying of the Spirit, Matthew speaks of the Holy Spirit. There is no case to be made for the dependence of either passage on the other. The best explanation of the similarity to each other which they show is that they both arose at a time when Father, Son, and Spirit were being linked together in Christian thought and devotion.

1 Pet. 1.2 carries no implication of a doctrine of the Trinity. Nothing is said about the relationship between Father, Son, and Spirit.

> But when the kindness of God our Saviour, and his love toward man, appeared, not by works done in righteousness, which we did ourselves, but according to his mercy he saved us, through the washing of regeneration and renewing of the Holy Spirit, which he poured out upon us richly, through Jesus Christ our Saviour (Titus 3.4–6).

Here the three persons are said to be active in baptism and salvation.

> Of how much sorer punishment, think ye, shall he be judged worthy, who hath trodden under foot the Son of God . . . and hath done despite unto the Spirit of grace? (Heb. 10.29).

The Father is not mentioned in this passage but Son and Spirit occur in parallel clauses. This passage is evidence that the author was aware of the triadic pattern.

---

[1] E. G. Selwyn, *First Epistle of Peter*, p. 247.   [2] Ibid., p. 248.

> But ye, beloved, building up yourselves on your most holy faith, praying in the Holy Spirit, keep yourselves in the love of God, looking for the mercy of our Lord Jesus Christ unto eternal life (Jude 20.21).

This verse comes from an epistle written in the second century, when it was a regular practice to use triadic formulae.

> Grace to you and peace, from him which is and which was and which is to come; and from the seven Spirits which are before his throne; and from Jesus Christ, who is the faithful witness . . . (Rev. 1.4,5).

Although the author spoke of seven spirits rather than the Holy Spirit, this passage shows that he was influenced by the triadic pattern, which for him becomes: God—seven spirits—Jesus Christ.

Other passages which bear traces of the threefold pattern are: 1 Pet. 4.14; Heb. 6.4 ff. Another passage, Acts 20.28, has a threefold form if "his own" refers to Christ as God's own Son. Then the passage would read:

> Take heed unto yourselves, and to all the flock, in which the Holy Spirit hath made you bishops, to feed the church of God, which he purchased with the blood of his own.

But this may not be the correct interpretation.[1]

Nor can the version of 1 John 5.7,8 which refers to Father, Word, and Spirit, be regarded as part of the authentic text. The Byzantine text reads:

> There are three who bear witness in heaven; the Father, the Word, and the Holy Spirit; and these three are one.

This is a gloss which may have arisen in Spain. Westcott points out that the words are not found in any independent Greek manuscript, in any independent Greek writer, in any early Latin Father, or in any ancient version except the Latin, and not in the earliest form of that.[2]

Even when we have disregarded these unreliable texts, there remains a strong body of evidence which shows that the writers of the New Testament were influenced in thought and expression

---

[1] See pp. 73–4 for a discussion of the text.
[2] Westcott, *The Epistles of John*, pp. 202–9.

by the triad "Father, Son, and Holy Spirit". In none of these passages, however, are there any clear doctrinal implications about the relationship between Father, Son, and Spirit.

Attempts have been made to trace the development of triadic formulae. Cullmann makes a distinction between confessions of faith and liturgical formulae.[1] He argues that in the New Testament there are no tripartite confessions of faith. The triadic formulae which are found in the New Testament are, according to him, formulae of a liturgical character but not confessions of faith. He claims that the original confessions of faith were single-membered formulae referring to Christ, or bipartite formulae referring to God and Christ. These two types of formulae probably existed alongside each other from the beginning, but originally the single-membered Christological confessions were the more widespread. Certainly this is the impression which is given by the New Testament. There is plenty of evidence for the confession "Jesus is Lord" or "Jesus is the Son of God". There are also bipartite formulae such as 1 Cor. 8.6 and the frequent phrase "God the Father and our Lord Jesus Christ". But probably, as Cullmann says, the single Christological formulae predominated.

Although the tripartite forms in the New Testament are not actually credal confessions, they show that the Christians believed in the Father and the Son and the Spirit. The threefold formula is used for baptism, and records the deepest experiences of individual Christians. By Father, Son, and Spirit the activities of the Christian Church are directed (1 Cor. 12.4–6). As the Christian bows his knee to the Father, he is strengthened with power through the Spirit, and Christ dwells in his heart (Eph. 3.14 ff). In prayer and worship Father, Son, and Spirit are in the foreground (Rom. 15.30; Phil. 3.3).

This triadic pattern has been traced in Paul, Hebrews, the First Epistle of Peter, the Pastoral Epistles, Jude, Revelation, and Matthew. In the next chapter it will be traced even more clearly in the Fourth Gospel. The pattern was used, it seems, by many sections of the Church, and was not confined to the teaching of any

[1] O. Cullmann, op. cit., p. 36.

one writer. As Chase says, "The writers speak without hesitation or misgiving. They assume that their friends to whom they write will at once understand their words about the Father, the Son, and the Holy Spirit."[1] On the other hand, Kelly goes too far when he says: "If Trinitarian creeds are rare, the Trinitarian pattern which was to dominate all later creeds was already part and parcel of the Christian tradition of doctrine."[2] The trinitarian pattern was influencing the worship of the Church and the way in which the apostolic writers expressed themselves. But it was not yet "part and parcel of the Christian tradition of doctrine". It could only become part of that tradition when the trinitarian problem arose and an attempt was made to answer it. As we shall argue in the next chapter, the trinitarian problem arose in the New Testament chiefly in the Fourth Gospel, and only partially in other writings.

[1] F. H. Chase, op. cit., p. 510.
[2] J. N. D. Kelly, *Early Christian Creeds*, p. 23.

CHAPTER 14

THE TRINITARIAN THOUGHT OF THE NEW TESTAMENT

The threefold pattern of thought about God is not confined to the trinitarian formulae which were discussed in the last chapter. In the first century A.D. there was a definite movement in the direction of a triadic conception of God. Often it seems to have been unconscious, for few of the New Testament writers betray any awareness of the problem of the Trinity or even of the problem of Christ's relationship to the Father. In some of the writings, however, there are signs of a consciousness of the trinitarian problem.

The most important part of the trinitarian problem is the explanation of the relationship between Father and Son. In an earlier chapter it has been shown that Paul, John, and the author of the Epistle to the Hebrews were aware of the difficulties of explaining this relationship, and used the Father-Son terminology to interpret it. All three writers acknowledged that Christ was God, and that he performed divine functions. They hailed him as Lord, and applied to him Old Testament quotations which were used by the Jews only of Yahweh. At the same time they recognized his humanity and described how he prayed to the Father and obeyed him. Moreover, when they discussed his relationship with the Father, they spoke as if he were in some sense less than the Father, even after his resurrection. In acknowledging the priority of the Father, however, they did not deny the Son's divinity. The writer who deals most fully with the problem of Father and Son is the Fourth Evangelist, and he is the writer who emphasizes that Jesus is God. When Paul and the author of Hebrews call Jesus God, they do so in passing, as though this were not an integral part of the argument. But the recognition that Jesus is God is deliberately interwoven into the Fourth Gospel, which begins with the statement that the Word is God, and reaches its climax in chapter 20.28 where Thomas calls Jesus "my God". There is nothing incidental about these references. The evangelist intends to state that Jesus is God, and in various passages attempts to show how the only-begotten Son of God who is also the only-begotten God is related to God the Father.

A second part of the trinitarian problem is the question of the relationship between the Spirit and Christ and between the Spirit and God the Father. This has been discussed in another chapter. It has been shown that the New Testament writers regarded the Spirit as a person, but did not call him God. They did not ascribe him divine functions with the same consistency and regularity with which they ascribed them to Christ. Nevertheless the Spirit was both the Spirit of God and the Spirit of Christ. The Spirit was believed to guide worship, and the possession of the Spirit was one of the main characteristics of the Christian life. There is, however, almost no indication that there was a problem of the Spirit, or that the writers felt any difficulty about the relationship between the Spirit and the Father or between the Spirit and the Son. Even Paul, who describes the Spirit as an intercessor to God, does not show any clear awareness of a problem about the relationship of the Spirit either to Father or to Son. The question is clearly present only in the Fourth Gospel, where an attempt is made to show that Father, Son, and Spirit are different from each other. The Father, says the evangelist, sends the Son, and the Son must go away that the Spirit may come. Thus an answer is given to the threefold problem. It is indeed only the beginning of an answer but it is evidence that the problem was in the author's mind.

The problem of the Spirit was not the main problem for New Testament writers any more than for later theologians. The main issues at stake in the doctrine of the Trinity are the unity of God and the deity of Christ. Few of the controversies of the Church have been provoked by disputes about the person of the Spirit. The real stumbling-block has been the divinity of Christ. In New Testament times little was done to explain the relationship of Spirit to the Father and Son. The problem of Christ was more urgent than that of the Spirit, for Christ had appeared to the Jews as a man. He was not just an emanation from the Godhead. He had lived a life of temptation, struggle, and prayer. He had fought the battle of faith, and learned obedience by the things which he suffered. He had humbled himself, becoming obedient unto death, even the death of the cross. On the cross he had cried in despair to God, and in spite of this dreadful experience had risen from the grave. These were the actions of one who not only came from God but also faced him, sought him, and found him. For this reason the problem of Christ's divinity was much greater than that of the Spirit's.

In earlier chapters the relationships between Father and Son, Father and Spirit, and Son and Spirit have been discussed. Now we must ask how far the New Testament writers were aware of the problem as a single whole, as a problem of the mutual relationship of Father, Son, and Spirit. Already a number of threefold formulae have been examined. These do not prove that the writers made a conscious effort to establish a triadic conception of God. They show, however, that the writers' thoughts about God were moving in the direction of a threefold conception.

The Fourth Evangelist is the only New Testament writer who clearly understands the threefold nature of the problem. Other writers, however, show trends in the direction of a threefold pattern of thought, which are not confined to the formulae which have already been discussed. The development of thought about the subject can be traced at three levels. The first is the level of the threefold formulae, where a writer reveals something about his background of worship and thought. At this level the threefold nature of the formulae is not integral to the writer's argument. A second level is that at which the triad, Father, Son, and Spirit, is deliberately stressed without any attempt to answer the problem of their relationship. And a third level is that which is found in the Fourth Gospel, where the problem is seen and an explanation attempted. The first level of thought, which is represented by the threefold formulae, has been discussed. In this chapter the second and third levels will be examined.

The level at which the triad is stressed without attempts to solve the full problem is found in the synoptic gospels. None of

Jesus' own sayings reveals any awareness of the threefold problem. He is deeply conscious of his relationship to the Father, and speaks occasionally about the Spirit. But nothing which he says suggests that the close association of Father, Son, and Spirit is prominent in his thinking. The only exception is Matt. 28.19, a post-resurrection saying the authenticity of which has been widely questioned.

The narratives of the gospels, however, show clearer traces of the threefold pattern. In the story of Jesus' life the pattern is seen in his baptism by John, when the Father names him Son, and the Spirit descends upon him. This is not Trinitarianism, for nothing is said about the divinity of Son and Spirit, and there is no question of interaction between Father and Spirit or even between Son and Spirit. But the event itself is one which has a threefold pattern. It is not just a formula but an important story in which the triad is prominent. The story is present in all four gospels—directly reported in the synoptic gospels, and indirectly reported in the Fourth Gospel.

Mark records the baptism of Jesus by John and also John's prophecy about the coming of one who would baptize with Spirit. In Mark's gospel there is no record of the fulfilment of this prophecy. It is found neither in the main body of the gospel nor in the three different endings (the Longer, the Shorter, and the Freer Endings). It is possible that the true ending of the gospel was lost, and contained a reference to Spirit-baptism. In the gospel as it survives there is no further reference to the triad after the story of Jesus' baptism.

Matthew is more conscious than Mark of the threefold nature of the divine revelation. His gospel begins with the Infancy Narrative, according to which Jesus was "conceived of the Holy Spirit" (Matt. 1.20). It ends with Jesus' command to evangelize and to baptize: " . . . baptizing them into the name of the Father and of the Son and of the Holy Spirit" (Matt. 28.19). In Matthew's version of a saying of Jesus which Luke also records, Father, Son, and Spirit are mentioned together: "If I by the Spirit of God cast out demons, then is the kingdom of God come upon you" (Matt. 12.28). Luke's version, which has "finger of God" for "Spirit of God", probably represents the actual words of Jesus. But Matthew has preferred a version which stresses the joint action of Son and Spirit.

These triadic references do not form a dominating theme in the Gospel according to St Matthew, but their importance ought not to be minimized. The threefold pattern occurs at crucial moments in the gospel story. It can be traced in the birth of Jesus, who was sent by God and conceived of the Holy Spirit. And it is found in the story of the baptism of Jesus, which is set in stronger relief by Matthew than by the other evangelists, because Matthew includes a paragraph in which John the Baptist confesses his reluctance to baptize Jesus (Matt. 3.14).

The stories of Jesus' infancy and baptism stand at the beginning of Matthew's gospel. At the end is the threefold formula "In the name of the Father and of the Son and of the Holy Spirit" (Matt. 28.19). This formula has itself no trinitarian doctrinal implication but is proof that the threefold pattern was accepted and valued when the gospel was written. Its position at the very end of the gospel is important. The evangelist has not only allowed the formula a place within the gospel but has allowed it a very prominent place. A saying of this nature at the end of a gospel is much more memorable than a saying of comparable importance in the middle. It is true that this saying could only be placed after the resurrection. But it is significant that the evangelist should choose a threefold formula to set at the end of the story, when he could have chosen many other endings. Now Matthew's gospel is a carefully planned gospel. And the hand of the literary artist is seen in the presence of the threefold idea at the beginning and the end. Yet although Matthew accepted and gave prominence to the triad, he shows no sign of being aware of a trinitarian problem. He does not attempt to explain how Father, Son, and Spirit are related to each other. He does not think that an explanation of the unity of God is required. Not even the central problem of relationship between Father and Son is a problem for him. He quotes Jesus' words about his Sonship and includes both the story of the Virgin Birth and that of the proclamation of Sonship at Jesus' baptism. But he does not see the Father-Son relationship as a problem.

Luke and Acts, which will be considered together, contain

several traces of the threefold pattern. Like Matthew, Luke begins
with the story of the Virgin Birth. The angel says to Mary at the
Annunciation: "The Holy Spirit shall come upon thee, and the
power of the Most High shall overshadow thee: wherefore also
that which is to be born shall be called holy, the Son of God"
(Luke 1.35).

An element of explanation, absent from Matthew at this point,
is included by Luke. The activity of the Spirit, says the angel,
is necessary to ensure the uniqueness and holiness of Christ.

Luke includes several other hints of the triad in his account of
the early part of Jesus' ministry. He tells the story of the baptism
and then, like Matthew, describes how Jesus was led by the Spirit
into the wilderness where he was for forty days tempted by the
devil. The questions put to Jesus twice mention that he is Son of
God. The Sonship of Jesus and the activity of the Spirit are linked
together in the fight against evil. In one respect Luke gives more
prominence to the Spirit than does Matthew. Both evangelists say
that Jesus was led by the Spirit into the wilderness, but Luke also
says that after the temptation "Jesus returned in the power of the
Spirit into Galilee" (Luke 4.14). He describes how Jesus opened
the book of the prophet Isaiah in the synagogue and read: "The
Spirit of the Lord is upon me" (Luke 4.17–8). Luke is emphasizing
that Jesus' victory over the devil was a victory of the Spirit, by
whose power Jesus was able to begin his ministry.

Luke records the fulfilment of the prophecy of the "Coming
One". In a prominent place almost at the end of the gospel (Luke
24.49) Jesus says:

> And behold, I send forth the promise of my Father upon you: but tarry ye
> in the city, until ye be clothed with power from on high.

"The promise of my Father" is the gift of the Spirit prophesied
by Joel and John the Baptist. "The power from on high" is the
Holy Spirit himself. Thus the Gospel according to St Luke ends,
as it began, with the activity of Father, Son, and Spirit.

In the Acts of the Apostles the promise of the Father which has
already been mentioned in Luke 24.49, is said to be Baptism with
the Holy Spirit (Acts 1.4,5). When the disciples receive the power

of the Spirit they will be witnesses of Christ (Acts 1.8). The actual fulfilment of the prophecy of Spirit-baptism is not limited by Luke to Pentecost. Peter sees its fulfilment in the descent of the Spirit upon Cornelius and his friends. In Acts 11.15,16 he says:

> And as I began to speak, the Holy Spirit fell on them, even as on us at the beginning. And I remembered the word of the Lord, how that he said, John indeed baptized with water; but ye shall be baptized with the Holy Spirit.

The fulfilment of the prophecy is not confined to what happened "at the beginning" but is extended to later acts of the Spirit.

The most important fulfilment of the prophecy, however, was at Pentecost. In two sections of Peter's speech at Pentecost the three members of the triad are mentioned together.

> Being therefore by the right hand of God exalted, and having received of the Father the promise of the Holy Spirit, he hath poured forth this, which ye see and hear (Acts 2.33).

> Repent ye, and be baptized every one of you in the name of Jesus Christ unto the remission of your sins; and ye shall receive the gift of the Holy Spirit. For to you is the promise, and to your children, and to all that are afar off, even as many as the Lord our God shall call unto him (Acts 2.38–9).

These are not just formulae in which Father, Son, and Spirit happen to be mentioned. They are passages in which a deliberate account is given of the activity of the three. The exalted Jesus who himself received the Spirit at baptism, pours out the Spirit upon his followers. Those who are baptized in the name of Jesus will receive the Spirit, and those who receive the Spirit are called by God. A slightly different account is found in Acts 11.17 where the gift of the Spirit is said to follow not after baptism but in response to faith:

> If then God gave unto them the like gift as he did also unto us, when we believed on the Lord Jesus Christ, who was I that I could withstand God?

Other passages in which there are traces of the threefold form are:

> The words of Ananias to Saul: Brother Saul, the Lord, even Jesus, who appeared unto thee in the way which thou camest, hath sent me, that thou mayest receive thy sight, and be filled with the Holy Spirit (Acts 9.17).

So the church throughout all Judaea and Galilee and Samaria had peace, being edified; and, walking in the fear of the Lord and in the comfort of the Holy Spirit, was multiplied (Acts 9.31).

A reference to the story of Jesus' baptism: . . . how that God anointed him with the Holy Spirit and with power (Acts 10.38).

Although the Father, Son, and Spirit are linked together prominently in the early part of Acts, the theme of the triad does not dominate the whole work. There is no trinitarian formula and no threefold pattern in the latter half of the book. When Luke mentions Father, Son, and Spirit in the first part of Acts, however, he does not just mention them in passing. The evidence of Peter's speech at Pentecost and the conversion of Cornelius and the prominence given to the narrative of Pentecost show that Luke linked Father, Son, and Spirit in his thought. He goes further than Matthew in so far as he describes the fulfilment of the prophecy of Spirit-baptism, but he does not see any problem in the relationships between the members of the triad.

In the last chapter threefold formulae were quoted from several writings of the New Testament, but in very few of them is there any insistence upon the actual triadic pattern of Father, Son, and Spirit. Indeed apart from the synoptic gospels and Acts only John and Paul appear to have given real prominence to the pattern. The threefold pattern is notably absent from the Epistle to the Hebrews. Apart from 6.4-6 the only possible reference is 10.29 in which "Son of God" and "Spirit of Grace" appear in parallel clauses. The Book of Revelation speaks of seven spirits before the throne of God, but nothing is said of the relation of these seven spirits to Christ. 1 Peter opens with a threefold formula, and in 1.11 claims that the Spirit of Christ testified beforehand of the sufferings of Christ. In 2.5 Christians are said to "offer up spiritual sacrifices, acceptable to God through Jesus Christ". This is not enough to warrant the assumption that the writer intended to record any thoughts about the relations between Father, Son, and Spirit.

In most of these writings the absence of the threefold pattern is not surprising, but the lack of it in Hebrews needs comment. The author of Hebrews is clearly aware of the central problem of the doctrine of the Trinity—the relationship between the Son of God and his Father. For the author calls Jesus God and Lord, speaks of him as creator, and treats him as the object of worship. The detailed discussion of his work and office as Son and High Priest shows that the writer knew there was a problem and attempted to answer it. But he does not tackle the problem of the Spirit, and does not recognize a threefold problem.

The Pastoral Epistles also fail to recognize the problem. One threefold formula has been quoted from them (Titus 3.4–6), and this speaks of the relationship between Father, Son, and Spirit. God saved us, says the writer, through the renewing of the Holy Spirit, which he "poured out upon us richly, through Jesus Christ our Saviour". The author of the Pastoral Epistles also describes Jesus as God (Titus 2.13). Christ shares with God the functions of judgement and salvation. At the same time God is one (1 Tim. 2.5) and as such is different from Christ the mediator. Here indeed is the material for a problem but no indication that the author was aware of it or attempted to solve it.

Although the Pauline Epistles do not fully face the threefold problem, they contain many statements which have a threefold pattern of Father, Son, and Spirit. Fourteen of these have been quoted in the previous chapter. Not all of them reveal that Paul had devoted great thought to the relationship between the members of the triad. Yet several passages show an appreciation of the importance of the threefold pattern.

Thus in Gal. 3.13–14, Paul writes:

> Christ redeemed us from the curse of the law, having become a curse for us: for it is written, Cursed is everyone that hangeth on a tree: that upon the Gentiles might come the blessing of Abraham in Christ Jesus; that we might receive the promise of the Spirit through faith.

According to this passage the purpose of the crucifixion is that men might receive the Spirit. This causal connection between the two events is a sign of thought about the relationship between Christ and the Spirit.

Again when in Gal. 4.6 he says:

> And because ye are sons, God sent forth the Spirit of his Son into our hearts, crying Abba, Father,

he has been thinking about the relationship of the members of the triad. In the same context Paul says that it was God who sent both the Spirit (Gal. 4.6) and the Son (Gal. 4.4).

The threefold pattern is found in the outline of some of Paul's writings as well as in isolated formulae. The first eight chapters of Romans may be divided as follows:

Introduction, 1.1–17.

The judgement of God upon Gentiles and Jews, 1.18—3.20.

Justification through faith in Jesus Christ, 3.21—8.1.

Life in the Spirit, 8.2–30.

Concluding paragraph, 8.31–9.

Paul's aim is not to describe the relationship between Father, Son, and Spirit. His purpose is to trace the pattern of man's salvation, the wrath and judgement of God, the saving work of Christ, and the new life of the adopted children of God who live by the Spirit. Nevertheless, this account of the plan of salvation fits into the threefold pattern. God the Father dominates the first section, Jesus Christ the second and the Holy Spirit the third.

The importance of both Christ and the Spirit is evident in the first three chapers of 1 Corinthians in which Paul is pleading for unity in the Church. These chapters have no strict outline. One theme grows out of another. The argument develops as follows:

Introduction, 1.1–9.

Pleas for harmony in the church, 1.10–17.

Christ, the power and the wisdom of God, 1.18–2.9

The instruction given by the Spirit, 2.10–16.

The functions of Paul and Apollos in the church at Corinth, 3.1–9.

Jesus Christ, the foundation for men's work, 3.10–15.

Men are God's temple in which the Spirit dwells, 3.16,17.

Conclusion to opening section, 3.18–23.

In these chapters Paul does not try to work out the relationship between Christ and the Spirit. His accounts of their work often intermingle and overlap. But he shows a definite tendency, after he has spoken of the Son, to move on to the Spirit.

The Epistle to the Galatians also has traces of the threefold idea. Its outline in brief is as follows:

Introduction, 1.1–5.

Paul's defence of his conduct, 1.6—2.21.

Justification through faith in Christ, 3.1–29.

Adoption into sonship through the redemption wrought by Christ and the sending of the Spirit, 4.1–7.

The bondage of the law and the freedom given by Christ, 4.8—5.15.

Life in the Spirit, 5.16—6.10.

Conclusion, 6.11–18.

There is no rigid triadic pattern in this epistle. The thought of God is present throughout, and often Son and Spirit are mentioned together. But by the natural turn of his thought Paul speaks first of the Son and then of the Spirit.

Few of Paul's letters are carefully planned. But the three which have been mentioned, Romans, 1 Corinthians, and Galatians, are more carefully planned than the others. And in their outlines there are clear traces of the triad of Father, Son, and Spirit. Even when the order of thought is "Son and Spirit" rather than "Father, Son, and Spirit", it is clear that God the Father has priority, since in the opening of each epistle Paul speaks of God the Father and the Lord Jesus Christ.

Mention must be made of the Epistle to the Ephesians. Although the threefold pattern does not dominate the thought of the epistle, there are several formulae in which the pattern can be found, and attention is given to the relationships of Father, Son, and Spirit. There is a special emphasis on the unity of the Church, to which both Christ and the Spirit are essential.

The ideas are found as follows:

CHRIST	THE HOLY SPIRIT
The Church is his body (1.22,23) of which he is head (4.15).	The Church is a habitation of God in the Spirit (2.22).
The Church has Christ as chief corner stone (2.20).	
Christ brought unity to the Church, making peace (2.14 ff).	The Church has unity in the Spirit (4.3; 2.18).

These two aspects of Christian unity are linked together in certain passages. In 2.20–2 Christ is the corner stone and the Church is a habitation of God in the Spirit. In 3.16–17 Paul prays that his readers may be strengthened through the Spirit in the inward man and that Christ may dwell in their hearts. And in 2.18 he says of Jews and Gentiles "Through him we both have our access in one Spirit unto the Father".

The most impressive passage is 4.4–6:

> There is one body and one Spirit, even as also ye were called in one hope of your calling; one Lord, one faith, one baptism, one God and Father of all, who is over all, and through all, and in all.

This appears to be a sixfold, or (if "one hope" is included) a sevenfold formula. But it divides naturally into three groups: body and Spirit—Lord, faith, baptism—God and Father. Such a division shows the influence of the triadic pattern on the writer. In this passage he does not intend to stress the triad, or the threefold character of the formula would have been more apparent. But the passage shows how the threefold pattern persisted in Paul's thought.

This survey of Paul's epistles does not reveal a conscious attempt to answer a threefold problem. In earlier chapters it has been shown that Paul was aware of some of the ingredients of trinitarian thought. He acknowledged Jesus as God, but this confession was not interwoven into his theology. It was something which belonged to his personal belief and to his ways of worship, but it was not part of his public thinking. He admitted without reservation that Jesus was creator, saviour, and judge. Jesus belonged to the order of Godhead, although he was in some sense secondary to the Father. Paul's continual emphasis on God the Father and Christ the Lord, and his lofty conception of Christ's person is evidence that he was aware of the problem of the unity of God and the deity of Christ. It is this problem with which he is wrestling when he says: "There is one God the Father and one Lord Jesus Christ" (1 Cor. 8.6). It is this problem which is before him in 1 Cor. 15 when he says that Christ hands over the Kingdom to the Father, and in Philippians when he describes Christ as receiving the adoration of all creatures "to the glory of God the Father". Here is the Christological core of the trinitarian problem and here is an attempt at an answer.

As for the Spirit, Paul speaks of him as a person, and even as an intercessor. But there is not always a clear distinction between the indwelling Christ and the indwelling Spirit (see Rom. 8.9–11). Although he never identifies Christ with the Spirit, he has not clarified the relation of the Spirit to the Father and the Son.

The threefold pattern, however, was in the background always, and Paul probably thought about it more than his writings reveal. For, with the possible exception of Romans and Ephesians, his epistles were not intended as theological treatises, but as advice and instruction for particular situations. He was also more concerned about the work than the person of Christ, about God's plan of salvation than God's nature. It would be rash to suppose that he never thought about a subject because he did not mention it in the epistles. But we can only speculate about his unwritten thoughts. In the epistles, although he writes of Christ's relationship to the Father, he does not recognize a threefold problem. He accepts a threefold pattern of Father, Son, and Spirit by which he describes the activity of God, but he does not show any awareness of a threefold problem.

The supreme biblical pattern of trinitarian thought is found in the Fourth Gospel. Other writers touched on parts of the problem but the Fourth Evangelist sees it in its threefoldness. His answer does not cope with all its complexities. When he had finished, there was much room for development and explanation. But although he never uses the word "Trinity" he sees the triadic nature of the problem.

In several passages from the Johannine writings Father, Son, and Spirit are mentioned together:

> But he that sent me to baptize with water, he said unto me, Upon whomsoever thou shalt see the Spirit descending, and abiding upon him, the same is he that baptizeth with the Holy Spirit. And I have seen, and have borne witness that this is the Son of God (John 1.33-4).

> And I will pray the Father, and he shall give you another Paraclete, that he may be with you for ever, even the Spirit of truth (John 14.16).

> But the Paraclete, even the Holy Spirit, whom the Father will send in my name, he shall teach you all things, and bring to your remembrance all that I said unto you (John 14.26).

> Jesus therefore said to them again, Peace be unto you: as the Father hath sent me, even so send I you. And when he had said this, he breathed on them, and saith unto them, Receive ye the Holy Spirit (John 20.21-2).

> All things whatsoever the Father hath are mine: therefore said I, that he (i.e. the Spirit) taketh of mine, and shall declare it unto you (John 16.15).

> Hereby know ye the Spirit of God: every Spirit which confesseth that Jesus Christ is come in the flesh is of God (1 John 4.2).

> Hereby know we that we abide in him (God), and he in us, because he hath given us of his Spirit. And we have beheld and bear witness that the Father hath sent the Son to be the Saviour of the world (1 John 4.13-14).

Two passages should be added which do not mention God the Father but speak of the relation between Son and Spirit:

> But this spake he of the Spirit, which they that believed on him were to receive: for the Spirit was not yet given; because Jesus was not yet glorified (John 7.39).

> It is expedient for you that I go away: for if I go not away, the Paraclete will not come unto you; but if I go, I will send him unto you (John 16.7).

Like the synoptic evangelists John refers to the baptism of Jesus (John 1.33-4). He does not give as detailed an account of it as the other evangelists do. He refers to it only in passing. But all those features of the Baptist's teaching which are concerned with Son and Spirit are concentrated in John 1.33-4. The Spirit descends on Christ, who will himself baptize with the Spirit. Indeed the Fourth Evangelist makes a definite link between the descent of the Spirit on Jesus and the Spirit-baptism, which Jesus was to give to others, a link which is not made in the other gospels where John's prophecy about the Spirit is kept distinct from the descent of the Spirit on Jesus.

In the Fourth Gospel John the Baptist says: "I have seen, and have borne witness that this is the Son of God." Now although the other gospels record that the voice from heaven said, "This is my Son", none of them says that the Baptist recognized the event as a sign of Jesus' Sonship. The Fourth Evangelist has been very selective in his description of this incident. He does not even mention that Jesus was baptized. He records those aspects of the incident and of the Baptist's teaching which stress the connection between Father, Son, and Spirit. His selectivity is probably caused by a desire to counteract excessive veneration of the Baptist,[1] but he seizes the opportunity to draw out the threefold nature of the divine life. The Father sends the Baptist. The Spirit descends upon the Son who will himself baptize with the Spirit.

The Paraclete sayings which have been quoted (John 14.16,26; 16.15) show the activity of Father, Son, and Spirit. It is implied (14.16) that Jesus as well as the Spirit is Paraclete (cf. 1 John 2.1). The Father will send the Spirit as Paraclete, indeed as "another Paraclete", who will teach the disciples all things and remind them of what Jesus has said. In virtue of this the Spirit is rightly called "the Spirit of truth". But the Spirit cannot come until Jesus goes away (John 16.7). Apart from the descent of the Spirit on Jesus at the beginning of his ministry, the Spirit's activity is placed after the resurrection of Jesus. Only when Jesus has been glorified through crucifixion and resurrection can he send the Spirit upon men. "The Spirit was not yet given; because Jesus was not yet glorified" (7.39). These sayings about the coming of the Spirit are fulfilled in John 20.21-2 when Jesus gives the Holy Spirit to his disciples. As he does this he says that he has been sent by the Father, and is himself sending those to whom he gives the Spirit.

Six passages from the gospel have been mentioned in this discussion. They are important because they form a consistent pattern. Barrett rightly says that "a simple consecutiveness of thought is not to be looked for in John's writing",[2] but there is sufficient con-

---

[1] C. K. Barrett, *St John*, p. 142.   [2] Ibid., p. 76.

secutiveness in his account of the relationship of Father, Son, and Spirit, for it to be regarded as one of the major themes of the gospel. The consistency of the remarks which have been discussed proves beyond doubt that he had reflected upon the matter, and was aware of the threefoldness of divine activity in Father, Son, and Spirit. The two passages from the First Epistle (1 John 4.2,13–14) add little information about the evangelist's thought but confirm the basic ideas. The Spirit leads men to confess divine truth, namely that Jesus Christ is come in the flesh and is of God, and that he is the Son whom God sent to be Saviour of the world.

The Fourth Gospel has been shown to have approached more nearly to the trinitarian position than any other writing of the New Testament. It emphasizes deliberately and clearly that Jesus is God. There is nothing accidental or unpremeditated about John's account of the words of Thomas, "My Lord and my God" (John 20.28). He deliberately says, "The Word was God" (John 1.1) and the best reading of John 1.18 contains the words "only-begotten God". The writer deliberately places acknowledgements of the divinity of Christ at the beginning and end of the gospel—for chapter twenty probably concluded the first edition of the gospel. In addition to this the Lord whom Isaiah saw in the temple is said by John to be the Christ (John 12.41).

The "I am" sayings of the gospel imply that Jesus is identified with Yahweh of the Old Testament who was called "I am that I am". And the evangelist makes it clear that Jesus shared the divine functions of judgement, creation, and salvation.

The Father-Son relationship is very prominent in the Fourth Gospel. More than any other New Testament writer John calls Jesus the Son of God. He writes about the relationship because he knows that a mystery must be explained. The Father is greater than the Son, and the Father sends the Son, but the Father and the Son are one, for the Son is in the bosom of the Father. John knows that there is a paradox, for the Word was with God and yet the Word was God. The way in which he presents the paradox, first through the idea of Word, and then through the idea of Father and Son, shows that he was attempting a solution. The idea of Father and Son was the most fitted to account for an interaction within the Godhead. It could also express how both Father and Son were God. It could give point to the priority of the Father without detracting from the divinity of the Son. And finally it could account for the unity of the two persons.

The Fourth Gospel also gives prominence to the doctrine of the Spirit. It has already been argued that the Spirit was regarded as a person by the evangelist, a fact which is specially clear from his use of the word Paraclete. Although his account of the Spirit's work is not as vivid and exhilarating as that of Paul, a more consistent distinction of the Spirit from Father and Son is found in the gospel than in Paul's epistles. The Spirit is quite definitely not the same as Christ, for the Spirit is "another Paraclete" and is given by the risen Christ. Although the Pauline emphasis on life in the Spirit is lacking, clarity and precision is gained by the more consistent distinction between Father, Son, and Spirit which is made in the Fourth Gospel.

It is true that some of the activities of Christ and the Spirit are similar, but the very fact that John attempts to distinguish the functions of the Spirit both temporally and qualitatively from those of Christ is evidence that he was trying to account for the threefold-ness of the Deity.

John does not actually call the Spirit God. He speaks, however, of the Spirit as passing judgement. And he more than any other New Testament writer makes it clear by his use of the word Paraclete that he regards the Spirit as a person.

The Fourth Evangelist goes further than any other New Testa-ment writer in stressing the fact that Jesus is God, and that the Spirit is a person whose functions are not wholly identical with those of Father and Son. Moreover he works out more fully than any other New Testament writer the relationship between Father and Son. All these matters lay the foundation of trinitarian theology. And when this is considered together with the passages in which the problem is clearly seen as threefold, it is reasonable to claim that John was aware of the trinitarian problem. As Barrett says, "more than any other New Testament writer he lays the founda-tions for a doctrine of a co-equal Trinity".[1] There is no doctrine

[1] Ibid., p. 78.

of a co-equal Trinity in the gospel but only the foundations. There is the doctrine as far as the relationship between Father and Son is concerned, for John maintains that both are God, that they are one, and that the Father has priority over the Son. Even though there are no technical metaphysical terms, there is a doctrine. Indeed there is the essence of the later doctrine. Here is not merely an awareness of the problem but an answer to it. In his discussion of the Spirit in relation to Father and Son the evangelist has not fully formulated his problem, for he does not actually say that the Spirit is God. He is moving in that direction. Once a plurality within the Godhead is admitted, it is not difficult to include the Spirit as well as the Son. For the Spirit does not create as serious difficulties in this connection as does the Son. John's concern with the problem as threefold would be caused partly by his own experience of the Spirit and partly by the growing tendency of Christians to link Father, Son, and Spirit together. He was not inventing a triad. He was explaining an association which was already recognized in the Christian community.

In his perception of the problem of the Trinity John seems to have been ahead of the other New Testament writers. Because he was the writer of a gospel he was impelled to concentrate on the question of the person of Christ. It is possible also that he knew what Paul had written, and sought to advance into realms of thought which Paul had not explored. But the main reason for John's distinctive contribution to trinitarian thought is his own genius, which led him to investigate the nature of God.

It is now possible to answer the question, "Is the doctrine of the Trinity to be found in the Bible?" The answer is that there is no formal statement of doctrine but an answer to the problem of the Trinity. This problem did not first occur when later generations of thinkers reflected upon the scriptures. At least three New Testament writers, Paul, John, and the author of Hebrews, were aware of a problem. Paul and the author of Hebrews did not see the problem as threefold. They concentrated on the relationship between Christ and God. Paul was conscious of the threefold pattern, but only grasped the problem as twofold. The Fourth

Evangelist, however, was conscious of a threefold problem of the mutual relationships of Father, Son, and Spirit.

These writers, in so far as they saw a problem, attempted to answer it. Their answers are not the main theme of their writings, but the way in which they speak of the divine persons shows that they have an answer. Other writers who did not see a problem, but attached importance to the threefold pattern, were Matthew and Luke. Their references to the triad are placed in such key positions that it is obvious that they were regarded as important.

It has been our purpose to consider how the trinitarian problem was first asked and answered. The answer which was given was neither complete nor definitive. But its lack of formal metaphysical vocabulary helps us to gain fresh insight into the trinitarian problem. A biblical doctrine of God can begin with an account of the names and title of Father, Son, and Spirit, and their divine functions and mutual relationships. Such an account of the Three in One cannot be summarized in a pithy formula, but its lack of rigid technical vocabulary and the absence of the word "Trinity" do not rob it of the status of doctrine.

This explanation of the matter cuts across the debate between Barth and Brunner about whether the doctrine of the Trinity is implicit in the New Testament. Instead of trying to find when charismatic theology became formal doctrine—an impossible task —we have shown how a problem was raised and answered. It is a matter of private taste whether to use the description "Doctrine of the Trinity" for the teaching contained in certain parts of the New Testament or to reserve this description for later writings. One thing is certain. The problem of the Trinity was being raised and answered in the New Testament. It arose because of the development of Christian experience, worship, and thought. It was rooted in experience, for men were conscious of the power of the Spirit and the presence and Lordship of the risen Christ. It was rooted in worship, because men worshipped in the Spirit, offered their prayers to God the Father through Christ, and sometimes worshipped Christ himself. It was rooted in thought, because the writers tackled first the Christological problem, and then, at any rate in the Fourth Gospel, the threefold problem. The whole matter was based on the life and resurrection of Jesus himself, who received the Spirit during his earthly life and imparted the Spirit to others after his resurrection.

For many centuries the Christian Church has interpreted its doctrine of God in terms of Greek metaphysics. But the biblical writers presented the doctrine in terms of their own experience, interpreted by the Hebrew names of God and the Hebrew ideas of divine functions. It is a salutary discipline to examine the biblical teaching and to observe how the nature of God was expounded without the patristic categories. The writers did not make it their chief aim to unravel all the complexities of the divine nature. Their chief aim was to show God as revealed in Christ and as present in the Spirit. They did not fully succeed in their task any more than later generations of Christian writers have succeeded. The divine nature was to biblical writers as to later Christians a tremendous and wonderful mystery.

O the depth of the riches both of the wisdom and the knowledge of God! how unsearchable are his judgements, and his ways past tracing out! For who hath known the mind of the Lord? or who hath been his counsellor? (Rom. 11.33–4).

The writers of the New Testament knew their limitations. They knew that they could but dimly discern and even more dimly interpret the nature of divine life. This did not deter them. Although they had not been schooled in systematic methods of philosophy, they did not shirk the task of interpretation. Their freedom from philosophical traditions, their down-to-earth Hebrew approach to heavenly things, enabled them to give an account of the work of God through Christ in the Spirit, which must ever provide the basis for Christian thought about the Triune God.

INDEXES

OLD TESTAMENT

NEW TESTAMENT

INDEX

NAMES AND SUBJECTS